# The Poverty of
# "The Poverty Rate"

# The Poverty of "The Poverty Rate"

## Measure and Mismeasure of Want in Modern America

By Nicholas Eberstadt

The AEI Press

*Publisher for the American Enterprise Institute*

WASHINGTON, D.C.

Distributed to the Trade by National Book Network, 15200 NBN Way, Blue Ridge Summit, PA 17214. To order call toll free 1-800-462-6420 or 1-717-794-3800. For all other inquiries please contact the AEI Press, 1150 Seventeenth Street, N.W., Washington, D.C. 20036 or call 1-800-862-5801.

Library of Congress Cataloging-in-Publication Data

Eberstadt, Nick, 1955-
  The poverty of "the poverty rate" : measure and mismeasure of want in modern America / by Nicholas Eberstadt.
      p. cm.
  Includes bibliographical references.
  ISBN-13: 978-0-8447-4246-5
  ISBN-10: 0-8447-4246-5
  1. Poverty—United States. 2. Poor—United States. 3. Income distribution—United States. I. Title.
  HC110.P6E24 2008
  362.5'20973—dc22

                                                            2008033682

  12 11 10 09 08          1 2 3 4 5 6 7

*Printed in the United States of America*

*To Christopher C. DeMuth*

*Mentor, role model, friend*

# Contents

LIST OF ILLUSTRATIONS     ix

ACKNOWLEDGMENTS     xiii

INTRODUCTION     1
   Why This Book   3
   A Road Map for This Study   5

1. WHAT IS THE OFFICIAL POVERTY RATE, AND WHAT DOES IT
   ACTUALLY MEASURE?     6

2. POVERTY TRENDS IN MODERN AMERICA, ACCORDING TO
   THE OFFICIAL POVERTY RATE     12

3. THE OFFICIAL POVERTY RATE VERSUS OTHER STATISTICAL
   INDICATORS BEARING ON MATERIAL DEPRIVATION IN AMERICA:
   GROWING DISCREPANCIES AND CONTRADICTIONS     17

4. SYSTEMATIC DIFFERENCES BETWEEN INCOME AND EXPENDITURES
   AMONG POORER HOUSEHOLDS IN MODERN AMERICA:
   A BLIND SPOT FOR THE OFFICIAL POVERTY RATE     28
      Unresolved Technical Criticisms of the Federal Poverty
      Measure   29
      Contrasting Measures of Material Standing: Income versus
      Consumption, Consumer Expenditures, and Consumer
      Outlays   33
      Income versus Expenditures for Lower-Income Americans:
      Evidence from the Consumer Expenditure Survey   36
      Do Reported Expenditures *Understate* Consumption Levels
      for Lower-Income Households?   40

The Declining Reliability of Income as a Predictor of
Household Budgets for Poverty-Level Families   *44*

5. ACCOUNTING FOR THE WIDENING REPORTED GAP BETWEEN
   INCOME AND CONSUMPTION FOR LOWER-INCOME AMERICANS   **48**
   Unsustainable "Overspending" by the Poor?   *49*
   Changes in CE Survey Methods and Practices   *57*
   Income Underreporting   *59*
   Increased Year-to-Year Income Variability   *63*
   A Continuing Puzzle   *73*

6. TRENDS IN LIVING STANDARDS FOR LOW-INCOME AMERICANS:
   INDICATIONS FROM PHYSICAL AND BIOMETRIC DATA   **76**
   The Principal Categories of Expenditures for Low-Income
   Consumers   *78*
      *Food and Nutrition*   80
      *Housing and Home Appliances*   82
      *Transportation*   86
      *Health and Medical Care*   88
   Living Standards for America's Poor: Constant Progress
   under a "Constant" Measure   *95*

CONCLUSION: WANTED—NEW POVERTY MEASURE(S) FOR MODERN
   AMERICA   **98**
   The Case against the Official Poverty Rate   *98*
   Don't "Mend" It—End It   *102*
   New Directions   *107*

APPENDIX   **111**

NOTES   **127**

BIBLIOGRAPHY   **153**

INDEX   **167**

ABOUT THE AUTHOR   **175**

# List of Illustrations

FIGURES

2-1   United States Poverty Rate, 1959–2006   *13*

2-2   No Progress for Three Decades? United States Poverty Rate, 1973–2006   *14*

3-1   Median Household Income vs. Non-Elderly Poverty Rate, 1973–2005   *19*

5-1   Median Household Net Worth, Lowest Income Quintile: Federal Reserve Board vs. United States Census Bureau, 1984–2004   *50*

5-2   Mean Value of Assets, Liabilities, and Net Worth, Lowest Income Quintile, 1989–2004   *51*

5-3   Mean Value of Assets, Liabilities, and Net Worth, Lowest Income Quintile, 65+, 1989–2004   *52*

5-4   Mean Value of Assets, Liabilities, and Net Worth, Lowest Income Quintile, Household Heads Ages 18–64, 1989–2004 *53*

5-5   Mean Value of Assets and Housing, Lowest Income Quintile, Household Heads Ages 65+, 1989–2004   *54*

5-6   Mean Value of Assets and Housing, Lowest Income Quintile, Household Heads Ages 18–64, 1989–2004   *55*

5-7   Percent of Households with No Assets, 1989–2004   *56*

5-8   Percent of Households with No Assets, Lowest Income Quintile, 1989–2004   *57*

5-9   Average Reported Annual Expenditures and Income, Lowest Income Quintile, 1984–2005   *60*

5-10  Episodic vs. Chronic Poverty: Measured Poverty for One Month vs. 48 Straight Months, 1996–99   *64*

5-11   Duration of Poverty Spells, 1996–99  *65*

5-12   Long-Term Probability of Staying in Poverty by Age, 1996–99  *65*

5-13   Total Income Variance and Transitory Income Variance, United States Families, 1969–1998  *67*

5-14   Absolute Annual Income Variability, Median Income Families, 1970–2000  *68*

5-15   Proportional Variability of Annual Income by Family Income, 1970–2000 (20th Percentile, 50th Percentile, 90th Percentile)  *70*

5-16   Mean Net Worth for All Reporting Households, First and Second Income Quintiles, 1989–2004  *72*

6-1   Percentage of Household Spending Allocated to Food by Reported Annual Income, 1960–61  *80*

6-2   Percentage of the United States Population Underweight, 1960–62 to 2001–4  *81*

6-3   Percentage of Medically Examined Low-Income Children Short of Stature or Underweight, 1973–2005  *82*

6-4   Percentage of Medically Examined Low-Income Children with Low Hemoglobin Count, 1973–2005  *83*

6-5   Age-Adjusted Mortality Rates: United States Population Ages 25–64, 1950–2004  *89*

6-6   Poverty Rates vs. Infant Mortality Rates: United States, White Children, 1959–2003  *90*

6-7   Infant Mortality vs. Low Birth Weight: United States, White Children, 1950–2004  *91*

6-8   Proportion of Adult Population with Untreated Dental Caries, 1960–62 to 1999–2002  *92*

6-9   Proportion of 65+ Population with No Remaining Natural Teeth, 1960–62 to 1999–2002  *93*

6-10   Percent of Children under 18 Years without a Reported Health Care Visit in the Past Year, by Percent of Poverty Threshold, 1982–2005  *94*

**TABLES**

3-1  Poverty Rate and Other Possible Indicators of Progress against Poverty, 1973 vs. 2001  *21*

3-2  Do United States Economic, Labor Force, and Antipoverty Policy Trends Correspond with the "Poverty Rate"? Regressions for 1973–2004  *24*

4-1  Percent of Families "Overspending" among Socio-economic Groups, Consumer Expenditure Survey  *38*

4-2  Overall Consumer Expenditure Patterns for the United States, 1960–61 vs. 2005  *40*

4-3  Consumer Expenditure Patterns for Low-Income Americans, 1960–61 to 2005  *41*

6-1  Percent Composition of Consumer Expenditures for the United States, 1960–61 vs. 2005  *79*

6-2  Percent Composition of Consumer Expenditures for Low-Income Americans, 1960–61 to 2005  *79*

6-3  Selected United States Housing Characteristics: Poor and Other Households, 1970–2001  *84*

6-4  Percent of Poor and Other United States Households with Selected Housing Appliances, 1970–2001  *86*

6-5  Motor Vehicle Patterns for Low-Income Americans, 1972–73 to 2003  *88*

**TABLES IN APPENDIX**

A-1  Simple Correlations among the Poverty Regression Variables from Table 3-2  *113*

A-2  Regressions among Variables from Table 3-2, Introducing a Time-Series Variable  *115*

A-3  Correlations of Poverty Regression Variables from Table A-2  *118*

A-4  Census Bureau Estimates of Poverty Rate According to Alternative Income Definitions  *120*

A-5  Correlations among Alternative Poverty Measures for Table A-4, 1980–2003  *122*

A-6  Do "Alternative Poverty Rates" Perform Better? Results for 70 Regression Equations for the 1980–2003 Period  *124*

# Acknowledgments

This study represents the endpoint of an inquiry I have been pursuing for more than two decades. Over such an extended outing I have naturally accumulated many debts.

First and foremost is my debt to friends and colleagues at the American Enterprise Institute—my haven and my home these past twenty-three years. This book might not have been written but for Michael Novak, who invited me aboard AEI in 1985 and then, in 1986, introduced me to the study of poverty in the United States through the memorable, and quite remarkable, Working Seminar of Family and Welfare Policy that he chaired. More recently, AEI scholars Douglas J. Besharov, Gordon Green, and Charles Murray provided generous help and valued counsel as I attempted to shape a manuscript into a book. What you see before you is much improved thanks to their wisdom and guidance. This book also owes immensely to the formidable and talented young research assistants I have been privileged to work with over the years. I fondly salute these "Team Eberstadt" all-stars. David Stetson, Lisa Howie, Heather Dresser, Courtney Meyers, Assia Dosseva, and Megan Davy will all recognize their hands in this work. Special thanks are due Megan Davy, "line officer" during the final push toward completion; her contributions were truly exemplary. (Any remaining errors or shortcomings in the work, of course, are mine and mine alone.)

Warm thanks are also in order to the dedicated specialists within the federal government who kindly took the time to review earlier drafts, or to answer arcane (and sometimes obtuse) questions about the technicalities of poverty measurement, the history of the official poverty rate, and the capacities of the U.S. statistical system for measuring various trends arguably bearing upon deprivation and poverty. In preparing this book I have benefited from the expertise of Katherine K. Wallman and Richard Bavier of the Office of Management and Budget; Daniel H. Weinberg and David S. Johnson of the Census Bureau; William D. Passero of the Bureau of Labor Statistics; Jennifer H. Madans of the National Center for Health Statistics; Stephanie Shipp of the National Institute of Standards and Technology; and Gordon M. Fisher of the Department of Health and Human Services. Let the record note that Gordon Fisher went well above and beyond the call of official duty with his meticulous tutorials on the genesis of the current federal poverty measure.

I am also happy to acknowledge the incisive comments, helpful suggestions, and constructive criticisms I received from scholars and poverty policy experts from the academy and the public policy research community. Dean Rebecca M. Blank of the Ford School of Public Policy at the University of Michigan; Professor Dale W. Jorgenson of Harvard University; Professor Bruce D. Meyer of the Harris School of Public Policy at the University of Chicago; Professor Lawrence H. Mead of New York University; Richard M. McGahey of the Ford Foundation; and Barbara Boyle Torrey of the Population Reference Bureau all enriched this study of poverty with penetrating insights. While some of these experts were by no means in sympathy with my argument or my analysis, I can truly say that I value their candid insights and our civil conversations all the more, precisely because of our differences in perspective.

This study has profited from the gracious provision of unpublished or proprietary data by Peter G. Gosselin of the *Los Angeles Times*, by Professor Jacob S. Hacker of Yale University, by John L. Czajka of Mathematica Policy Research, and by Professor Robert F. Schoeni of the University of Michigan and his colleagues. I would also be remiss if I did not mention the unflagging help I obtained from the research staff of the Georgetown University Library, whose government documents division, ably and knowledgably headed by Ms. Kristina Bobe, attended remarkably well to my wide-ranging queries and requests.

Much of the research in this book was initially presented at the Seminar on Reconsidering the Federal Poverty Measure, an undertaking jointly sponsored by AEI and the University of Maryland's Welfare Reform Academy, chaired by Douglas J. Besharov, and encouraged by the active interest of then undersecretary of commerce Kathleen B. Cooper. Further useful feedback on this work came from seminars at Princeton University's James

Madison Program and the Center for Studies in Demography and Ecology at the University of Washington.

Earlier versions of this study have been published in part by *Policy Review* and *Economic Affairs*—my thanks are due both journals for their interest.

Finally, I must thank the Bodman Foundation and Achelis Foundation for the support that helped turn my argument in these pages into a book— and to Joseph S. Dolan, executive secretary of the foundations, who made the case to me that a book on this theme would serve a public purpose.

# Introduction

For well over a century, with ever-expanding scale and scope, the United States government has been generating statistics that might illuminate the plight of society's poorest and most vulnerable members. From the beginning, the express objectives of such efforts have always been to abet purposeful action to protect the weak, better the condition of the needy, and progressively enhance the general weal.

America's official quest to describe the circumstances of the disadvantaged in quantitative terms began in the 1870s and '80s, with the initial efforts of the Massachusetts Bureau of Statistics of Labor and the U.S. Bureau of Labor Statistics to compile systematic information on cost of living, wages, and employment conditions for urban working households in the United States.[1] Statistical capabilities for describing the material well-being of the nation's population through numbers have developed immensely since then.

Today the United States government regularly compiles an array of hundreds upon hundreds of social and economic indicators that bear on poverty or progress on the domestic scene. Within that now vast compendium, however, a single official number on the magnitude of deprivation and need in modern America is unquestionably more important than any of the others, and has been so regarded for the past four decades. This is the federal "poverty rate."

First unveiled in early 1965, shortly after the launch of the Johnson administration's "War on Poverty," the poverty rate is a measure identifying the proportion of families with incomes falling below a "poverty threshold"— a level based on family size and composition, and subsequently set to be fixed and unchanging over time. Almost immediately upon its invention, this calculated poverty rate was accorded a special significance in the national conversation on the U.S. poverty situation and in policymakers' response to the problem.

In May 1965, just months after the debut of this new statistical measure, the War on Poverty's new Office of Economic Opportunity (OEO) designated the measure as its unofficial working definition of poverty. By August 1969, the Bureau of the Budget (the forerunner of today's Office of Management and Budget) had stipulated that the thresholds used in calculating American poverty rates would constitute the federal government's official statistical definition for poverty. The standard has remained so ever since.[2]

The authority and credibility enjoyed by the official poverty rate (or OPR) as an especially telling indicator of American domestic want are revealed in its unique official treatment. The OPR is regularly calculated not only for the country as a whole, but for every locality down to the level of the school district.[3] (It is even available at the level of "census tracts"—enumerative designations that demarcate the nation into subdivisions of as few as one thousand residents.)

Furthermore, U.S. government antipoverty spending has come to be calibrated against, and made contingent upon, this particular measure. Everywhere in America today, eligibility for means-tested public benefits depends on the relationship between a household's income and the apposite "poverty threshold." In fiscal year 2002, by one estimate, over $300 billion in public funds were allocated in accordance with the criterion of "poverty guidelines," the version of poverty thresholds used by the Department of Health and Human Services.[4] Many billions of dollars of additional public spending not directly earmarked for antipoverty programs are currently also contingent upon the OPR, which may, for example, serve as a component in the complex formulas through which "Community Development Block Grants" (formerly referred to as "revenue-sharing" programs) dispense funds to local communities.

No estimate for the total volume of annual government outlays allocated with reference to the "poverty rate" appears to be currently available from any official U.S. source.[5] A recent study by the Congressional Research Service, however, indicates that in fiscal year 2004 (the latest period for which such figures are readily available), no less than $380 billion in official expenditures at the federal, state, and local levels were distributed through mechanisms wherein the federal poverty measure came into play as a criterion for disbursement.[6]

Given its unparalleled importance—both as a touchstone for informed public discussion and a direct instrument for public policy—the reliability of the OPR as an indicator of material deprivation is a critical consideration. How accurately—and consistently—does the OPR reflect changing patterns of hardship in modern America, or changes in the living standards of the poor population? How faithfully, in other words, does our nation's OPR describe trends in the condition that most Americans would think of as "poverty"?

The disturbing, but incontrovertible, answer to these questions is: The official poverty rate appears to be inconstant, deeply flawed, and increasingly biased. Our country's official measure of poverty looks to be a very poor measure indeed.

## Why This Book

In the following pages we will be examining the official poverty rate and its performance as a poverty indicator. This is by no means the first foray into this territory. To the contrary, the OPR has already been examined, and critiqued, extensively. A tremendous amount has been written over the years about the federal poverty measure, and enough exacting and highly technical analysis has been conducted to fill a small library.[7]

As it happens, however, most of these works have concerned themselves with the possibility of *revising* the official poverty rate. Some propose updating or overhauling poverty thresholds in accordance with changing standards of living, for example, or replacing the index's existing metric of "income" with a broader and more comprehensive measure (that is, annually reported income excluding noncash benefits, returns imputed from home ownership, and so on). Others recommend revamping this index in accordance with purportedly more realistic household or consumer "equivalence scales" (metrics to adjust for differences in budgetary requirements according to household size or composition).[8] By contrast, this study focuses on the much more limited objective of merely *evaluating* the official poverty rate—of examining the reliability of the OPR as an unbiased, long-term indicator of want in modern America. Perhaps surprisingly, the more mundane question of just how this statistical indicator actually fares in discharging the specific task assigned to it has, to date, attracted strangely little attention.[9] Here we will attempt to remedy this curious oversight.

Our official poverty rate is now by and large taken for granted, having become widely regarded with the passage of time as a "natural" method for calibrating the prevalence of material deprivation in American society. It is necessary to remember, however, that the measure itself was originally an ad hoc improvisation—and, arguably, a fairly idiosyncratic one. Although the OPR has been in use for fully four decades, and although considerable poverty research has been undertaken in that interim by official statistical agencies throughout the rest of the world, no other contemporary government or international institution has elected to calculate its own domestic poverty rate by the sorts of techniques the U.S. government uses.

In practical terms, the OPR appears to be a problematic descriptor of poverty trends and levels. For one thing, its reported results do not track well with other indicators that would ordinarily be expected to bear directly on living conditions across the nation. In fact, over the past three decades, relationships between the OPR and these other indicators have been perversely discordant.

While the OPR suggests that the proportion of the American population living below a fixed poverty line has stagnated—or increased—in this period, data on U.S. expenditure patterns document a substantial and continuing increase in consumption levels for the entire country, including the strata with the lowest reported income levels. And while the poverty threshold was devised to measure a fixed and unchanging degree of material deprivation (that is, an "absolute" level of poverty) over time, an abundance of data on the actual living conditions of low-income families and "poverty households" contradicts that key presumption, demonstrating instead that the material circumstances of persons officially defined as "poor" have improved broadly and appreciably over the past four decades.

In short, America's most relied-upon metric for charting a course in our national effort to reduce and, ultimately, eliminate poverty appears to offer unreliable—and, indeed, increasingly misleading—soundings on where we are today, where we have come from, and where we might be headed.

At this point, we might as well state the obvious: This study will make the case that the official poverty rate is incapable of accurately representing long-term trends for material want in modern America. It will also attempt to demonstrate that standards of living for the official poverty population are far higher today than they were in 1964 or 1965, at the start of the War on Poverty. But these findings obviously do not mean—nor should they be taken to suggest—that all is well for America's poorest and most vulnerable citizens today. They do not herald a final "mission accomplished" celebration for our long national struggle to improve the weal of our country's poorest members, nor are they intended to suggest that, either.

There is a motive for this study, however, and we might as well declare it here. The unavoidable fact is that the official yardstick that informs and guides our antipoverty efforts is broken. We desperately need a better replacement for it—not least for the sake of our continuing quest to form a more perfect union.

## A Road Map for This Study

A brief road map of what lies ahead for the reader: In chapter 1, we will describe the genesis of the official poverty rate, explain how it is constructed, and examine exactly what it is intended to measure. Chapter 2 will review the poverty trends in the United States for the period since 1959, the era for which official poverty rates have been calculated. Chapter 3 will look at the correspondence between the OPR and other macroeconomic indicators bearing on material deprivation in modern America, focusing especially on the decades since 1973 (the long period during which the incidence of poverty in the United States has been worsening, according to the OPR). Following a discussion in chapter 4 of the growing divergence between reported income levels (the benchmark for OPR calculations) and reported expenditure levels for American households at the lower end of the income spectrum, chapter 5 will attempt to explain this major and portentous discrepancy. As devised, the official poverty rate presumes to measure a fixed and unchanging living standard over time; chapter 6 presents evidence on actual trends in "poverty-level" living standards over the past four decades. The conclusion offers a recapitulation of the findings of this study and some suggestions for improving our nation's measurement of material deprivation in the future.

# 1

# What Is the Official Poverty Rate, and What Does It Actually Measure?

The current conception of the U.S. federal poverty measure was introduced to the American public in January 1965 in a landmark study authored by Mollie Orshanky, an economist and statistician at the U.S. Social Security Administration.[1] President Lyndon B. Johnson had announced a "War on Poverty" in his January 1964 State of the Union address—but, as one history of American poverty research has noted, "There was no official definition of poverty when [he] made [t]his declaration of war."[2]

The same month as that presidential declaration, the President's Council of Economic Advisers (CEA) had presented an analysis of "The Problem of Poverty in America" that offered a benchmark of $3,000 in annual income for determining whether a family was in need; but this was a crude, and highly imprecise, measure.[3] As Orshansky later observed, "This original [CEA] standard led to the odd result that an elderly couple with $2,900 income for the year would be considered poor, but a family with a husband, wife and 4 little children with $3,100 income would not be."[4] Orshansky's own method for measuring poverty promised results that would be more nuanced, discriminating, and commonsensical.

Drawing upon her own earlier work, in which she had experimented with household income thresholds for distinguishing American children living in impoverished conditions,[5] Orshansky's 1965 study proposed a countrywide set of annual income criteria for identifying families and unrelated individuals in poverty based upon money income requirements set "essentially on the amount of income remaining after allowance for an adequate diet at minimum cost."[6]

6

As devised, Orshansky's poverty thresholds were established as scalar multiples of the annual cost of a nutritionally adequate—but humble—household diet. For the base food budget, Orshansky used the U.S. Department of Agriculture (USDA) Economy Food Plan (the predecessor of today's USDA Thrifty Food Plan)—the lower of two such budgets prepared by the USDA for nonfarm families of modest means and specifically issued "for temporary or emergency use when funds are low."[7]

The selection of a particular poverty-level food budget immediately begged the question of the appropriate multiplier for an overall poverty line for total annual income for the officially poor. The specific factor to choose for a multiplier was by no means obvious. While the cost of the Economy Food Plan could be justified in terms of sheer empirical exigency—people must eat to survive, and food costs money—the choice of a food budget multiplier was a much more subjective affair.

From the pioneering work of the German statistician Ernst Engel in the 1850s onward, a century of household budget studies around the world had demonstrated that food did *not* account for a fixed percentage of household expenditures. Rather, the share of food in total spending steadily and predictably declined as household income levels increased. In impoverished low-income countries, 60 percent or more of the household budget was allocated to food, while a much smaller fraction of total income went to food in the richest countries in the postwar era.[8] What was the correct proportion to use in constructing an official poverty threshold?

In the event, Orshansky used a multiplier of roughly three to calculate poverty thresholds from the costs of the food plan. While readily noting that her proposed multiplier was normative,[9] Orshansky also argued that her coefficient had a solid grounding and, indeed, reflected the norms in U.S. contemporary living standards. A USDA national food consumption survey, conducted in the United States for the spring of 1955 (the most recent such survey available at the time of Orshansky's study), had indicated that nonfarm families of two or more were devoting an average of roughly one-third of their after-tax money incomes to food. Orshansky seized upon this three-to-one relationship for the general guideline for the OPR she computed, and, accordingly, established her poverty thresholds as a multiplicative product of, on the one hand, a nutritionally adequate (but stringent) food budget otherwise suggestive of poverty conditions and, on the other, the then-prevailing ratio of total food costs to total after-tax money income for "Main Street" Americans.

But not all civilian noninstitutional households were accorded a poverty threshold of exactly three times their corresponding Economy Food Plan budgets. Orshansky tailored these thresholds further to take into account variations in family size and the presumed impact of these demographic factors on the "Engel coefficient" (the proportion of family income spent on food). Poor families of two persons, for example, were posited to allocate a higher share of their income to nonfood costs than three-person families, and unrelated individuals were implicitly presumed to require an even higher share of their incomes for nonfood expenses than two-person families.[10] Thus, poverty thresholds for two-person families were set at 3.7 times their corresponding food costs from the Economy Food Plan, and the poverty threshold for unrelated individuals at approximately 5.3 times.

The USDA Economy Food Plan offered separate budgets for nineteen types of family configurations. For her part, Orshansky created poverty thresholds for sixty-two separate types of nonfarm homes—fifty-eight varieties for different sorts of families, and an additional four for persons living alone (differentiated by age and gender). She also estimated the sixty-two corresponding poverty thresholds for the U.S. farm population, for a nationwide total of one hundred twenty-four poverty thresholds.

In devising what she described as a "matrix" of poverty thresholds, Orshansky also, perforce, developed an "equivalence scale" for American families of varying size and composition (albeit implicitly). In addition to USDA Economy Food Plan budgets, Orshansky drew upon U.S. Bureau of Labor Statistics (BLS) expenditure surveys and 1960 census returns from the U.S. Census Bureau as background "reality checks" for her calculations. In effect, she accepted USDA budgets for estimated minimal food needs in diverse family structures and then adjusted these in accordance with Engel coefficients actually observed in contemporary America—in accordance with her own judgments about the role that economies of scale—or sheer deprivation—had played in influencing observed outcomes.

Using these newly calculated poverty thresholds (all initially benchmarked against the January 1964 USDA Economy Food Plan), Orshansky calculated the total population below the poverty line for the United States as a whole and for regional and demographic subgroups within the country for calendar year 1963, relying upon Census Bureau data on pretax money income for that same year to determine whether or not a family and its residents were living below the poverty line. The statistical distinction between pretax income—the figures used in practice for determining whether a family fell below the poverty threshold—and after-tax money income—the theoretical criterion against which those same poverty thresholds had originally been constructed—was finessed through a presumption that the poor would not be paying out much, or anything, in taxes.[11]

Although Orshansky's study did not actually use the term "poverty rate"—talking instead about the "incidence of poverty"—the poverty rate quickly came to mean the proportion of persons or families below the poverty line in the apposite reference group, and has been understood so ever since.

The schema and framework for estimating official poverty rates in the United States today are basically the same as in 1965. Annual OPRs are still determined on the basis of poverty thresholds maintained and updated by the U.S. Census Bureau (currently calculated for "only" forty-eight family subtypes), and official poverty status is still contingent upon whether a family's measured annual pretax money income exceeds or falls below that stipulated threshold. While a number of minor revisions have been introduced (such as the elimination of Orshansky's farm/nonfarm differentials and her differentials between male- and female-headed families), the original Orshansky approach of computing poverty rates on the basis of poverty thresholds and annual income levels of families or unrelated individuals remains entirely intact.

The most significant change to the original poverty thresholds is their annual upward adjustment to compensate for changes in general price levels. In 1969, the Bureau of the Budget directed that the poverty line would thenceforth be pegged against the Consumer Price Index (CPI), and ruled that the CPI deflator would also be used to establish official poverty thresholds back to 1963, the base year for Orshansky's original study. (CPI-scaled adjustments were subsequently utilized to calculate poverty thresholds, and thus OPRs, as far back as 1959.)

To this writing, official U.S. poverty thresholds continue to be annually updated in accordance with changes in the CPI[12]—and with CPI changes alone. Implicit in this decision is the important presumption that America's

OPR should be a measure of *absolute poverty* rather than *relative poverty*. Whereas a relative measure might take some account of general improvements in living standards in assessing "material deprivation," the determination to hold poverty thresholds constant over time, adjusting only for inflation, is to insist upon an absolute conception of poverty—a standard of deprivation held as constant over time as the "index problem" will permit.

In her seminal 1965 study, Orshansky acknowledged that her measure of poverty was arbitrary, although she also vigorously defended it as "admittedly arbitrary, but not unreasonable."[13] Though she did not dwell on the point, a considerable amount of this apparent arbitrariness was conditioned by the imperative of fashioning a serviceable and regularly "update-able" index from the limited data sources then readily at hand.

Whatever the intellectual merits of representing material deprivation in terms of a nationwide standard based on annual reported pretax money incomes—a practice to which a variety of objections could be drawn from basic tenets in microeconomics[14]—the singular virtue of such a poverty indicator was that the Census Bureau was already producing detailed and continuous data of just this sort through its P-60 (that is, "Consumer Income") series of *Current Population Reports*.[15] As Orshansky would later explain of her own poverty measure, "The index is arbitrary in that it relies only on income as the criterion of poverty, but income statistics happen to be the only ones available on a regular basis . . . We have no choice but to base [our index] on whatever kind of statistics are available."[16]

By the same token, Orshansky's poverty thresholds were open to criticism on a number of conceptual and empirical grounds, as she herself recognized; but those constructs also happened to represent concoctions—arguably quite insightful and ingenious ones—based upon the somewhat haphazard ingredients then at hand in the statistical larders of the USDA, the Census Bureau, and the BLS.

The OPR is the single longest-standing official index for assessing deprivation and material need in any contemporary country. That fact alone makes it unique. But America's OPR is also unique in another sense: Although a multitude of governments and international institutions have pursued quantitative efforts in poverty research over the past two decades and have even fashioned particular national and international poverty indices, *none* has elected to replicate the Orshansky approach to "counting the poor."[17] While this curious fact is not often remarked upon by U.S. statistical authorities, it is worth not only bearing in mind, but also pondering, as one evaluates the OPR and its long-term performance.

# 2

# Poverty Trends in Modern America, According to the Official Poverty Rate

Estimates of the official poverty rate for the United States are available from the year 1959 onward—a time series of forty-eight years at this writing. The long-term trends from this index are shown in figure 2-1. For the total population of the United States, the OPR declined by nearly half over this period, from 22.4 percent in 1959 to 12.3 percent in 2006, and the OPR for U.S. families dropped by roughly similar proportions, from 20.8 percent to 9.8 percent. Measured progress against poverty was more pronounced for older Americans (the OPR for persons sixty-five years of age and older fell from 35.2 percent to 9.4 percent), but more limited for children under eighteen (27.3 percent versus 17.4 percent). For African Americans, the OPR declined by almost three-fifths—by over thirty percentage points—between 1959 and 2006; but in 2006 it remained still over twice as high as the rate for whites.

America's recent immigration experience can also be viewed through the lens of the official poverty rate. On average, the rate for the foreign-born tends to be higher than that for native-born Americans (15.2 percent versus 11.9 percent in 2006, for example), and for undocumented immigrants, it is presumably higher still. The large influx of new immigrants after the changes in U.S. immigration laws in 1965 has thus, perforce, meant that an increasing fraction of the officially poor in America are foreign-born. According to the official numbers, just under a sixth of America's poor were foreign-born in 2006, and the foreign-born, who were estimated to account for about a thirteenth of America's noninstitutionalized population, reportedly comprised just under an eighth of the poor population.[1]

One particularly noteworthy feature of the trends in figure 2-1 is that most of the reported reduction in overall U.S. poverty rates occurred at the very

FIGURE 2-1
UNITED STATES POVERTY RATE, 1959–2006

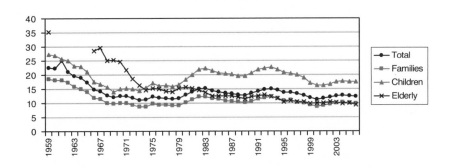

SOURCES: U.S. Bureau of the Census, "Poverty Status of People by Family Relationship, Race, and Hispanic Origin: 1959 to 2006," *Historical Poverty Tables*, table 2, http://www.census.gov/hhes/www/poverty/histpov/hstpov2.html (accessed August 29, 2007); U.S. Bureau of the Census, "Poverty Status of People, by Age, Race, and Hispanic Origin: 1959 to 2006," *Historical Poverty Tables*, table 3, http://www.census.gov/hhes/www/histpov/hstpov3.html (accessed August 29, 2007); U.S. Bureau of the Census, "Poverty Status of Families, by Type of Family, Presence of Related Children, Race, and Hispanic Origin: 1959 to 2006," *Historical Poverty Tables*, table 4, http://www.census.gov/hhes/www/poverty/histpov/hstpov4.html (accessed August 29, 2007).

beginning of the series—that is to say, during the first decade for which numbers are available. Between 1959 and 1968, the poverty rate for the total population of the United States fell from 22.4 percent to 12.8 percent, or by more than a percentage point per year. In 2006, by contrast, the OPR was lower than it had been in 1968, but just barely, and it was actually ever so slightly higher than it had been back in 1969.

Indeed, to judge by the OPR, the United States has suffered more than a generation of stagnation—or even retrogression—in its quest to reduce poverty. Figure 2-2 illustrates the situation. For the entire U.S. population, the lowest OPR yet recorded was for the year 1973, when the index bottomed out at 11.1 percent. Over the subsequent three decades, the OPR nationwide remained steadily above 11.1 percent, often substantially. In 2006, the rate reported was 12.3 percent.

This long-term rise in the official poverty rate for the United States as a whole was not a statistical artifact—not, in any event, an arithmetic consequence of averaging in some particularly grim trends for some smaller

FIGURE 2-2

NO PROGRESS FOR THREE DECADES? UNITED STATES POVERTY RATE,
1973–2006

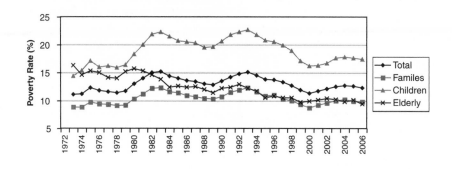

SOURCES: U.S. Bureau of the Census, "Poverty Status of People by Family Relationship, Race, and Hispanic Origin: 1959 to 2006," *Historical Poverty Tables*, table 2, http://www.census.gov/hhes/www/
poverty/histpov/hstpov2.html (accessed August 29, 2007); U.S. Bureau of the Census, "Poverty Status
of People, by Age, Race, and Hispanic Origin: 1959 to 2006," *Historical Poverty Tables*, table 3,
http://www.census.gov/hhes/www/poverty/histpov/hstpov3.html (accessed August 29, 2007); U.S.
Bureau of the Census, "Poverty Status of Families, by Type of Family, Presence of Related Children, Race,
and Hispanic Origin: 1959 to 2006," *Historical Poverty Tables*, table 4, http://www.census.gov/
hhes/www/poverty/histpov/hstpov4.html (accessed August 29, 2007).

subpopulations within the nation. To the contrary, long-term increases in
OPRs were characteristic for the overwhelming majority of U.S. demographic
groups during the period in question. Between 1973 and 2006, the official
poverty rate did decline for older Americans as a whole (16.3 percent versus
9.4 percent), and for persons living alone (25.6 percent versus 20.0 percent);
it also declined for African Americans overall (31.4 percent in 1973 versus
24.3 percent in 2006).

But for the rest of the country, the official poverty rate was, in general,
higher at the start of the new century than it had been in the early 1970s.
Measured poverty rates, for example, were higher in 2006 than they had
been in 1973 for both children under eighteen (14.4 percent in 1973 versus 17.4 percent in 2006) and people of working age—that is, eighteen to
sixty-four (8.3 percent versus 10.8 percent). The nationwide OPR for families likewise rose over those years (from 8.8 percent to 9.8 percent). Except
for the South, where the OPR registered a slight decline (15.3 percent versus 13.8 percent), poverty rates were higher in every region of the country

in 2006 than in 1973. Overall poverty rates for non-Hispanic whites—
so-called "Anglos"—were also higher than they had been in 1973 (8.2 percent versus 7.5 percent). No less strikingly, the overall poverty rate for Hispanic Americans was scarcely lower in 2006 than in 1973 (20.6 percent
versus 21.9 percent), implying that the circumstances of this diverse but
often socially disadvantaged ethnic minority had improved hardly at all
over the course of over three decades.[2]

Taken at face value, these stark numbers would seem to be a cause for
dismay, if not outright alarm. To go by the OPR, modern America has failed
stunningly to lift the more vulnerable elements of society out of deprivation—
out from below the income line where, according to the author of the federal poverty measure, "everyday living implied choosing between an
adequate diet of the most economical sort and some other necessity because
there was not money enough to have both."[3]

This statistical portrait of an apparent long-term rise in absolute poverty
in the contemporary United States evokes the specter of profound economic, social, and political dysfunction in a highly affluent capitalist
democracy. All the more troubling is the near-total failure of social policy
implied by such numbers. Despite the War on Poverty and all subsequent
governmental antipoverty initiatives, official poverty rates for the nation
have mainly moved in the wrong direction over the past three decades.

If these numbers cast a disturbing and unfamiliar picture of their country for American citizens and policymakers, it is worth remembering that
they would be regarded as utterly unsurprising by many of the most con-
vinced critics of the American system, who would regard such results as
exactly what they would expect. The apparent paradox of steady economic
growth and persistent or increasing poverty, for example, conforms rather
well with some of the Marxian and neo-Marxist critiques of industrial and
global capitalism, which accused such systems of inherently generating
"immiserating growth."[4] Among non-Marxists, these contours of the U.S.
tableau are viewed today as affirming the critique of what is known inter-
nationally as "neoliberal reform," and providing powerful particulars for
vigorously rejecting the "American model."[5]

But, as we shall demonstrate in the following chapters, the social and
economic portrait afforded by America's official poverty statistics is woefully
distorted—almost bizarrely miscast. In reality, the prevalence of absolute

deprivation in the United States has declined dramatically over the decades since the debut of the official poverty rate. In reality, the purchasing power of lower-income households is far higher today than it was in the 1960s or '70s. In reality, the standard of living of the poverty population itself has improved manifestly, decade by decade, since the federal poverty measure was first introduced. The problem is, the statistical measure our democracy has devised for charting our national performance against poverty does not register these basic realities—and worse, cannot even recognize them.

# 3

# The Official Poverty Rate versus Other Statistical Indicators Bearing on Material Deprivation in America: Growing Discrepancies and Contradictions

Although the official poverty rate is currently accorded a special status (in both practice and in law) as an indicator of poverty conditions in modern America, it is by no means the only statistical measure that casts light on poverty and material deprivation in the country. To the contrary, quite a few other official statistical indices bearing upon poverty and want are readily available today. Perhaps the most important of these are macroeconomic and/or demographic in nature; they include the nation's per-capita income level, the civilian unemployment rate, and the country's educational profile, to name but a few. By and large, these other data series share three characteristics: They predate the OPR by many decades; their meaning is conceptually clear and self-evident; and their basic accuracy and reliability are not a matter of serious question.

All other things being equal, one would expect the OPR to track, at least in broad terms, with the trends revealed by the major macroeconomic indicators (and the other major statistical indicators) bearing on poverty in America. It would certainly be reasonable to presume that the government's preferred index for assessing the scope and distribution of domestic poverty should correspond with information provided by other prospective indicators of material need. As it happens, a great many students of the poverty problem seem to be under the impression that the OPR reflects—and perhaps refines—information that is found in other major statistical indicators on

social and economic conditions in our country. As we will see in the following pages, however, any such impression is fundamentally mistaken.

When we compare trends in the official poverty rate and other statistical
indicators bearing upon want and deprivation in modern America, two striking and peculiar findings immediately jump out. First, the official poverty rate
today does not at all exhibit what one might describe as a "normal and cus-
tomary relationship" with any of the other important macroeconomic or
demographic "poverty proxies" one would ordinarily wish to examine; to the
contrary, against the backdrop of those other indicators, the soundings from
the OPR often appear erratic, if not positively perverse. As our analysis will
attest, nothing like a "normal" relationship exists today between the OPR and
what should ordinarily be the main drivers of poverty reduction: economic
growth; employment; education; anti-poverty spending.

Second, the mismatch between reported trends for the official poverty
rate and practically all the other indicators bearing on poverty and want has
been especially pronounced since 1973—the very decades for which the
OPR has been reporting that the prevalence of poverty in the United States
has been stagnating, or actually increasing.

Specialists on the poverty question commonly presume that the official
poverty rate is strongly influenced by the state of the U.S. economy (that is to
say, by macroeconomic conditions). This is not only a commonsensical prem-
ise; it is a notion confirmed in the past by empirical research. In a series of
influential publications in the mid-1980s, for example, Harvard economists
David Ellwood and Lawrence Summers argued that changes in the official
poverty rate were mainly determined by "general economic developments."
In "reviewing trends in poverty, poverty spending, and economic performance," they argued, ". . . it is immediately apparent that economic performance is the dominant determinant of the measured poverty rate over the past
two decades."[1] Presenting a persuasive graphic that compared changes in the
poverty rate and changes in median family income over time, Ellwood and
Summers explained in words what the trend lines demonstrated visually:
*"Almost all of the variation in the measured poverty rate is tracked by movements
in median family income"* [emphasis in the original].[2]

Ellwood and Summers accurately described the correspondence
between trends in the official poverty rate and real median family income—
*at the time of their writing.* But that work was published over two decades

FIGURE 3-1

MEDIAN HOUSEHOLD INCOME VS. NON-ELDERLY POVERTY RATE, 1973–2005

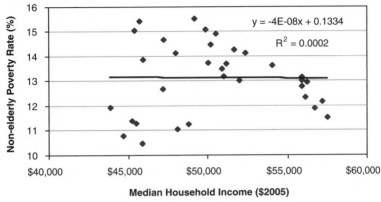

SOURCES: U.S. Bureau of the Census, "Poverty Status of People, by Age, Race, and Hispanic Origin: 1959 to 2006," Historical Poverty Tables, table 3, http://www.census.gov/hhes/www/poverty/histpov/ hstpov3.html (accessed August 29, 2007); U.S. Bureau of the Census, "Race and Hispanic Origin of Householder—Households by Median and Mean Income: 1967 to 2006," Historical Income Tables—Households, table H-5, http://www.census.gov/hhes/www/income/histinc/h05.html (accessed March 17, 2008).

ago. The time series data they were examining only ran from 1959 through the year 1983. Moreover, even back then they found it worth mentioning that "one does see a slight divergence of the trends in the eighties."[3] By now, that "divergence" amounts to a virtually complete disconnection.

Indeed, over the decades the correspondence between the official poverty rate and median family income appears to have broken down altogether. We can see this by comparing trends since 1973 for the official poverty rate of the nonelderly population, on the one hand, and real median family income, on the other, as shown in figure 3-1. These are the same variables for which Ellwood and Summers found such a powerful association over the years 1959–83. For the period 1973–2005, there is no discernable relationship whatever between the measured poverty rate and median family income. In fact, over the past three-plus decades, the "correlation coefficient" for these two trends has been approximately zero. In other words, over the past generation, data on the median income for American families have basically provided no clue about the numbers that would be registered for the official poverty rate.[4]

If the true prevalence of poverty in the United States is indeed affected by "general economic developments"—as it is commonly taken to be—then this uncoupling of the official poverty rate and the median family income, their pronounced and dramatic transition to a new relationship characterized by utter randomness, should in itself raise serious questions about the reliability of the country's primary poverty index. But this is hardly the worst of it. A quick review will confirm that the OPR has, for the period since 1973, severed what might be regarded as a commonsensical relationship with all of the other major statistical indices bearing on poverty and deprivation in contemporary America. Even worse: For the period since 1973, the behavior of the official poverty rate looks increasingly aberrant and perverse, registering retrogression when the other indices commonly record progress.

Table 3-1 illustrates the problem. It contrasts results for the years 1973 and 2001 for the OPR with several other indicators widely recognized as bearing directly upon the risk of poverty in any modern urbanized society. (The choice of these two specific end-years is admittedly and deliberately selective, but it is a selection that highlights the underlying contradictions discussed below.)

Consider the "general economic developments" that characterized the United States in the nearly three decades between 1973 and 2001, as shown by four indicators: per-capita income, unemployment, educational attainment, and official "antipoverty" outlays.

From 1973 to 2001, per-capita income in the United States rose very significantly in real (inflation-adjusted) terms—by roughly 60 percent, according to estimates from the Census Bureau's Current Population Survey (CPS) series. Other official U.S. data suggest the gains over those years may have been even more substantial. The National Income and Product Accounts from the Bureau of Economic Analysis (BEA), for example, estimate an increase in per-capita output of about 67 percent for 1973–2001.[5]

By the same token, the measured rate of unemployment for persons ages sixteen and over was somewhat lower in 2001 (4.7 percent) than it had been in 1973 (4.9 percent). Alternative measures of the availability of remunerative employment also indicate that a higher fraction of the American population was gainfully occupied in 2001 than in 1973. Labor force participation rates for those sixteen and older, for instance, were over six

TABLE 3-1

POVERTY RATE AND OTHER POSSIBLE INDICATORS OF PROGRESS
AGAINST POVERTY, 1973 VS. 2001

| Year | Poverty rate (%) | Unemploy- ment rate (%) | Per capita income (2004 U.S. $) | Adults 25 and over with a high school degree (%) | Total nonmedical means-tested government spending (million 2004 U.S. $) |
|------|------|------|------|------|------|
| 1973 | 11.1 | 4.9 | 15,250 | 59.8 | 136,992 |
| 2001 | 11.7 | 4.7 | 24,384 | 84.1 | 241,489 |

SOURCES: U.S. Bureau of the Census, "Poverty Status of People by Family Relationship, Race, and His-panic Origin: 1959 to 2006," *Historical Poverty Tables*, table 2, http://www.census.gov/hhes/www/poverty/histpov/hstpov2.html (accessed August 29, 2007); U.S. Bureau of the Census, "CPS Popula-tion and Per Capita Money Income, All Races: 1967 to 2004," *Historical Income Tables—People*, table P-1, http://www.census.gov/hhes/www/income/histinc/p01ar.html (accessed August 31, 2006); U.S. Department of Labor, Bureau of Labor Statistics, "Unemployment Rate—Civilian Labor Force," Labor Force Statistics from the Current Population Survey, http://www.bls.gov/data/home.htm (accessed September 21, 2006); U.S. Bureau of the Census, "Percent of People 25 Years and Over Who Have Completed High School or College, by Race, Hispanic Origin and Sex: Selected Years 1940 to 2006," *Historical Tables: Current Population Survey*, table A-2, http://www.census.gov/population/www/socdemo/educ-attn.html (accessed September 21, 2006); Congressional Research Service, "Cash and Noncash Benefits for Persons with Limited Income: Eligibility Rules, Recipient and Expenditure Data, FY2002–FY2004," CRS Report RL33340, March 27, 2006.

percentage points higher in 2001 (66.9 percent) than they had been in 1973 (60.5 percent), and the employment-to-population ratio for the sixteen-plus group was almost seven points higher in 2001 (63.7 percent) than in 1973 (56.9 percent).[6]

In terms of educational attainment, America's working-age adults clearly had completed more years of schooling in 2001 than in 1973. In 1973, about 40 percent of adults twenty-five or older had no high school degree; by 2001, the corresponding fraction was under 16 percent. Among youth and young adults, the profile for access to schooling also improved between 1973 and 2001, if less dramatically; whereas the ratio of net enroll-ment in high school for children fourteen to seventeen years of age had been 91.0 percent in 1973, it was a projected 94.8 percent for 2001.[7]

Finally, we can also consider the trends in spending by government at the federal, state, and local levels on means-tested benefit programs—that is to say, public antipoverty outlays. Between fiscal years 1973 and 2001, real spending on such programs more than tripled, leaping from $163 billion to $507 billion (in 2004 dollars), or by over 130 percent on a per–capita, inflation-adjusted basis. One can make arguments for excluding the medical and health-care component from the measure of antipoverty program spending; even so, nonhealth antipoverty spending would still rise in constant 2004 terms, from $116 billion in 1973 to $241 billion in 2001, or by about 55 percent per capita.[8]

These outlay data, one must emphasize, account for just the government's share of antipoverty monies; private charitable donations provide additional resources for meeting the needs of America's poor, and these resources are considerable. In the year 2001, total private philanthropic giving was estimated at $239 billion—in real terms, 156 percent more than in 1973 and, in real per-capita terms, an increase of over 90 percent.[9] Although we cannot know the exact proportion of these private funds earmarked for alleviating poverty, it seems safe to say that antipoverty spending by both the public and private sectors increased very significantly on a real per-capita basis between 1973 and 2001.

As it was constructed, the OPR was meant to measure only pretax money incomes; in-kind benefits, such as food or housing, would be excluded from this calculus automatically, and by design. Given the prevailing perceptions that cash aid accounts for only a small fraction of U.S. antipoverty spending—and the common belief that means-tested cash aid has been substantially reduced in the United States since the "welfare reform" laws of 1996—one might assume that antipoverty spending ought not have too much of an influence on long-term trends in the official poverty rate. Yet cash transfers through official antipoverty policies are by no means trivial today, nor has the rise over the past three decades in such spending been insignificant. In 2001, cash aid and credit programs provided by federal and state governments for the poor dispensed over $100 billion—78 percent more in real terms than in 1973, and 32 percent more on a real per-capita basis.[10] If we were to factor in private-sector cash aid, the total for antipoverty transfers for 2001 would be that much higher.

Per-capita income, unemployment, educational attainment, and antipoverty spending are all factors we would expect to exert an independent and important influence on the prevalence of poverty in a modern industrialized society—in *any* modern industrialized society. When trends for all four of these measures move conjointly in the direction favoring poverty reduction, we would, as a matter of course, strongly expect that the prevalence of measured poverty should decline as well (that is, so long as poverty were being measured against an absolute rather than a relative benchmark). Yet, curiously and most improbably, the official poverty rate for the U.S. population was actually reported to be *higher* for 2001 (11.7 percent) than for 1973 (11.1 percent).

Needless to say, such a discordant and counterintuitive result demands explanation. Further examination, unfortunately, reveals that the paradoxical relationship between the poverty rate and these other indicators of material deprivation highlighted in table 3-1, while perverse, is not at all anomalous. To the contrary: For the period since 1973, the U.S. poverty rate has ceased to correspond with these other broad measures of poverty and progress in any regular and commonsense fashion. Instead, the poverty rate seems to have become possessed of a strange but deeply structural capriciousness, for while it continues (in a technical, statistical sense) to maintain a predictable relationship with the other indicators, the relationship is by and large precisely the opposite of what one would normally expect.

Table 3-2 illustrates the curious behavior of the OPR in relation to these four other important measures as revealed by simple econometrics, using "regression equations" in which these other measures are utilized in an attempt to "predict" the poverty rate for a period of thirty-one years (1973–2004).

Under any ordinary circumstances, we would expect unemployment and poverty to be positively associated (the higher the unemployment level, the higher the poverty level), while per-capita income, educational attainment, and antipoverty spending should all correlate negatively with any absolute measure of poverty. Such expectations, however, are sharply confuted by our calculated results.

Consider, to begin with, the table's "equation 1," which attempts to track the official poverty rate against per-capita income and per-capita antipoverty spending. All other things being equal, we would expect a strong association here, with increased incomes and higher antipoverty spending both pressing the true prevalence of poverty downward. Yet equation 1 discerns no systematic relationship whatever between the OPR and these two quantities. Even taken together, per-capita income and per-capita

TABLE 3-2

## DO UNITED STATES ECONOMIC, LABOR FORCE, AND ANTIPOVERTY POLICY TRENDS CORRESPOND WITH THE "POVERTY RATE"? REGRESSIONS FOR 1973–2004

|  | Equation 1 | Equation 2 | Equation 3 | Equation 4 | Equation 5 |
|---|---|---|---|---|---|
| N | 31 | 31 | 31 | 31 | 31 |
| Adjusted RSq. | −0.04 | 0.51 | 0.51 | 0.71 | 0.91 |
| Ln PCI | −0.21 | 0.41 | 0.57 |  | −1.89 |
|  | (−0.81) | (3.88) | (2.58) |  | (−7.97) |
| Ln UNEM |  | 0.43 | 0.45 | −0.35 | −0.01 |
|  |  | (5.82) | (5.71) | (7.38) | (−0.21) |
| Ln HS25+ |  |  |  | 1.17 | 3.33 |
|  |  |  |  | (5.54) | (11.30) |
| Ln ANTIPV | 0.13 |  | −0.09 | −0.024 | −0.16 |
|  | (0.84) |  | (−0.81) | (−2.90) | (−3.37) |

SOURCES: U.S. Bureau of the Census, "Poverty Status of People by Family Relationship, Race, and Hispanic Origin: 1959 to 2006," *Historical Poverty Tables*, table 2, http://www.census.gov/hhes/www/poverty/histpov/hstpov2.html (accessed August 29, 2007); U.S. Bureau of the Census, "CPS Population and Per Capita Money Income, All Races: 1967 to 2004," *Historical Income Tables—People*, table P-1, http://www.census.gov/hhes/www/income/histinc/p01ar.html (accessed August 31, 2006); U.S. Department of Labor, Bureau of Labor Statistics, "Unemployment Rate—Civilian Labor Force," Labor Force Statistics from the Current Population Survey, http://www.bls.gov/data/home.htm (accessed September 21, 2006); U.S. Bureau of the Census, "Percent of People 25 Years and Over Who Have Completed High School or College, by Race, Hispanic Origin and Sex: Selected Years 1940 to 2006," *Historical Tables: Current Population Survey*, table A-2, http://www.census.gov/population/www/socdemo/educ-attn.html (accessed September 21, 2006); Congressional Research Service, "Cash and Noncash Benefits for Persons with Limited Income: Eligibility Rules, Recipient and Expenditure Data, FY2002–FY2004," CRS Report RL33340, March 27, 2006.
NOTES: Parenthetical numbers are "t-statistics," year 1974 excluded (lack of ANTIPV data). Antipoverty spending is deflated using the CPI-U-RS, while the poverty rate is based on a poverty threshold calculated against the CPI-U; ANTIPV data are for fiscal year, not calendar year. PCI = U.S. per capita money income in thousand U.S. \$; UNEM = civilian unemployment rate; HS25+ = percent of U.S. population 25 and older with at least a high school education; ANTIPV = per capita U.S. means-tested spending in thousand 2004 U.S. \$. The dependent variable is the poverty rate for the total civilian noninstitutional population (transformed into natural logarithm).

antipoverty spending offer no help at all for predicting changes in the official poverty rate for the post-1973 period; this is the meaning of the "zero" value for the calculated "r-squared" here.[11] In other words, as far as statistical analysis is concerned, there is no association whatever between the OPR and these other two trends; their "relationship," such as it is, seems to be governed entirely by chance. (To the extent that there is any discernible tendency here at all, incidentally, higher antipoverty spending seems to track with *increasing* official poverty rates!)

Now consider equation 2, which attempts to relate changes in the official poverty rate to changes in per-capita income and the unemployment rate. Taken together, per-capita income and unemployment seem to provide us with a fair amount of information about the official poverty rate. In tandem, their movements correspond with about half of the change in the OPR over the post-1973 period, and each of these variables meets the test of "statistical significance," which is to say that the associations detected look to be meaningful rather than random in nature. But now, absurdly, the poverty rate and per-capita income appear to be *positively* associated—with an 18 percent increase in per-capita income presaging a 1 point *rise* in the poverty rate as of 2004!

Equation 3 adds antipoverty spending into the mix from equation 2. This extra variable provides no additional explanatory power for understanding movements in the official poverty rate. Per-capita income and unemployment retain their statistically significant association with the poverty rate, but per-capita income and the OPR retain as well the perverse and counterintuitive positive relationship already witnessed in equation 2. According to this correspondence, in fact, a $3,200 *decrease* in per-capita income in 2004 would have *lowered* the OPR by 1 percentage point!

Equation 4 attempts to explain changing trends in the official poverty rate through another combination of major macroeconomic and socioeconomic indices, this time the unemployment rate, adult educational attainment, and antipoverty spending. In one sense, this effort is fairly successful, since all of the associations are statistically significant, and the three variables together can predict almost three-fourths of the overall variation in reported poverty levels. But, here again, our variables behave perversely. By this regression, a 1.3 point *rise* in the unemployment rate is associated with a 1 point *drop* in the official poverty rate in 2006—and a 6 point increase in the proportion of adults with high school degrees would mean a *rise* in the OPR of roughly 1 point.

Finally, in equation 5, we consider these four potential explanators of the poverty rate simultaneously. Taken together, these four variables can track over 90 percent of the variation in the official poverty rate for the period since 1973. At last the commonsense (that is, negative) relationship between per-capita income and poverty emerges, and it is statistically strong. But, once again, some of the important calculated relationships come through as perverse. Unemployment again correlates negatively (albeit very weakly) with the poverty rate—meaning that declining unemployment correlates with a very slight rise in the official poverty rate—while higher levels of adult education track with sharply increased OPR levels. That calculated association between increasing education and increasing poverty, incidentally, is extremely strong from the standpoint of statistical significance: It implies that a 1 point improvement in high school graduation rates for American adults would make for a 0.5 point *increase* in the official poverty rate.

Clearly, something is badly amiss here. From the five regressions in table 3-2, we have econometric evidence that every one of the four major indices under consideration—all of them "poverty proxies" that one would routinely expect to help explain true poverty trends for modern America—can be shown to "point the wrong way" in association with the OPR for the period since 1973. How, then, to explain the lack of normal and regular association—actually, the positive disassociation—of the official poverty rate with per-capita income, the unemployment rate, educational attainment, *and* public antipoverty spending over the past three-plus decades?

We could, of course, begin an analysis of the calculated results in table 3-2 by suspending disbelief and pretending that they might really speak to new underlying relationships—that is, that the prevalence of poverty might truly be declining when the civilian unemployment rate rises, and so on. But we should recognize these findings for what they are: nonsensical results from officially calculated U.S. government statistics. To what can we attribute results that lack credibility on their very face? The first obvious working hypothesis would be that something is seriously wrong with some of the data series under consideration here—and the burden of proof would, perforce, fall on the OPR. After all, official U.S. estimates for per-capita income, unemployment, educational attainment, and public antipoverty spending are used in myriad separate settings on a daily basis—typically without setting off the statistical equivalent of alarm bells. Moreover, the interrelationships of all these other major macroeconomic and demographic indicators for the decades since 1973 continue, by and large, to look robust and plausible—which is to say, their correlations with one another remain strong, and the signs for these correlations "point in the right direction." Unless and until someone can propose a plausible storyline to explain why we might expect U.S. data series on per-capita incomes, unemployment rates, adult educational attainment, *and* antipoverty spending to be collectively flawed and deeply biased for the post-1973 period, the simplest explanation for the jarring results in tables 3-1 and 3-2 would be that the officially measured poverty rate offers a highly misleading, even dysfunctional, measure of material deprivation for American society—and has, moreover, been doing so for some considerable period of time.

The regressions in table 3-2 will raise a number of technical points for the statistician or the econometrician that will not be of interest to the more general reader. A more detailed discussion of method and results in the preceding pages is, therefore, attached as an appendix at the end of this study. Here let us note simply that our demonstration of the strangely inconstant relationship of the OPR with other, perhaps more intuitively obvious, indicators of want and plenty is by no means unique or novel. Quite the contrary: A number of economic studies have already observed and commented upon this curious disassociation.[12] As one of these studies vividly phrased it, "macroeconomic performance" during the post-1973 period seemed to have lost "its antipoverty bite."[13]

That would only be the case, however, if the official poverty rate were, indeed, faithfully representing macroeconomic fundamentals over the decades in question. Every one of the studies just cited takes the reliability of the official poverty rate for granted, and consequently presumes that the detected breakdown of the association between it and these other indicators is telling us something real about changing life conditions for the poor in modern America. What has not been accorded serious consideration in studies on the official poverty rate, at least to date, is the possibility that the evident divorce between macroeconomic performance and trends in the OPR in recent decades might instead simply be a statistical artifact, largely or entirely explained by systematic flaws embodied in the official poverty index itself.

# 4

## Systematic Differences between Income and Expenditures among Poorer Households in Modern America: A Blind Spot for the Official Poverty Rate

In the previous chapter we detailed the jarring disjuncture that has emerged since the early 1970s between trends in the official poverty rate and trends for other major socioeconomic indicators: median family income, per-capita income, the unemployment rate, educational attainment, and even antipoverty spending. The increasingly implausible reported correspondences between the OPR and these other basic data series, as we have noted, should immediately raise questions about the reliability of the official poverty rate as a measure of actual want and deprivation in contemporary America.

Such questions cannot be answered without looking at the actual design of the federal poverty measure itself. Are there evident and identifiable flaws, limitations, or shortcomings in this statistical construct that might impair its capacities to report the true prevalence of poverty and want in our country today—built-in errors, so to speak, that might themselves account for, among other things, the strange behavior of the OPR documented in the previous chapter?

Many technical problems with the official poverty rate have been noted by specialists over the years since its inception. Yet, as we shall see in the following pages, one particular defect lies at the very heart of this statistical construct. This defect is not just central to the entire conception of the existing federal poverty measure; under the current approach, it is also impossible to correct.

Simply put, the official poverty rate posits that the spending power (or consumption levels) of low-income Americans is accurately represented by their reported incomes. Yet that assumption is far from correct. In reality, lower-income Americans report annual expenditures that far exceed their annually reported incomes. For the lowest income quintile in the United States, reported expenditures are, in fact, almost twice as high as reported incomes nowadays. The difference between the reported incomes and reported spending of poorer Americans, furthermore, has widened tremendously over the decades since the official poverty rate made its debut.

In practical terms, this means that income figures are also an ever less reliable predictor of true consumption patterns for households near the bottom of the income distribution. As may also be immediately appreciated, the derailing of any presumed tight correspondence between income and consumption for poorer Americans poses more than incidental difficulties to a poverty measure that relies upon reported income levels for its metric in benchmarking national trends in domestic want.

### Unresolved Technical Criticisms of the Federal Poverty Measure

One should not imagine that the official poverty rate has somehow escaped technical scrutiny over the many decades since its initial debut. The very opposite would be closer to the truth. Ever since it was formally embraced as the U.S. government's official statistical index for determining who is poor in America, the federal poverty measure has been subject to continuing and almost continuous examination and critique by economists and statisticians, both within the U.S. government and outside it.

Emblematic of the expert controversy that would be fated always to attend the OPR was the very first *New York Times* news account to appear on the new poverty standard, back in May 1965. After noting that the Office of Equal Opportunity had adopted "a new yardstick today for determining which United States families were poor," the story went on to report that the U.S. Chamber of Commerce's Task Force on Economic Growth and Opportunity was working on a study of its own that would propose an alternative poverty metric—one "that would gauge what it costs to live a decent life in different parts of the country and under different circumstances."[1] (The contending approaches, needless to say, were never reconciled.)

Although the method by which it is calculated has gone essentially unchanged since the 1960s, the official poverty rate itself has been the focus of what are by now decades of careful, extensive, and exacting technical review—and criticisms. The ledger of technical criticisms lodged against the federal poverty measure, and the official poverty rate that is calculated from it, includes (but is not limited to) the following objections or assertions:

- The OPR takes no account of regional differences in U.S. price levels.

- The OPR embraces an inappropriate deflator for its intertemporal adjustments in price levels for its poverty thresholds.

- The OPR takes no account in "money income" of either personal taxes paid or capital gains and tax credits reaped—quantities that have been on the rise over the past generation.

- The OPR takes no account of total assets or net worth, even though common sense would seem to require such means to be considered in determining any family's poverty status.

- The OPR takes no account of the noncash benefits that households consume (including means-tested public benefits and such private services as employer-provided health insurance).

- The OPR makes no imputation for the implicit rental "income" homeowners enjoy through occupying their own properties.

- The OPR makes no adjustment to income for work expenses (including transportation and daycare), despite increasing sensitivity of official poverty counts to these quantities.

- The OPR makes no adjustments to income for a family's out-of-pocket medical expenses (health-care expenditures and health-insurance premiums), even though the burden of health costs falls unevenly on families.

- The OPR measures only family or unrelated individuals' income and, therefore, ignores the impact of cohabitation on household finances.

- Finally, the OPR utilizes "equivalence scales" for determining the poverty thresholds for families of varying size and demographic composition that are highly arbitrary and quite possibly inappropriate.

Ever since the 1960s, the job of compiling and publishing the nation's official poverty statistics has been delegated to the U.S. Census Bureau. As a purely administrative matter, it is important to understand that the Census Bureau computes the annual poverty thresholds, and calculates the official poverty rate, by a methodology it is expressly instructed to utilize (by federal law, or by specific directives from the President's Office of Management and Budget). Thus, while the Census Bureau is responsible for the release and maintenance of the OPR data series, it does not actually have the authority to alter or adjust the method by which the country's official poverty figures are derived.

Nevertheless, the Census Bureau is known to be mindful of, and responsive to, technical criticisms of the official poverty rate. Officials and researchers at the Census Bureau have, of course, long been cognizant of the technical objections enumerated above. And they have attempted to deal with most of these—within the channels and under the accepted parameters established for this kind of government work.[2] Census Bureau inquiries into the potential impact on the calculated poverty rate of various proposed technical changes have been presented for several decades under the format of studies and papers offering "alternative," "experimental," or "exploratory" poverty-rate calculations.

Thus, a series of Census Bureau studies have calculated "alternative poverty estimates" for the United States, using both a different price index for poverty thresholds (CPI-U-RS, whose calculated tempo of increase has been somewhat slower than that of CPI-U)[3] and a variety of more inclusive measures of "income," and the associated permutations for the two.[4] These "alternative" measures of income brought factors such as taxes, capital gains, tax credits (the EITC, or earned income tax credit), noncash public program benefits, and the imputed value of homeownership all into consideration.

Further, for several decades, studies by the Census Bureau have regularly reported on the asset holdings and net worth of American families by income, age, and ethnicity of household head.[5] Other Census Bureau papers have begun an assessment of the potential implications of revising poverty thresholds to reflect the impact of such unevenly distributed expenses as out-of-pocket medical charges and daycare needs, and offered a preliminary look at different methods and approaches to calculating "equivalence scales," or metrics to adjust for differences in budget requirements according to household size or composition.[6] Some census-supported work, moreover, has attempted to indicate the impact on child poverty rates of counting the total income of cohabiting adults in households with children.[7] Census Bureau researchers have even attempted to make allowances for geographic differences in price levels among the fifty states to suggest the potential effect of such variations on calculated poverty rates—although this work should probably be regarded as illustrative.[8] (In the final analysis, the Census Bureau has not been able to calculate regional poverty thresholds for different parts of the United States, due mainly to a lack of necessary detailed data on local price levels.)

In effect, the Census Bureau's "alternative," "experimental," and "exploratory" work on the poverty data has provided a fair amount of "sensitivity analysis" on how a variety of technical tweaks to the existing federal poverty measure would affect the level, trend, and distribution of the official poverty count. Taking taxes into account, for example, would naturally raise the estimated prevalence of poverty. Conversely, including the value of capital gains, tax credits, returns to home equity, and means-tested public benefits would each tend to reduce the calculated prevalence of poverty. Over time, a somewhat lower price deflator for poverty thresholds would gradually result in ever lower poverty totals than those estimated by the OPR. Measuring the combined incomes of cohabiting adults in households with children would clearly reduce the calculated prevalence of child poverty, especially for children in single-parent families.[9] And so on.

But we should also recognize what this collection of Census Bureau studies and papers does not do. While "alternative," "experimental," and "exploratory" poverty calculations offer welcome additional perspective on the official poverty rate and its performance, they do not in themselves resolve any of the many underlying technical issues that remain in contention regarding this particular statistical measure. Further, it is not clear that any selection of "tweaks" to the existing poverty measure derived from the menu of technical issues discussed above would be capable of resolving the strange and counterintuitive misalignment between the official poverty rate and other major indicators of macroeconomic performance that was described in the previous chapter. That much is suggested by the materials in the appendix at the end of this book; even with fourteen "alternative" measures of income, it is still not possible to establish a robust, plausible association between the poverty rate and all the macro indicators we would normally expect to correspond with it.

### Contrasting Measures of Material Standing: Income versus Consumption, Consumer Expenditures, and Consumer Outlays

Although the technical criticisms just reviewed cover a wide terrain of intellectual concerns, they also share one common thread. All of these technical questions about, or objections to, the official poverty rate *accept* the basic framework by which the federal poverty measure estimates the incidence of poverty in the United States. While proposing particular adjustments to the poverty threshold or the definition of income, every one of these criticisms presumes, if implicitly, that the proper method for gauging poverty is, indeed, an income metric—that is, a comparison of individual, family, or household income relative to some designated poverty line.

But there is a more fundamental and far-reaching problem with the existing conception of the federal poverty measure, and thus with the official poverty rate—one left unaddressed in the many technical issues considered above and, indeed, all too seldom addressed by any of the technical reviews of that measure in the many decades since its official launch. This is its implicit assumption that the income level and the consumption level of a poverty-status family should automatically be identical.

The original Orshansky methodology estimated its poverty thresholds to designate expenditure levels consonant with poverty status, and matched these against annually reported household money incomes. But it made no effort to determine the actual consumption levels of those low-income households. Instead, it simply posited an identity between reported money income and expenditures for these families. In Orshansky's words, "the standard" for counting a family as poor "is based essentially on the amount of income remaining after allowance for an adequate diet at minimum cost"[10]—that is, a one-to-one mapping of reported annual money income with total presumed consumption expenditures on the part of Americans in need.

Over four decades later, the method by which the official poverty rate is calculated continues to presume an identity between measured annual money incomes and annual expenditure levels for low-income families and unrelated individuals. Yet this presumption is dubious in theory, and it is confuted empirically by virtually all available data on spending patterns for America's poorer strata.

From the standpoint of economic theory, a literature extending back to the early postwar period and including the contributions of at least two Nobel laureates in economics (Milton Friedman and Franco Modigliani) has outlined the entirely logical reasons for expecting consumption to exceed income for the typical consumer who ends up in the lowest income stratum in any given year.[11] Both the "permanent-income hypothesis" and the "lifecycle-income hypothesis" tell us that families and individuals base their household budgets not just on the fortunes (and uncertainties) of a single year, but against a longer life-course horizon, stabilizing their long-term living standards (and smoothing their consumption trajectory) against the vagaries of short-term income fluctuations. Such behavior naturally suggests that the marginal propensity to consume will tend to be disproportionately high for lower-income households. For the perhaps considerable number of households where expected "permanent income" exceeds current income— that is, "transitory income"—current consumption will likewise exceed current income if financial arrangements permit.[12] This economic formulation of consumer behavior theory suggests that annual incomes would equate to annual expenditures in the lowest income stratum only where those low income levels were, in fact, consonant with a household's expectations of its long-term financial outlook—or where institutional barriers prevented the household from financing additional near-term consumption.[13]

From the standpoint of empirics, U.S. survey data demonstrate that annual expenditures significantly exceed annual incomes for poorer Americans; moreover, as will be seen, the discrepancy between consumption levels and income levels appears to have increased substantially over the decades during which the official poverty rate has been in use. Later in this chapter, we will underscore and illustrate these distinctions, largely with the assistance of data compiled by the "Consumer Expenditure Survey," a data source maintained by the Bureau of Labor Statistics. Before delving into these empirical data, however, we should first formally spell out the differences between measured consumer "expenditures" or "outlays" on the one hand and the economic concept of "consumption" on the other.

Some readers may implicitly regard consumer expenditures as if they were a proxy for consumption levels. But for purposes of clarity, it is necessary to emphasize that "consumption" and "consumer expenditures" are *not* entirely interchangeable terms, and "consumer expenditures" differ from "consumer outlays" in some key respects, as well. Outlining the similarities and differences among "consumption," "expenditures," and "outlays" is necessary to avoid unnecessary confusion over, or unwarranted conflation of, these three separate measures in the coming pages.[14]

The economic concept of "consumption" refers to the entire flow of goods and services that are acquired and absorbed (or used up) by an individual, a family, a household, or some other population unit over some period of time. By contrast, "consumer expenditures" refer only to the purchases of goods and services over some time period. "Consumer outlays," in turn, are distinguished from consumer expenditures in that the former entail all purchase commitments, while the latter cover only the actual out-of-pocket spending advanced on those commitments.

In practice, spending on services and nondurable goods, respectively, are commonly included and similarly treated in all three of these frameworks. But big differences arise with respect to spending on durable goods (typically, "big-ticket" expenditures on items that are kept for a number of years—cars, refrigerators, furniture, and the like). From an economic perspective, the consumption of durable goods involves the flow of services from these products (quantities not ordinarily measured in real life). Consumer expenditures, by contrast, would cover the full purchase price and the loan interest costs involved in acquiring such goods while, for their part, consumer outlays would track just the principal and interest payments on such goods when they were financed rather than purchased outright.

There are additional distinctions among "consumption," "expenditures," and outlays," not all of which need concern us here.[15] "Expenditures" and "outlays," for example, could include work expenses and gifts given to others outside the household, whereas the concept of consumption would not. Similarly, life insurance premiums and annuities would logically be counted in household expenditures and outlays, but would not necessarily be included under the concept of consumption, per se.

On the other hand, "consumption," should properly include the value of barter and in-kind receipts, both of which are excluded from accountings of household expenditures and outlays.

By the same token—perhaps most significantly, for the purposes of this study—consumption would cover the value of noncash transfers of goods and services provided by means-tested government programs, whereas these quantities would be excluded from the ledger of household expenditures and outlays. We should keep this last distinction very much in mind as we examine trends over the past decades in consumer expenditures for lower-income Americans.

### Income versus Expenditures for Lower-Income Americans: Evidence from the Consumer Expenditure Survey

Of the various data sources available today for tracking the spending patterns of the American consumer, the longest standing and most comprehensive is, without question, the Consumer Expenditure (CE) survey, which is produced by the U.S. Bureau of Labor Statistics.[16] The CE provides an alternative window into conditions in America from that offered by the Census Bureau's P-60 series on money incomes of U.S. families and unrelated individuals, against which the official poverty rate has always been calculated.

There are differences in coverage and methodology between these two important data series. Whereas the Census Bureau's annual P-60 series has been prepared continuously since the late 1940s, the CE surveys have, until fairly recently, been episodic, taking place about once a decade between the end of World War II and the start of the 1980s.[17] From 1984 onward, the CE survey has been published and released annually. Like the P-60 series, the CE survey in principle measures pretax money income, inclusive of government cash payments, but exclusive of capital gains or tax credits (thus excluding the EITC).[18] But unlike P-60, which by design offers no regular information on family or individual spending patterns, CE cross-references reported annual income against a detailed breakdown of reported out-of-pocket expenditures (net of reimbursement) for the surveyed households (which are "consumer units" in the CE, as opposed to families and unrelated individuals in the P-60 series).[19]

On the basis of the CE survey data, we can make several points about income and consumption that bear both upon living conditions for lower-income Americans on the one hand, and the accuracy of the official poverty rate on the other.

First, it is by no means exceptional for reported expenditures to exceed reported income in the United States today. Quite the contrary: That circumstance nowadays very nearly appears to define the norm. Table 4-1 underscores this fact.

According to a recent unpublished analysis of CE data, reported expenditures exceeded reported income for nearly two-fifths of American households in 2001.[20] (There is no indication, furthermore, that the year 2001 was anomalous in this particular respect. CE data for the entire decade 1992–2002 reveal that an average of roughly 40 percent of all households were reporting annual spending levels in excess of annual income levels throughout this period.) While poorer households are more likely to report expenditures in excess of income—a critical point in our analysis, to which we will presently be turning—the fact of the matter is that a surfeit of expenditures over income is not only characteristic of Americans at the very bottom of the income scale; it is also commonplace for more affluent Americans. According to these CE data, an average of over 15 percent of the households in the top income quartile reported higher spending than income in any given year during the 1992–2002 period.[21]

Second, the presumption that annual expenditures are limited to annual reported pretax money income for poorer households is flatly refuted by the CE data. Indeed, it is totally contradicted. In actuality, in any given year, the overwhelming majority of lower-income households in the United States report their spending to be higher than their income. For the years 1992–2002, according to the CE survey, over 70 percent of households in the lowest quartile reported annual expenditures in excess of annual incomes.

TABLE 4-1

PERCENT OF FAMILIES "OVERSPENDING" AMONG SOCIOECONOMIC GROUPS, CONSUMER EXPENDITURE SURVEY

| | Race | | Education | | | |
|---|---|---|---|---|---|---|
| Year | White | Nonwhite | Dropout | High School | College | College + |
| 1992 | 39.4 | 40.3 | 47.4 | 39.9 | 38.6 | 33 |
| 1995 | 39.7 | 44.3 | 50.7 | 38.5 | 41.9 | 34.4 |
| 1998 | 39.6 | 43.7 | 51.4 | 40.3 | 41.8 | 31.1 |
| 1999 | 39.2 | 42.4 | 46.7 | 40.4 | 40.5 | 33.8 |
| 2001 | 36.6 | 40.5 | 44.8 | 37.3 | 37.8 | 32.5 |
| All years | 38.8 | 41.7 | 46.1 | 39.8 | 40 | 32.9 |

SOURCE: Kerwin Kofi Charles, Geng Li, Robert Schoeni, "Overspending—Who, Why, and How?" conference paper, National Poverty Center, Gerald R. Ford School of Public Policy, University of Michigan, May 2006, http://www.npc.umich.edu/news/events/consumption06_agenda/charles-li-schoeni.pdf (accessed February 25, 2007).

Third, for lower-income households in the United States as a whole, mean reported annual income fails to offer an accurate proxy for mean annual expenditures. Instead, CE data now document a tremendous discrepancy between reported annual expenditure levels and reported annual income levels for poorer households in the United States. That disproportion, moreover, seems to have been widening over the decades since the OPR was first devised. This is evident in tables 4-2 and 4-3 (see pages 40 and 41), which present income and expenditure levels for America as a whole and for poorer U.S. households from 1960–61 to 2005, as reported in CE surveys.

In one very important respect, trends for poorer households were strikingly similar to those of the rest of the country over these four and a half decades: Rich and poor alike appear to have registered significant long-term increases in their spending power. Between 1960–61 and 2005, the level of inflation-adjusted expenditures in the United States rose overall by roughly 66 percent on a per-household basis—but since average household size declined over those years from 3.2 persons to 2.5 persons, unweighted, real per-capita expenditures rose by about 110 percent.[22] Over those same years, real expenditures rose just as substantially for lower-income Americans. In 2005, inflation-adjusted expenditures for the poorest fifth (lowest income quintile) of U.S. households were reported to be 64 percent higher

| Marital status | | Income quartile | | | |
|---|---|---|---|---|---|
| Married | Unmarried | Bottom | 2nd | 3rd | Highest |
| 34 | 47 | 71.5 | 46.3 | 30.3 | 15.2 |
| 36.9 | 45 | 72.4 | 46.3 | 27.9 | 18.6 |
| 35.9 | 46 | 72.8 | 46.3 | 29.4 | 13.1 |
| 35.2 | 45.8 | 69.9 | 45.7 | 28.7 | 16.6 |
| 33.1 | 42.8 | 71.3 | 40.1 | 28.2 | 13.6 |
| 35 | 44.9 | 71 | 44.4 | 28.9 | 15.5 |

than they had been for the poorest fourth (lowest quartile) in 1960–61. Correcting for changes in household size, unweighted per-capita expenditure levels would have been about 112 percent higher in real terms for the poorest fifth of U.S. households in 2005 than they were for the poorest fourth in 1960–61.[23]

In another critical respect, however, spending patterns for poorer Americans diverged strikingly from overall U.S. patterns between the early 1960s and 2005. In 1960–61, according the CE surveys, households in aggregate devoted 81 percent of their pretax money income to consumer expenditures. Over the intervening decades, that ratio remained fairly stable, and in 2005 it was 79 percent—very close to the fraction reported more than four decades earlier. By contrast, reported spending has regularly exceeded reported income for poorer American households—but the margin by which spending has surpassed income has moved gradually upward over time. In the early 1960s, the reported ratio of spending to pretax money income was 112 percent for the lowest income quartile. In 1972–73, that ratio was 140 percent for the lowest income quintile. Between 1972–73 and 2005, the ratio of expenditures to income for the bottom quintile jumped from 140 percent to 198 percent. According to the CE survey, consumer expenditures are now nearly twice as high as pretax

TABLE 4-2
OVERALL CONSUMER EXPENDITURE PATTERNS FOR THE UNITED STATES,
1960/61 VS. 2005

|  | 1960/61 (all families) | 2005 (all consumer units) |
|---|---|---|
| Persons per unit | 3.2 | 2.5 |
| Reported annual current consumption expenditures (constant 2005 U.S. $) | $28,290 | $46,409 |
| Reported annual pretax income (constant 2005 U.S. $) | $35,010 | $58,712 |
| Reported consumption as percent of reported income | 81% | 79% |

SOURCES: U.S. Department of Labor, Bureau of Labor Statistics, *Handbook of Labor Statistics 1975—Reference Edition*, BLS Bulletin 1865 (Washington, D.C.: U.S. Department of Labor, 1978), table 137; U.S. Bureau of Labor Statistics, "Consumer Expenditures in 2005," Report 998 (Washington, D.C.: U.S. Department of Labor, February 2007), available at http://www.bls.gov/cex/csxann05.pdf (accessed 08/21/07).
NOTE: 1960/61 survey results deflated by CPI-U-RS index. See U.S. Bureau of the Census, "Annual Average Consumer Price Index Research Series Using Current Methods (CPI-U-RS) All Items: 1947 to 2006," available at http://www.census.gov/hhes/www/income/income06/AA-CPI-U-RS.pdf (accessed August 29, 2007). Mean value of 1960 and 1961 used.

money incomes among the poorest fifth of households. We will have more to say about the possible explanations and implications of this growing imbalance in the following chapter. Whatever else that imbalance may signify, however, it appears incontestable that reported income is not only a badly inadequate descriptor of the spending power of America's poorer strata, but also a progressively less reliable one.

### Do Reported Expenditures *Understate* Consumption Levels for Lower-Income Households?

Table 4-3 documents the considerable rise in real spending levels for the poorest fifth of American households over the period between 1972–73 and 2005, as reported in the CE survey. There are strong reasons, furthermore,

TABLE 4-3

CONSUMER EXPENDITURE PATTERNS FOR LOW-INCOME AMERICANS,
1960/61–2005

|  | 1960/61 (families, lowest quartile) | 1972/73 (families, lowest quintile) | 2005 (consumer units, lowest quintile) |
|---|---|---|---|
| Persons per unit | 2.2 | 1.6 | 1.7 |
| Reported annual current consumption expenditures (constant 2005 U.S. $) | $11,679 | $13,330 | $19,120 |
| Reported annual pretax income (constant 2005 U.S. $) | $10,436 | $9,553 | $9,676 |
| Reported consumption as a percent of family income | 112% | 140% | 198% |

SOURCES: U.S. Department of Labor, Bureau of Labor Statistics, *Handbook of Labor Statistics 1975—Reference Edition*, BLS Bulletin 1865 (Washington, D.C.: U.S. Department of Labor, 1978), table 137; U.S. Department of Labor, Bureau of Labor Statistics, *Consumer Expenditures Survey: Interview Survey 1972–73*, BLS Bulletin 1997 (Washington, D.C.: U.S. Department of Labor, 1978), volume 1, table 10; U.S. Bureau of Labor Statistics, "Consumer Expenditures in 2005," Report 998 (Washington, D.C.: U.S. Department of Labor, February 2007), http://www.bls.gov/cex/csxann05.pdf (accessed 08/21/07).
NOTE: Earlier surveys deflated by CPI-U-RS index; mean value of reported years used for 1960/61 and 1972/73.

to believe that these numbers in fact understate both the true rise in consumption for the lower-income strata of the United States since 1973 and the actual levels of consumption for poorer Americans today.

Two problems are in play here. First, the CE survey currently appears to underreport consumer expenditures very substantially—and to have been missing a greater share of total consumer spending over time. This problem is highlighted by the growing gap between CE-based estimates of aggregate consumer spending on the one hand and, on the other, estimates of "personal consumption expenditures" (PCE) drawn from the National Income and Product Accounts (NIPA, the country's detailed gross domestic product and gross national product series), maintained by the U.S. Commerce Department's Bureau of Economic Analysis.[24] As Kevin Hassett and Aparna Mathur recently noted,

In 2005, the aggregate consumption reported by the [CE] survey
was about 6 trillion dollars, whereas [PCE data from NIPA indicated that] aggregate consumption was closer to 9 trillion dollars.
In fact, these divergences have tended to increase over time.[25]

We should not, of course, presume that the $3 trillion gap to which Has-
sett and Mathur refer is entirely attributable to an underestimation of consumer expenditures on the part of the CE survey.[26] Some of this divergence
can be explained in terms of intentional differences in coverage in the two
series. The CE survey, for example, tracks only out-of-pocket medical and
health-care expenses, net of reimbursements, while the PCE is meant to estimate the consumption of all health-care services—and health care accounts
for a large and rapidly growing share of the national economy. By the same
token, the CE is charged with following expenditures by individuals and
households, and thus excludes outlays by nonprofit organizations (a large
share of whose growing disbursements are, incidentally, for health care).

Yet even when one attempts to standardize for comparability and coverage, the relative gap between the PCE and CE appears to have been rising steadily over the past decade. A recent BLS effort to reconcile PCE and
CE expenditure data found that even after making adjustments for population coverage and expenditure categories to achieve methodological comparability, the ratio of the CE to the PCE consumption series still fell over
time, with an overall drop from 86 percent to 81 percent in the period
1992–2002. Even steeper were declines in estimates for coverage of spending on durable goods (down to 76 percent in 2002 from 88 percent as
recently as 1992) and nondurable goods (63 percent in 2002 versus 69 percent a decade earlier). Only in the realm of services did the CE and PCE
estimates remain close to identical.[27]

Earlier work by BLS researchers had concluded that the CE and PCE
series on aggregate consumption seemed to match fairly well back in the
1980s.[28] If that was correct, then the degree of underreporting in the CE
(whether through sampling or nonsampling error, or both) has markedly
increased over the past decade and a half. By 1992, a 16 percent upward
adjustment would have been needed to bring CE survey estimates of overall consumer spending into line with NIPA's PCE series; by 2002, the
required upward adjustment would have been over 23 percent. While we
cannot know the incidence of this apparent underestimate of consumer

spending with respect to households by income, either for 2002 (the end-point year) or over time, it would be reasonable to expect that significant and gradually increasing underestimates of consumer expenditures characterized the CE survey's figures for lower-income households, just as for the rest of the surveyed population.

A second problem is that the CE survey by design excludes most non-cash, means-tested benefits. Yet, by any criterion we might choose, the consumption of in-kind goods and services is a nontrivial component of total consumption for lower-income households in America today. Disbursements of noncash, means-tested public benefits, furthermore, have risen appreciably since 1973.

Estimates of public expenditures on means-tested benefit programs prepared by the Congressional Research Service, many of which are published in the House Ways and Means Committee's *Green Book*, provide a sense of scale here. In fiscal year 2004 (the most recent date for which such estimates are currently available) total public outlays for means-tested, noncash benefit programs exceeded $470 billion (in constant FY 2004 dollars). And between fiscal years 1973 and 2004, public expenditures on in-kind, means-tested benefits rose by $368 billion (in constant FY 2004 dollars), or over 350 percent.[29]

Most of that surge, to be sure, was due to health-care programs—and within academic and public policy circles, there is no general consensus today on how to factor in appropriately the value of in-kind transfers of health and medical services for lower-income Americans.[30] Yet even if we *completely exclude* health and medical benefits from this tally, and we further exclude the value of food stamps (since this quantity is already estimated in CE tabulations), we are still left with a rather sizable residual. After subtracting all health and medical outlays, all cash transfers, and the entire food stamp program from means-tested program expenditures, for example, public spending on the remainder of in-kind, means-tested programs still would have amounted to $124 billion in FY 2004. Over the years between FY 1973 and FY 2004, moreover, the real increment in such means-tested outlays (goods and services, which, as we have mentioned, by definition do not show up in the ledgers of CE surveys, even for qualifying households) would have worked out to over $76 billion in constant FY 2004 dollars. In real terms, that would make for a jump of over 160 percent.[31]

By comparison with the measured expenditures of the lowest quintile of U.S. households in the CE survey, the means-tested benefits that go unmeasured in CE surveys are sizable quantities. In 2004, the CE survey's aggregate estimated expenditures for the bottom fifth of American households came to just $414 billion (in current dollars). As pure orders of magnitude, the noncash, means-tested benefits (exclusive of health care and food stamps) from FY 2004 would have equaled fully 30 percent of that total—and the absolute increase between FY 1973 and FY 2004 in those very same benefits would have equaled 18 percent of total measured spending for the lowest quintile of households in 2004.

Here again, as with the rise in underreporting of consumer spending, we do not have at hand the data to allow us to estimate the precise incidence of these benefits as they would accrue within the lowest quintile of households in the CE survey.[32] But when one considers that the total increase in such noncash, means-tested benefits averaged $3,200 per recipient household, whereas the measured increase in real expenditures for the lowest quintile in CE surveys between 1972–73 and 2002 was roughly $7,100 (in constant 2004 dollars), one begins to appreciate the scale of the underestimation of changes in consumption levels that may be entailed.[33]

Taken together, the underreporting of consumer expenditures within the CE survey and the survey's exclusion of means-tested public program benefits (other than cash and health care) make for what is, in all likelihood, a fairly major underestimate of the true increase in consumption levels between 1972–73 and 2005 by the bottom quintile of households in the Consumer Expenditure Survey. Without hazarding a specific guess about the exact magnitude of this underestimation, we cannot exclude the possibility that a comprehensive and accurate measure of consumption for the CE's bottom income quintile might as much as double the recorded increase registered in the CE survey itself.

### The Declining Reliability of Income as a Predictor of Household Budgets for Poverty-Level Families

Over the decades between 1973 and 2005, according to the official poverty rate, the United States made no long-term progress in reducing the prevalence of poverty among the general population; indeed, the OPR for the total population was higher in 2005 (12.3 percent) than it had been thirty-two years earlier (11.1 percent). These numerical results were a direct computational consequence of, first, the fact that the OPR relies upon an income-based yardstick in its measurement of poverty and, second, the fact that reported income has been stagnant, or worse, for the lower strata of the American society since the early 1970s.

Long-term income figures for the lowest income quintile tell the latter story (a story by now perhaps familiar to much of the reading public). According to the Consumer Expenditure Survey, real pretax income for the bottom fifth of households was barely 1 percent higher in 2005 than in 1972–73. By the same token, according to the Census Bureau's P-60 money income series, real pretax income for the bottom fifth of households rose by less than 10 percent between 1973 and 2005. Even those slight real income gains registered in the P-60 data series, moreover, were entirely dependent upon the use of a more "optimistic" price deflator for adjusting cost-of-living increases over those many decades. The CPI-U-RS, which replaced the CPI-U as the official deflator for Census Bureau household income estimates in 2000, offers slightly lower long-term estimates for the pace of inflation in the United States; if CPI-U were still the official deflator, measured real income for the lowest quintile of households in the United States would actually have declined over the decades between 1973 and 2005.

If the spending patterns of America's poor were, in fact, determined by, and determinatively constrained by, their income levels, these discouraging trends for reported income would have been matched by equally dismal data on long-term changes in purchasing power for the bottom fifth of households. Yet, as it happens, the spending power of the poorest households was *not* stagnant over those decades, as we saw in table 4-3. Quite the contrary: According to the Consumer Expenditure Survey, the mean level of real spending by the bottom fifth of households rose unmistakably, by about 45 percent between 1972–73 and 2005. As we have also noted, the true mean increase in consumption by these households was very likely higher than the CE numbers suggest—possibly quite significantly higher.

The discordance between long-term trends in income and spending for lower-income Americans subverts the entire methodology that undergirds the official poverty rate. With gradually escalating, and now major, discrepancies between income and spending being reported by lower-income households in the United States, our official, income-based poverty measure must, perforce, become an ever more biased and less reliable indicator of absolute poverty over time.

The measurement errors introduced by these biases are no longer small enough to gloss over, as may be illustrated by focusing on the households reporting under $10,000 in annual income in the 2005 Consumer Expenditure Survey. According to that survey, these lowest-income households accounted for 9.3 percent of the U.S. civilian noninstitutional population as of 2005. Going by the federal poverty measure, and using CE survey soundings on annual income, practically all the people in this grouping would officially be counted as "poor."[34] Yet, as of 2005, the average expenditure level for this same grouping of U.S. households was over $17,500—that is to say, almost 40 percent above the official 2005 poverty threshold for a two-person family, even though the average household size was well under two persons (1.6).[35] Most of these households, in other words, were spending at levels above their designated "poverty threshold" budgets (some of them well above it)—even though almost all of them reported incomes that fell below the poverty threshold (some of them far below it).

For well over a century, it has been conventional in economic research on the poverty question to use income-based yardsticks in measuring poverty, as the U.S. government does with the official poverty rate. Yet we should also remember that there is nothing intrinsically sacrosanct about income figures per se that should automatically dictate their selection as an essential ingredient in a poverty indicator. From both the theoretical and practical standpoints, the appeal of income in poverty studies is precisely its promise as a predictor of *consumption*, as a window on purchasing power. If we did not expect income to proxy consumption for poorer households—on a consistent and tolerably accurate basis—an income-based poverty indicator would have precious little rationale.

Unfortunately, we find ourselves at a juncture in America today where income can no longer be expected to serve as an accurate proxy for consumption—or even for consumer expenditures. As we have seen, the overwhelming majority of lower-income households in any given calendar year now report that their expenditures exceed their pretax money incomes. In the aggregate, reported spending is now almost twice as high as reported income for the bottom fifth of American households. And, over time, the gap between spending and income for poorer households looks only to have been growing. Under such circumstances, an income-based measure for tracking the incidence of poverty cannot help but fail in its assigned charge.

Ironically enough, the problems highlighted in this chapter would not have caught Mollie Orshansky by surprise. Her seminal study on "Counting the Poor," which is seldom read nowadays, actually opens with a declaration about the importance of tracking not just the income, but also the consumption, of poorer families. In her words:

> The method of measuring equivalent levels of income that is presented here is still relatively crude. [We are] attempting to develop more refined measures based on the relationship of income and consumption. Such studies will take time. Until they can be completed, the indexes used here will provide a more sensitive method than has hitherto been available of delineating the profile of poverty in this country and of measuring changes in that profile over time.[36]

Over four decades later, the official research on "the relationship of income to consumption" to which Orshansky referred has yet to be undertaken. Instead, the official methodology for "counting the poor" proceeds almost exactly as when Orshansky first introduced it, frozen in time, incognizant of Orshanksy's own caveats.

The divergence between reported income and reported expenditure levels for low-income households has always been a critical blind spot for the official poverty rate. With the gap between reported income and expenditures now assuming chasm-like proportions, that blind spot has come to obscure almost all of the landscape that the OPR is meant to survey.

It is one thing, of course, to recognize this immense gap in the budgets of America's lower-income households and quite another to explain it. How are we to make sense of this profound but puzzling development? In the next chapter we shall attempt to explore this paradox.

# 5

# Accounting for the Widening Reported Gap between Income and Consumption for Lower-Income Americans

A yawning gap between income and expenditures for lower-income households in the United States has come to be a central—and, arguably, a defining—feature of poverty in modern America. It also represents an unexpected development, to say the very least.

This development was unexpected, to begin with, from the standpoint of economic theory. Though it might not surprise economists to learn that aggregate reported expenditures have exceeded aggregate reported incomes for lower-income households at any given point in time in the postwar era, received economic theory does not prepare us for the ever-widening disparities between spending and income that have been recorded since the 1960s. Further, as a matter of pure empirics, this development was manifestly unexpected—for it is, as yet, generally unrecognized. All too few of the current academic and policy studies on the U.S. poverty problem demonstrate a familiarity with the basic fact that reported expenditures for poorer households have been on the rise, despite stagnant reported incomes[1]—an unfortunate consequence, perhaps, of an official methodology for measuring poverty that ignores evolving spending patterns altogether. Unexpected, unrecognized, and unfamiliar, the phenomenon has, by and large, gone unexplained.

Yet understanding this phenomenon is of self-evident importance to an overall assessment of the material situation of poverty-level Americans today. By any reckoning, the tale of the permanent, and ever-widening, imbalance between spending and income for poorer Americans is a big story. In the early 1960s—the period whose data Orshansky relied upon in devising her original poverty rate—a surfeit of reported expenditures over reported pre-tax income among low-income households was already evident. But that dis-crepancy, reported in the 1960–61 BLS Consumer Expenditure Survey, was relatively modest: about 12 percent for the lowest income quartile. By 1972–73, the poorest fifth of households in the CE survey was reportedly spending nearly 40 percent more than its annual income. And by 2005, the lowest income quintile in the Consumer Expenditure Survey was reportedly spending almost *double* its reported annual income.

The stark and increasing mismatch between reported annual incomes and reported annual expenditures for low-income households may go far in explaining why the official poverty rate—predicated as it is on reported annual money income—seems so very inconsistent with other data series bearing on the incidence of material deprivation in modern America. But how is this widening gap to be explained? How did the surfeit of expendi-tures over pretax income for low-income households reported in CE sur-veys vault from about 12 percent in the early 1960s to 98 percent in 2005?[2] In the following pages we will examine some of the factors that might help to unravel this economic mystery.

## Unsustainable "Overspending" by the Poor?

One hypothesis to account for this widening gap between spending and income would be that low-income Americans are "overspending"—that is, going ever deeper into debt. By this reasoning, the apparently widening gap between income and expenditures, far from being an artifact, would repre-sent an all too genuine phenomenon—an ominous, unsustainable "binge" which must eventually come to an end, with deleterious consequences for future living standards of the vulnerable and the disadvantaged.[3]

On its face, this hypothesis might seem plausible. In the event, how-ever, it appears to be confuted by a wealth of data on the net worth of poorer American households.

If expenditures for lower-income households were being financed through a steady drawdown of assets or accumulation of debt, we would expect the net worth of poorer Americans to decline steadily over time in absolute terms. No such trend is evident from the two government data

FIGURE 5-1

MEDIAN HOUSEHOLD NET WORTH, LOWEST INCOME QUINTILE: FEDERAL
RESERVE BOARD VS. UNITED STATES CENSUS BUREAU, 1984–2004

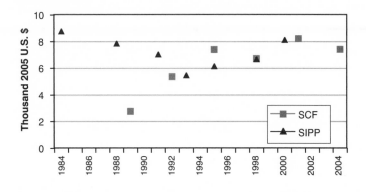

SOURCES: Federal Reserve Board, "2004 Survey on Consumer Finances Chartbook," http://www.federalreserve.gov/pubs/oss/oss2/2004/scf2004home.html (accessed September 17, 2007); U.S. Bureau of the Census, "Household Wealth and Asset Ownership: 1984," *Current Population Reports*, P70-7 (Washington, D.C.: U.S. Bureau of the Census, 1986), http://www.sipp.census.gov/sipp/p70-7.pdf (accessed May 17, 2007); Judith Eargle, "Household Wealth and Asset Ownership: 1988," *Current Population Reports*, P70-22 (Washington, D.C.: U.S. Bureau of the Census, December 1990), http://www.sipp.census.gov/sipp/p70-22.pdf (accessed May 17, 2007); T.J. Eller, "Household Wealth and Asset Ownership: 1991," *Current Population Reports*, P70-34 (Washington, D.C.: U.S. Bureau of the Census, January 1994), http://www.sipp.census.gov/sipp/p70-34.pdf (accessed May 17, 2007); T.J. Eller and Wallace Fraser, "Asset Ownership of Households: 1993," *Current Population Reports*, P70-47 (Washington, D.C.: U.S. Bureau of the Census, September 1995), http://www.sipp.census.gov/sipp/p70s/p70-47.pdf (accessed May 16, 2007); Michael Davern and Patricia Fisher, "Household Net Worth and Asset Ownership: 1995," *Current Population Reports*, P70-71 (Washington, D.C.: U.S. Bureau of the Census, February 2001), http://www.sipp.census.gov/sipp/p70s/p70-71.pdf (accessed May 16, 2007); Shawna Orzechowski and Peter Sepielli, "Net Worth and Asset Ownership of Households," *Current Population Reports*, P70-88 (Washington, D.C.: U.S. Bureau of the Census, May 2003), http://www.census.gov/prod/2003pubs/p70-88.pdf (accessed May 16, 2007)
NOTE: SIPP data deflated by CPI-U-RS. SCF deflated by PCE.

sources that attempt to estimate the net worth of poorer Americans—the Census Bureau's Survey of Income and Program Participation (SIPP) and the Federal Reserve Board's Survey of Consumer Finances (SCF).[4]

To be sure, poorer households do appear to have very modest means by comparison with the rest of contemporary America. At the turn of the twenty-first century, according to both the SIPP and the SCF, the median net worth for U.S. households in the bottom income quintile was less than $8,000 (2004 dollars). But the available data do not suggest that the

Figure 5-2

MEAN VALUE OF ASSETS, LIABILITIES, AND NET WORTH,
LOWEST INCOME QUINTILE, 1989–2004

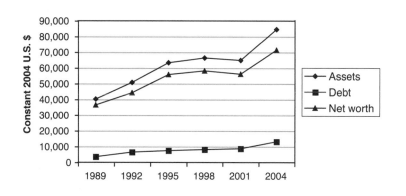

SOURCE: Federal Reserve Board, Survey of Consumer Finances, various years, http://www.
federalreserve.gov/Pubs/oss/oss2/scfindex.html (accessed September 19, 2007).

median net worth of poorer households is declining steadily over time. SIPP
data report that this figure dipped between the mid-1980s and the early
1990s, but then rose back close to its earlier levels by the turn of the century. The SCF data corroborate a rise over the 1990s.

A slightly more sophisticated version of the same "spend-down" thesis
might propose that net worth was only holding for low-income households
because fixed-value liabilities, such as mortgages or credit-card debt, were
being accumulated against nominal (and potentially transient) increases in
the values of such assets as housing or mutual funds. (We might term this
as a "second-order overspending hypothesis.") Available data argue against
this conjecture, as well.

The SCF provides estimates not only of mean net worth, but also of
mean assets and liabilities for the poorest fifth of U.S. households. Between
1989 and 2004, mean liabilities for the lowest quintile in the SCF survey
did, indeed, rise; in fact, they more than tripled in real terms, increasing by
over $9,000 per family (in 2004 dollars). But the estimated mean value of
these households' assets appreciated much more substantially than their
mean liabilities, increasing by an average of more than $44,000 over the

FIGURE 5-3

MEAN VALUE OF ASSETS, LIABILITIES, AND NET WORTH, LOWEST INCOME QUINTILE, 65+, 1989–2004

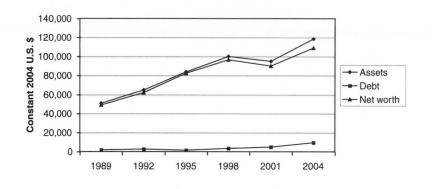

SOURCE: Federal Reserve Board, Survey of Consumer Finances, various years, http://www. federalreserve.gov/Pubs/oss/oss2/scfindex.html (accessed September 19, 2007).

same period. Consequently, the mean net worth of the poorest fifth of U.S. households roughly doubled in real terms, rising from about $36,000 in 1989 to over $71,000 in 2004 (all in 2004 dollars).

To judge by these data, poorer U.S. households, taken as a whole, may have been "spending down" a portion of their appreciating asset values, but only a portion—a pattern not so different from the "wealth effects" witnessed among more affluent households over those same years.

Just how meaningful should we take the trends in figure 5-2 to be? Skeptics will caution that mean wealth and assets for the lowest quintile of households are influenced heavily by patterns of home ownership and housing prices—and that housing prices witnessed an unusually sharp run-up during the years under consideration (1989–2004).[5] Furthermore, as the incidence of home ownership typically rises with the age of the head of household, skeptics might further infer the aforementioned gains from asset appreciation from owner-occupied housing would be disproportionately concentrated among the older households in this lowest income quintile. For these reasons, skeptics might argue that the reported SCF trends in mean assets and mean net worth for the lowest quintile could be unrepresentative

FIGURE 5-4

MEAN VALUE OF ASSETS, LIABILITIES, AND NET WORTH, LOWEST INCOME
QUINTILE, HOUSEHOLD HEADS AGES 18–64, 1989–2004

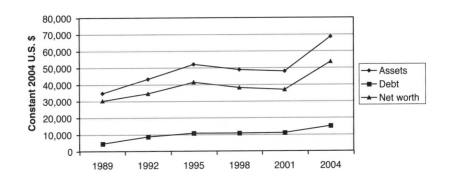

SOURCE: Federal Reserve Board, Survey of Consumer Finances, various years, http://www.
federalreserve.gov/Pubs/oss/oss2/scfindex.html (accessed September 19, 2007).

of, and potentially misleading about, actual wealth trends for most lower-
income Americans.

These are reasonable reservations, all—but the record suggests such
apprehensions and qualifications are empirically unfounded, at least for the
years in question here.

For the country as a whole, it is true that net worth is higher for households whose heads are sixty-five years of age or older than for other households;
this general relationship is just as true for the lowest quintile as for the rest
of the income spectrum. Within America's lowest income quintile, the mean
net worth of families with householders sixty-five or older was twice as high
as for those with householders eighteen to sixty-four years of age in 2004. But
for the lowest quintile, mean assets and net worth for both types of households progressively rose over the decade and a half under consideration—and
among lower-income households *not* headed by senior citizens, mean assets
roughly doubled, while mean net worth increased by over three-fourths, to
about $53,000.

By the same token, while the growing value of owner-occupied housing
played a very important role in overall asset appreciation for lower-income

FIGURE 5-5

MEAN VALUE OF ASSETS AND HOUSING, LOWEST INCOME QUINTILE,
HOUSEHOLD HEADS AGES 65+, 1989–2004

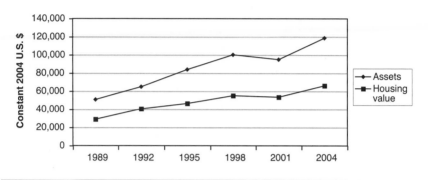

SOURCE: Federal Reserve Board, Survey of Consumer Finances, various years, http://www.federalreserve.gov/Pubs/oss/oss2/scfindex.html (accessed September 19, 2007).

households, it was by no means the only factor driving asset accumulation for either older or younger families. Increases in the value of the primary residence accounted for just over half (54 percent) of all asset appreciation among households headed by senior citizens in this lowest quintile between 1989 and 2004—meaning that just under half accrued from other types of assets, such as savings accounts, bonds, and stocks. Among lowest-quintile households headed by nonseniors, increased rates of home ownership and increased prices of owner-occupied housing accounted for just under half (47 percent) of overall asset appreciation over this same decade and a half.

In the early years of the twenty-first century, U.S. housing prices may well have been affected by a speculative bubble. The point here, however, is that wealth accumulation in the lowest quintile was hardly dependent on run-ups in home prices alone. Even if we were to exclude owner-occupied housing altogether, mean assets for households in the lowest quintile would still have risen between 1989 and 2004, by 63 percent for senior households in this grouping and by 50 percent for nonsenior households.

One other aspect of wealth and asset trends for lower-income Americans is highlighted by the SCF data and seems deserving of comment. This is the striking, if little noticed, decline in "propertyless-ness" among the

FIGURE 5-6

MEAN VALUE OF ASSETS AND HOUSING, LOWEST INCOME QUINTILE,
HOUSEHOLD HEADS AGES 18–64, 1989–2004

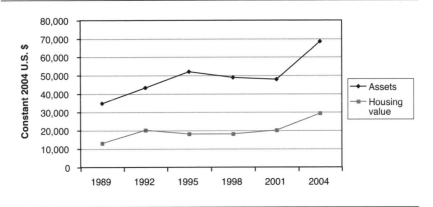

SOURCE: Federal Reserve Board, Survey of Consumer Finances, various years, http://www.
federalreserve.gov/Pubs/oss/oss2/scfindex.html (accessed September 19, 2007).

poorest quintile between 1989 and 2004. In 1989, 21 percent of the families in this lowest quintile reported owning no assets whatever; by 2004, the
corresponding proportion had dropped by nearly two-thirds, to under 8
percent. Not surprisingly, in this lowest quintile the proportion of households with no assets was much lower for families headed by seniors than
nonseniors. But even among the poorer households headed by persons
under sixty-five years of age, the trend was unmistakable: Whereas 27 percent of those families had no reported assets at all in 1989, the corresponding fraction was down to under 11 percent in 2004—that is to say, 11
percent of such households from within the lowest overall income quintile.
Asset ownership, to be sure, is not the same thing as net wealth—but the
apparent spread of property ownership among households at the lower
reaches of the income spectrum suggests, at the very least, a rather different dynamic from the one presumed by the "overspending" hypothesis.

Entirely overlooked in the ongoing public conversation on wealth and
economic inequality in America today is the critical fact that households
near the bottom of the income spectrum have also been party to our nation's
great recent surge in wealth. To go by the estimates of the Federal Reserve

FIGURE 5-7

**PERCENT OF HOUSEHOLDS WITH NO ASSETS, 1989–2004**

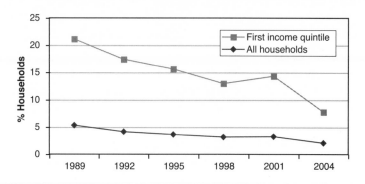

SOURCE: Federal Reserve Board, Survey of Consumer Finances, various years, http://www.
federalreserve.gov/Pubs/oss/oss2/scfindex.html (accessed September 19, 2007).

Board, aggregate inflation-adjusted assets for this bottom quintile of families
increased by nearly one trillion dollars ($995 billion in 2004 constant dollars)—
between 1989 and 2004 alone. Over this same period, even after excluding
home ownership from the reckoning, the value of personal assets still rose
almost half a trillion dollars ($487 billion). The estimated net worth for this
same quintile of Americans grew by over three-quarters of a trillion dollars
($780 billion), a jump of 95 percent over this decade and a half.[6]

This is not to say that some lower-income households may not have
been caught up in a syndrome of "overspending" during the decades in
which their reported income and reported consumption have so progressively and strikingly diverged. But the empirical record is unambiguous: On
the whole, far from having drawn down their assets to maintain personal
consumption, America's poorest fifth were richer by 2004 than ever before,
by the criteria of both asset ownership and net worth.

If the growing statistical discrepancy between incomes and expenditures for poorer Americans cannot be explained by a growing indebtedness
of lower-income households, how then can we account for it? Three partial
explanations suggest themselves: changes in CE survey methods and practices, income underreporting or misreporting, and increased year-to-year
income variability. Let us examine each of these in turn.

FIGURE 5-8
## PERCENT OF HOUSEHOLDS WITH NO ASSETS, LOWEST INCOME QUINTILE, 1989–2004

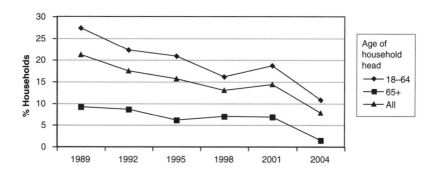

SOURCE: Federal Reserve Board, Survey of Consumer Finances, various years, http://www. federalreserve.gov/Pubs/oss/oss2/scfindex.html (accessed September 19, 2007).

## Changes in CE Survey Methods and Practices

Theoretically, the growing mismatch between reported income and reported expenditures for lower-income households could, in part, be an artifact of changes in the CE survey itself. As it happens, major modifications in design and method for the CE survey—potentially capable of affecting the comparability of results between surveys—were indeed implemented since 1960–61. For our purposes, three of these deserve special mention.[7]

First, sample size for the CE survey was drastically reduced after 1960–61. In the 1960–61 survey, close to 14,000 households were interviewed. In the 1972–73 survey, the sample comprised about 10,000 households. Sample size was cut further still, to about 5,000 households, for the CE surveys between 1984 and 1998, before being increased somewhat, to about 7,500 households per round, in 1999 (at which level it remains to this writing).

Second, whereas the 1960–61 survey in principle planned for a single interview with each sampled household about its annual income and expenditure patterns over the entire previous year, in 1972–73 and thereafter the CE carried out quarterly interviews on a panel basis—that is, with a selected group of households who would be asked about income and expenditures over the previous three months. (For CE surveys since the early 1980s, quarterly interviews have been conducted on a "revolving-panel basis," with sampled households interviewed for five consecutive quarters, the first interview being devoted to "bounding" and the subsequent four to gathering data for survey tabulation.)[8]

Finally, the 1960–61 survey relied upon intensive, in-depth interactions with respondents. The procedure, in the words of one government statistician, entailed "extremely lengthy interviews"[9] (typically six hours in duration), in which inconsistencies might be reconciled and oversights or omissions caught and corrected. By contrast, the interactive process became much less arduous for both interviewer and interviewee in subsequent CE surveys, usually involving a sixty- to ninety-minute battery of questions for each quarter—but, at the same time, incomplete responses emerged as a nonnegligible feature of the survey results. On average, about 10–15 percent of those interviewed for the CE panels do not provide what is regarded as complete responses about sources of income. (It should be noted, in addition, that roughly 15 percent of survey-contacted households decline to be interviewed in the first place.)[10]

The decades for which these increasingly extreme divergences between income and reported expenditures for poorer households are reported, in other words, also frame a period in which CE survey techniques and procedures were undergoing major, and at times abrupt, transition. Moreover, over the same decades in which CE surveys were registering ever-higher ratios of spending to income for lower-income households, the overall correspondence between reported household income and expenditures seems to have been in general decline.

In a trenchant study of U.S. poverty data, Daniel Slesnick of the University of Texas has noted that the correlation between reported income and reported expenditures on the CE surveys as a whole dropped substantially between the early 1960s and the 1980s.[11] By Slesnick's calculations, variations in reported pretax money incomes corresponded with almost 70 percent of the reported variation in household spending in 1960–61. By 1985, that correspondence had fallen to just over 46 percent. The correspondence between household income and household spending rose somewhat thereafter, but the correlation of variance was still below 50 percent as of 1995. Harvard University's Christopher Jencks, however, has counseled against imputing too much significance to that apparent decline. Jencks observes that the CE survey currently entails fewer built-in checks and safeguards than in the past. Whereas inconsistent or curious responses would have been likely to invite reinterviews—and emendations—in the 1960–61 survey, similarly suspicious data might simply have been entered into the official database in more recent surveys.[12] Neither Slesnick nor Jencks has volunteered an indication of the actual quantitative impact of these alterations in the conduct of the CE survey on the correspondence between reported income and expenditures in the United States as a whole, or for lower-income households in particular.

## Income Underreporting

Another explanation, perhaps directly related to the issues just reviewed, might be a tendency over time for increased misreporting of income in the CE surveys. Statisticians and economists at the U.S. Bureau of Labor Statistics caution that theirs is an expenditure survey, rather than an income and expenditure survey, and explicitly advise that "for users interested only in income information, data published by the Census Bureau of the U.S. Department of Commerce may be a better source of information."[13] Further, BLS staff responsible for the CE surveys carefully note that users should place more confidence in their expenditure estimates than their income estimates, especially for the lowest reported income deciles. The CE staff seems especially concerned by the relatively large number of respondents who report extremely low or even negative incomes but healthy spending patterns.[14]

Concerns about the reliability of the income measure in the CE survey have prompted BLS staffers to conduct some "sensitivity analyses" of the survey's reported results for income and expenditures. As a diagnostic, and possible corrective, for the survey's income underreporting, for example, CE researchers have proposed the ranking of households by current outlays rather than income.[15] Doing so radically changes the ratio of outlays to income for the bottom quintile; in the 1992 CE survey, for instance, that ratio drops from 2.05 (ranked by income) to a mere 0.67 (ranked by outlays).[16] Among its other implications, this reexamination of the income–expenditure

FIGURE 5-9

AVERAGE REPORTED ANNUAL EXPENDITURES AND INCOME,
LOWEST INCOME QUINTILE, 1984–2005

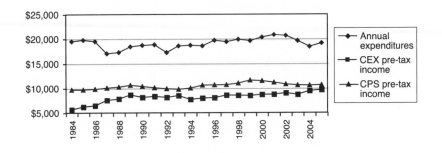

SOURCES: U.S. Bureau of the Census, "Mean Household Income Received by Each Fifth and Top 5 Percent, All Races: 1967 to 2005," *Historical Income Tables—Households*, table H-3, http://www.census.gov/hhes/www/income/histinc/h03ar.html (accessed August 22, 2007); U.S. Department of Labor, Bureau of Labor Statistics, "Quintiles of Income Before Taxes: Average Annual Expenditures and Characteristics," Consumer Expenditure Survey, Standard Tables 1984-2005, http://www.bls.gov/cex/csxstnd.htm (accessed August 22, 2007).
NOTE: Income and expenditures adjusted by CPI-U-RS. CEX and CPS use different definitions for households ("consumer unit" versus "families and unrelated individuals").

correspondence for U.S. consumer units might seem to suggest that many households designated as low-income in the CE survey are in reality simply misclassified income underreporters and, further, that a faithful estimate of true household income might dramatically reduce (or completely eliminate) the strange and extreme reported surfeit of expenditures over income for the lowest quintile of the income distribution in the CE survey.

This innovative exercise casts an interesting additional light on U.S. expenditure patterns, but as a corrective for income underreporting, it has some problems of its own. For one thing, a ranking of household incomes and expenditures based on outlays produces the entirely anomalous result that America's greatest "savers" are the quintile of households with the very lowest reported incomes (with a pretax income-to-outlays ratio of 1.50) while the greatest "dis-savers" are the very top quintile (with a ratio of only 0.88).

Accounting for the growing discrepancy between reported income and reported expenditures in the CE survey through income misreporting would require some evidence of *increased* misreporting of incomes for the lowest quintile of households. In actuality, the discrepancies between CE and Census Bureau estimates for pretax money incomes have been diminishing for the past two decades. As may be seen in figure 5-9, CE estimates for the money incomes of the lowest quintile were 42 percent below Census Bureau estimates in 1984, whereas the difference was 9 percent in 2005. The gradual reconciliation of CE and Census Bureau income estimates would not argue for *increasing* misreporting over time, unless the CPS data themselves were a primary source of the problem.[17]

In any case, even if we do happen to accord greater confidence to CPS than CE data on incomes for the bottom fifth of households, the puzzling discrepancy we have been discussing is by no means resolved by relying on Census Bureau rather than BLS income estimates for poorer Americans. We can see as much if we substitute Census Bureau estimates for the pretax money income of the poorest quintile for the CE's income figures for that same quintile, then calculate the ratio of spending to income with CE expenditure data.

As officially reported in CE surveys, we will recall, the ratio of spending to income for the lowest quintile was 140 percent in 1972–73, and 198 percent in 2005. Comparing the CE survey data on expenditures and the Census Bureau data on money incomes, reported expenditures for the lowest fifth of "households" (that is, the distinctly defined reference units from the two respective surveys) would likewise have been about 40 percent higher than pretax income in 1972–73. As for the year 2005, CE numbers on the bottom quintile's mean expenditures would have been nearly 80 percent higher than Census Bureau numbers on the bottom quintile's pretax money income. In this instance, using census rather than BLS reported-income data does, to a degree, mitigate the reported cleavage between levels of spending and income levels. But it hardly vitiates indications of an apparently widening gap between incomes and expenditures for poorer American households, whose ostensible dimensions and growth both remain striking in the face of this particular adjustment for potential income underreporting.[18]

Some officials intimately familiar with the CE and CPS series and their current limitations seem hopeful that a broader, more accurate measure of income and a more reliable measure of consumption by income might reduce the reported discrepancy between income and outlays at the lower end of the income spectrum in the United States.[19] In principle, improvements in survey design and implementation and increased coverage of income actually accrued might enhance a reconciliation of current income and expenditure patterns. Yet such improvements, welcome as they would be, seem nonetheless quite unlikely to bring income and spending into alignment.

At issue here is the sheer magnitude of the current imbalances. If we compare reported pretax income with reported expenditures for the bottom quintile in the 2004 CE survey, for example, we find the aggregate implied difference between these two quantities amounts to about $201 billion.[20] What would it take, as a practical matter, for improvements in coverage and accuracy for the income measure to close this tremendous gap?

For lower-income Americans, perhaps the most serious omission from the current measure of income is the earned income tax credit. In FY 2004, the EITC transferred a total of $34.7 billion in refunds to 19.2 million lower-income tax-return filers.[21] Sizable as it is, that transfer looks very small in relation to the gap between reported spending and reported income for the bottom quintile—indeed, if it happened that the EITC accrued *solely* to households in this bottom quintile, it would only be able to explain a little more than one-sixth of that gap.

In principle, the CE, like the CPS, is supposed to measure means-tested cash aid in pretax money income, but such funds are drastically understated in the CPS, where in 2001, for example, less than 60 percent of total transfers to households for income maintenance programs was reported.[22] But even if we were to presume to make an adjustment equal to half of all FY 2004 means-tested cash aid (apart from EITC, which has already been considered here) to help balance the ledgers for the lowest quintile, this would amount to just under $39 billion—and, taken together with the EITC, would account for only 36 percent of the reported income-expenditure gap. Nor should we forget that income is not the only quantity subject to underreporting here. As we saw in the previous chapter, the CE survey appears to underreport household expenditures as well.[23] Adjustments for these substantially underreported (or taxonomically excluded) sources of income, in short, cannot eliminate the tremendous gap between reported income and reported expenditures for lower-income households; indeed, such adjustments in themselves would not even take us to the halfway mark for reconciling this disparity.

## Increased Year-to-Year Income Variability

The third possible explanation for a secular rise in the expenditure-to-income ratio for households in the lowest annual income quintile, not necessarily inconsistent with the two just examined, is a long-term increase in year-to-year variations in household income. If U.S. consumer behavior comports with the "permanent-income hypothesis," and if the stochastic year-to-year variability (that is, "transitory variance") in American income patterns were to increase, then we would expect, all other things being equal, an increase in the ratio of reported annual expenditures to reported annual incomes for households in the lower deciles of the income distribution in any given year.

This ratio would be expected to rise because, at any given time, a higher proportion of effectively nonpoor households would be experiencing a "low-income year" due to intensified transitory variance—and, since their consumption levels would be conditioned by their permanent-income expectations, they would still be spending like nonpoor households, even if they were temporarily classified as poor by the criterion of current income. The greater the proportion of temporary poor in the total poor population, the greater the discrepancy between observed income levels and observed expenditure levels should be within that population.

If poverty is defined in terms of a particular income threshold, it should be readily apparent that poverty status is not a fixed, long-term condition for the overwhelming majority of those who are ever designated as "poor." Quite the contrary—since U.S. society and the American economy are characterized by tremendous and incessant mobility, long-term poverty status appears to be the lot of only a tiny minority of the people counted as poor at any point in time by the official U.S. poverty metric.

This may be seen in figures 5-10, 5-11, and 5-12, which draw on the Census Bureau's longitudinal Survey on Income and Program Participation. For the calendar year 1999, nearly 20 percent of the noninstitutionalized American population was estimated to have experienced two or more months in which their household income fell below the (prorated monthly) poverty threshold. And at some point during the four years 1996–99, fully 34 percent of the surveyed population spent two months or more below the poverty line. On the other hand, just 2 percent of the population spent all

FIGURE 5-10

**EPISODIC VS. CHRONIC POVERTY: MEASURED POVERTY FOR
ONE MONTH VS. 48 STRAIGHT MONTHS, 1996–99**

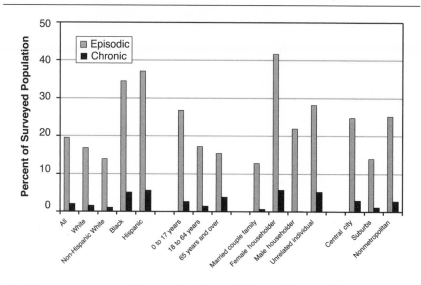

SOURCE: John Iceland, "Dynamics of Economic Well-Being: Poverty 1996–1999," *Current Population Reports*, P70-91 (Washington, D.C.: U.S. Bureau of the Census, July 2003), http://www.census.gov/prod/2003pubs/p70-91.pdf (accessed May 16, 2007).

forty-eight months of 1996–99 below the poverty line. The "long-term poor" (or "permanent poor"), in other words, accounted for barely one-tenth of those who passed through officially designated poverty at some point in 1999 and less than 6 percent of those who were counted as poor at any point between the start of 1996 and the end of 1999.

As might be expected, the incidence of chronic or long-term poverty varies according to ethnicity, age, household composition, and location. Whereas just 1 percent of the non-Hispanic white population is estimated to have spent all of 1996–99 below the poverty line, the rate was over 5 percent for both African Americans and Hispanic Americans; long-term poverty rates of over 5 percent also typified female-headed households and persons living alone. Yet even for the groups with the highest measured rates of long-term poverty, these permanent poor accounted for a very small fraction of the ever-poor. Fewer than a sixth of Hispanics who were counted

FIGURE 5-11

DURATION OF POVERTY SPELLS, 1996–99

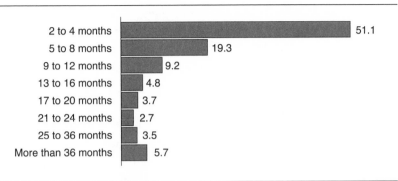

SOURCE: John Iceland, "Dynamics of Economic Well-Being: Poverty 1996–1999," *Current Population Reports*, P70-91 (Washington, D.C.: U.S. Bureau of the Census, July 2003), http://www.census.gov/prod/2003pubs/p70-91.pdf (accessed May 16, 2007).
NOTE: Percent excludes spells underway during the first interview month.

FIGURE 5-12

LONG-TERM PROBABILITY OF STAYING IN POVERTY BY AGE, 1996–99

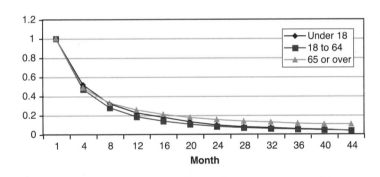

SOURCE: U.S. Bureau of the Census, "Spells of Poverty for Persons Who Became Poor During the 1996 SIPP Panel, by Selected Characteristics: 1996–1999," *Poverty—Poverty Dynamics 1996–9*, table 4, http://www.census.gov/hhes/www/poverty/sipp96/table04.html (accessed May 16, 2007).

as poor at any time during 1999, for example, had been below the poverty line throughout 1996–99.[24]

Given the high proportion of the temporarily poor within the overall population of the counted poor, it should not be surprising that reported expenditures would exceed reported income among America's lower-income strata, as they apparently do today. But while the dynamics illustrated in figures 5-10, 5-11, and 5-12 speak to high, steady, and rapid rates of transition into and out of "poverty status" for households in the late 1990s, those data do not indicate whether the longer-term trend in year-to-year household income variability has been increasing.

More extended longitudinal data series would be required for such calculations; fortunately, such data are currently available. Perhaps the most comprehensive of these is the Panel Study of Income Dynamics (PSID), an ongoing, in-depth socioeconomic survey that commenced in 1968 and currently follows 7,000 sampled families.[25] Several researchers have attempted to estimate longer-term trends for transitory variance in U.S. household income based on these data.

Given its own point of historical inception, the PSID cannot help us trace these trends back to the early 1960s—to the time of the 1960–61 CE survey—but PSID data can map out trends for the decades since the 1972–73 CE survey. Transitory variance estimates based on these PSID files seem to point to a general pattern—one of secular, and quite significant, increases in such variability between the early 1970s and the beginning of the twenty-first century. The patterns suggested by the PSID survey are illustrated in figures 5-13 to 5-15.

Although the concept of transitory income—and thus variance in transitory income—is clear enough in theory, the task of computing transitory variance is not straightforward in practice, owing to the nature of the observational problem. (After all, just how are outside observers supposed to distinguish the "permanent" component of a household's reported aggregate income from the "transitory" component at any given point in time?) Consequently, a variety of techniques have been advanced for decomposing permanent variance and transitory variance within the spectrum of overall income differences within a given population.

One approach to decomposing transitory variance and permanent variance was developed by Robert A. Moffitt of Johns Hopkins University and Peter Gottschalk of Boston College, who applied their method to PSID household earnings data.[26] Relying on this same technique, Jacob S. Hacker of Yale University calculated that the year-to-year variability of pretax money income for U.S. families rose dramatically over the last quarter of the twentieth

FIGURE 5-13

TOTAL INCOME VARIANCE AND TRANSITORY INCOME VARIANCE,
UNITED STATES FAMILIES, 1969–1998

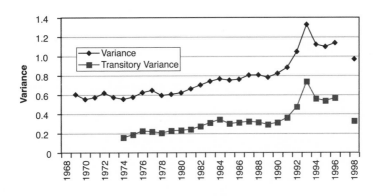

SOURCE: Jacob S. Hacker, "Table 1: Permanent and Transitory Variances of Log Income, 1969–1998," http://pantheon.yale.edu/~jhacker/PSID_Data_NYT.htm (accessed May 16, 2007).
NOTE: Pretax money income, constant 1997 U.S. $.

century, more than doubling between 1973 and 1998.[27] By those calculations, transitory variance (or what Hacker labels "income instability") rose quite steadily over the course of the 1970s and 1980s, then spiked upward in the early 1990s. It dropped off in the mid- and late 1990s, but nevertheless remained in 1998 well above the average level of the 1973–90 period.

Further work by Hacker updated those calculations to cover the 1973–2000 period, and changed the metric from pretax family income to post-tax, post-transfer family income (arguably, a more representative measure for permanent income). Those computations also indicated a substantial long-term rise in transitory variance for U.S. household income (along with a strong evident measure of cyclicality). Like Hacker's initial findings, these updated calculations in figure 5-13 report a curious and unexplained spike in transitory variance for the year 1993—but, even excluding that observation, there is an unmistakable secular increase in measured year-to-year variability over this period.

In a recent book, Hacker offered additional detail and perspective on trends in year-to-year income volatility, as reflected in the PSID. Between 1974 and 2002, for example, transitory variance in family income in households

FIGURE 5-14

ABSOLUTE ANNUAL INCOME VARIABILITY,
MEDIAN INCOME FAMILIES, 1970–2000

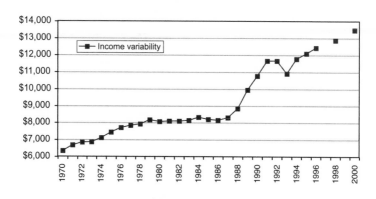

SOURCES: *Los Angeles Times*, "The Source of the Statistics and How They Were Analyzed," December 29, 2004, http://www.latimes.com/business/la-fi-riskshift3oct10-method,1,2775842.story (accessed May 17, 2007); calculations by Robert A. Moffitt and Peter Gottschalk. Raw numbers provided by Peter Gosselin, e-mail message to author, November 8, 2005.
NOTE: Variability defined statistically as one standard deviation of variance.

headed by persons between the ages of twenty-five and sixty-one reportedly more than doubled, irrespective of whether one examined pretax or after-tax money income; the spread between "best" income year and "worst" income year for such families in any ten-year stretch progressively widened over the course of the '70s, '80s, and '90s; and for those same families, the odds of seeing their income fall by 50 percent or more in the coming year rose almost constantly between 1970 and 2002, from about 7 percent in 1970 to about 16 percent in 2002.[28]

Other analyses of the PSID survey corroborated Hacker's general findings and expanded on them. For a special series of articles on economic insecurity in the United States today for the *Los Angeles Times*,[29] Robert A. Moffitt was commissioned to supervise an additional breakdown of trends in transitory variance in U.S. family income over the 1970–2000 period. Utilizing Moffitt-Gottschalk techniques, he and two graduate students calculated, among other things, the changes in transitory income variance for families at different rungs on the income ladder, and the absolute change in transitory variance for median-income households in the United States.

FIGURE 5-15

PROPORTIONAL VARIABILITY OF ANNUAL INCOME BY FAMILY INCOME:
1970–2000 (20TH PERCENTILE, 50TH PERCENTILE, 90TH PERCENTILE)

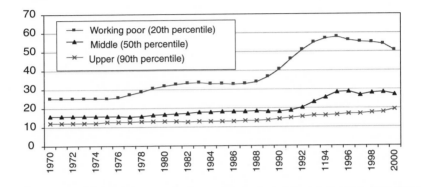

SOURCES: *Los Angeles Times*, "The Source of the Statistics and How They Were Analyzed," December 29, 2004, http://www.latimes.com/business/la-fi-riskshift3oct10-method,1,2775842.story (accessed May 17, 2007). Calculations by Robert A. Moffitt and Peter Gottschalk. Raw numbers provided by Peter Gosselin, e-mail message to author, November 8, 2005.
NOTE: 2001 constant U.S. $. Proportional variability is the coefficient of variation for random fluctuations.

According to those calculations, inflation-adjusted variations in annual U.S. family income registered a steady and consequential climb over the 1970–2000 period, as shown in figure 5-14. For a median-income American household—a family in the very middle of overall income distribution—the maximum expected random volatility in year-to-year income more than doubled over these years, rising from about $6,300 in 1970 to nearly $13,500 in 2000 (in 2003 dollars).[30] Since inflation-adjusted median family income (in the PSID data series) rose by just 28 percent over those same years, maximum random annual volatility in relation to annual income rose substantially— from about 16 percent in 1970 to about 27 percent in 2000. The correspondence between income shocks and family income levels, moreover, was not uniform across the income spectrum, as figure 5-15 attests.

Moffitt calculated what statisticians call the "coefficient of variation" (variance as a proportion of the sample's mean) for families at three separate positions in the income scale: the twentieth percentile (designated as "the working poor"), the fiftieth percentile (labeled "the middle class"), and the ninetieth percentile ("upper income"). In 1970, the coefficient of variation was lowest for the highest of these income groupings, and highest for the lowest income grouping; proportional income variability was about twice as high for families at the 20 percent mark in the overall income distribution as it was for those at the 90 percent threshold. Between 1970 and 2000, the coefficient of variation rose for families at all three spots in the overall U.S. income distribution—but it was measured as rising especially sharply for those bordering the bottom income quintile. Whereas proportional income variability increased by about three-fifths for the "upper-income" grouping, and by about three-fourths for the "middle-class" grouping, it fully doubled for the "working-poor" families at the boundary between the bottom income quintile and the second income quintile in the overall income distribution.

The long-term increase in proportional income variability for American households and the disproportionate increase in such variability for Americans at the lower rungs of the income ladder evident within the PSID data series are highly suggestive.[31] Certainly, the measured long-term increases in transitory income variance reflected in the PSID would be consistent with the by now generally accepted finding that secular differences in overall household earnings and overall household income both increased during the last quarter of the twentieth century in the United States.[32]

The causes of different socioeconomic factors and their relative contributions to the phenomenon of increased earnings and income dispersion in contemporary America are matters of extensive ongoing research and active debate among informed specialists, and stand beyond the scope of this inquiry. The social consequences of increased income inequality, and the policy implications of those trends, are likewise a matter of widespread interest and continuing, intense dispute that would take us far afield. For our limited purposes here, it may suffice to underscore a single statistical consequence of the measured rise in U.S. income inequality. If (as PSID data strongly suggest) the proportional variation in annual household income has been on the rise over the past generation, and if, moreover, such increases have been especially pronounced for the lower quintiles of the overall income distribution (as PSID data also strongly suggest), then we would expect a corresponding rise—possibly a sharp rise—in the discrepancy between reported annual incomes and reported annual expenditures for households in the bottom quintile of the income distribution.[33]

FIGURE 5-16

MEAN NET WORTH FOR ALL REPORTING HOUSEHOLDS,
FIRST AND SECOND INCOME QUINTILES, 1989–2004

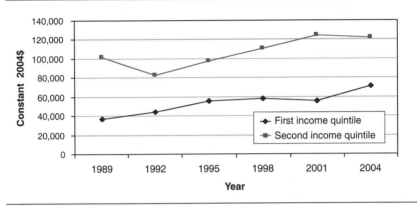

SOURCE: Federal Reserve Board, Survey of Consumer Finances, various years, http://www.federalreserve.gov/Pubs/oss/oss2/scfindex.html (accessed February 22, 2008).

The proposition that America has been experiencing a major long-term shift toward greater year-to-year income volatility—with disproportionate increases affecting the lower half of the income distribution—would be consistent not only with the otherwise curious divergence between income and spending trends for lower-income households, but also with some equally counterintuitive patterns that have been observed regarding wealth formation. According to the Federal Reserve Survey of Consumer Finance (see figure 5-16), differences in net worth for the bottom quintile and the next highest quintile of families actually narrowed between 1989 and 2004. In those years, the estimated ratio for the net worth of the bottom quintile in relation to the second quintile of families rose from 36 percent to 58 percent. Over that same period, furthermore, the absolute increase in estimated net worth for the bottom quintile exceeded that of the "wealthier" quintile immediately above it (roughly $35,000 versus roughly $21,000).

Needless to say, those are surprising results—especially given the prevailing understanding that income differences have been widening, not narrowing, in our country since the late 1960s. But they could, perhaps, be explained to some meaningful degree by increasing transitory variance in family incomes. If year-to-year volatility were on the rise, and especially marked for families in the lower half of the income distribution, we would expect an increasing share of "permanent" families from the second quintile to register temporarily in the bottom quintile in any given year—and conversely, we would also expect a rising share of "permanent" lowest-quintile families to appear in the second quintile in any given year. In effect, the rise in transient variance would increasingly blur the line between these two quintiles in any annual "snapshot" we might take—and the impact of such blurring on a point-in-time measurement of wealth could be to imply a narrowing of wealth differentials between these income quintiles, even during a prolonged period of increasing income differentiation. Income volatility, in short, could be a key to explaining the seemingly paradoxical behavior of lower-income households with respect to both spending and the accumulation of wealth.

Clearly, much more research is warranted on the issue of transitory income variance. The PSID is not the only data series that might be used to test the hypothesis of secular increases in income volatility in the years since 1973; the Census Bureau's Survey of Income and Program Participation is another longitudinal source that could permit us to probe, test, and perhaps corroborate the relationship that has emerged with such robustness from the PSID data.[34] If conclusively established, rising year-to-year income volatility would qualify as a truly major socioeconomic trend.

The possible ramifications of a secular increase in income volatility would be far-reaching and profound. Increases in income volatility might or might not presage secular increases in consumption inequality in America for the post-1973 period. In point of fact, a recent analysis of CE survey data by Dirk Krueger of the University of Pennsylvania and Fabrizio Perri of the University of Minnesota suggests that U.S. households experienced only a modest increase in consumption inequality between 1980 and 2003.[35] Yet even if per-capita consumption did increase after 1973 and consumption inequality did not, the implications of increased income inequality for consumer welfare would raise important questions. Basic economic reasoning suggests that if some households had preferred less uncertainty about annual fluctuations in their incomes, they would also have been willing, on some particular terms, to trade lower long-term streams of both income and consumption for reduced income volatility. As a consequence, without some sense of risk tolerance and risk preference in the population at large, the welfare implications of the unfolding trends for income and consumption cannot be comprehensively, or even adequately, assessed.

These weighty matters, however, are beyond the scope of this inquiry. For the limited purposes of this study, it will suffice here simply to note that the curious divergence between reported income and expenditure patterns that has been recorded in consumer expenditure surveys for the period since the early 1970s appears to be matched, and could possibly be largely explained, by the simultaneous rise in transitory income variance for U.S. families, as registered in the PSID survey, and by the particularly marked increase in proportionate year-to-year variations reported for families at the borderline of the bottom income quintile.

## A Continuing Puzzle

Let us summarize the findings of this chapter. A stark and growing surfeit of expenditure over income has been reported for poorer U.S. families over the past half-century. We have examined four factors that might help to account for this puzzling and seemingly paradoxical development.

The first possible factor—"overspending" through excessive (and potentially unsustainable) debt accumulation by lower-income households—sounds superficially plausible, but its existence is not supported by the empirical data on wealth formation. Quite the contrary: Available data point to an unprecedented aggregate upsurge in wealth and asset holdings on the part of the lowest income quintile during the very period when that same quintile has reported unprecedented imbalances between spending and income.

A second possible factor would be alterations in the design and conduct of the BLS's Consumer Expenditure Survey, the principal source for the data documenting the tremendous reported rise in the ratio of spending to pre-tax money income for poorer households. As it happens, important discontinuities in survey method and practice *have* marked the CE survey since the 1960–61 decennial survey; just how much of that reported widening should be ascribed to purely methodological factors, however, remains unclear.

Perhaps the most obvious methodological issue would be underreporting of income, which we treat as a third plausible factor for explaining the growing reported divergence between spending and income for poorer households. There is good reason to believe that income underreporting figures into the reported imbalances between spending and income in CE surveys, at least from the 1980s onward. But, as we have seen, income underreporting could explain only a relatively small proportion of the widening gap between spending and pretax money incomes for poorer households over the decades in question—and our reckoning takes no account of any possible increase in the underreporting of expenditures by lower-income households over those same years.

A fourth potential explanation for a widening mismatch between spending and income for poorer households would be rising year-to-year variations in household income—in more technical parlance, increasing transitory variance for household income. All other things being equal, greater transitory variance would be expected to increase the disparity between spending and income among households that happened to be on the lower rungs of the income distribution in any given year. As we have seen, there is intriguing, and accumulating, evidence to suggest that transitory variance for household incomes in the United States may have risen very substantially since at least the early 1970s—and, moreover, that year-to-year volatility may have risen disproportionately for households in the lower half of the income distribution. Rising year-to-year income volatility might well go far in explaining the sustained and increasingly extreme excess of reported spending over income among poorer households over the past generation or more. Clearly, much more research is warranted here: This corner of the American economy is in need of much more illumination. For now, however, we may safely say that available data on the measured rise in transitory variance appear to be generally consistent with the otherwise mysterious long-term rise in the reported ratio of spending to income for poorer households.

Our examination of the widening gap between income and consumption for lower-income households should be regarded as only a preliminary investigation into this deep mystery in modern America's social and economic contours. Many questions about this continuing mystery remain. What should be apparent by now, however, is that this gap is *not* merely a statistical artifact. The disconnection of income levels from spending levels in the lower deciles of our country's annual income distribution is genuine. It is not only enduring, but apparently growing. And for households with incomes at or below the poverty level, this disconnection is now immense—a stark and widening gap that has inescapable implications for the reliability of the official poverty rate. If reported income levels severely underpredict consumption for families near the official poverty threshold—and do so by ever-larger margins over time—the official poverty rate cannot hope to offer an accurate count of the population subsisting below a certain fixed living standard. We shall explore this problem in greater depth in the following chapter.

# 6

# Trends in Living Standards for Low-Income Americans: Indications from Physical and Biometric Data

The official poverty rate is a gauge for measuring absolute poverty—that is to say, for tracking the prevalence of need against an unchanging absolute criterion. This basic fact is central both to the method by which the OPR is calculated, and to the conventional interpretation of its reported results.

The official poverty rate formally became a measure of absolute poverty in the late 1960s, and it has been one ever since. The decision that permanently converted the OPR into an absolute poverty index was made in 1969, with the federal government's determination that the Orshansky matrix of poverty thresholds would thenceforth be adjusted regularly—but only to reflect changes in prevailing price levels.[1] By indexing annual changes in nominal poverty thresholds against the Consumer Price Index (as opposed, say, to adjusting for changes in both prices and incomes), the official poverty rate is, both in principle and in practice, devised to track over time a set of fixed and constant household income standards for distinguishing the poor from the nonpoor.

While there are conceptual justifications for both absolute and relative measures of poverty, the plain fact is that the OPR, for nearly four decades, has expressly been an *absolute* measure—one that would identify people living in conditions determined by a specific and already established budget constraint, as proxied by their reported pretax money incomes.[2] As Orshansky herself would write of the case for an absolute poverty measure, "Statistical nicety will be better served if there remains an invariant criterion."[3]

Given the manner in which the OPR has been constructed, contemporary specialists on the poverty question commonly and quite naturally understand it to identify the proportion of the population faced by, or trapped in, a condition of designated absolute want, defined over time at a constant level; hence the following description, by David Ellwood and Larry Summers, of what the OPR is and what it represents:

> The officially defined poverty rate [tracks] the fraction of the population living in families with incomes below the poverty line. It is important to understand that the poverty line is a fixed level of real income . . . It is adjusted each year only for changes in the cost of living. Changes in the poverty rate thus provide an indicator of society's success in alleviating hardship among those with relatively low incomes.[4]

Accordingly, when the OPR registers stagnation, or worse, over a number of successive decades, the inescapable interpretation is that hardship is *not* being alleviated. Since the OPR is an absolute indicator of poverty, the national trends that have been reported since the early 1970s are necessarily taken to suggest that the standard of living for the lower strata of American society has evidenced no long-run improvement—on the contrary, it may actually have been subject to some long-term deterioration.

Exactly that understanding was implicit in the comments of economist Sheldon Danziger of the University of Michigan, a leading authority on America's poverty problem, upon the annual release of the Census Bureau's poverty report in 2004. The report revealed that the OPR for the country was higher in 2003 than it had been thirty years earlier. In Danziger's words, "We have had a generation with basically no progress against poverty. . . . The economic growth is not trickling down to the poor."[5] Danziger's appraisal, we should emphasize, is in no sense exceptional; rather, that same assessment of the OPR data is widely shared by poverty experts in academic and policy circles.

But the notion that the OPR tracks a fixed and unchanging standard of living is patently contradicted by a wide array of physical and biometric indicators. These data demonstrate steady and basically uninterrupted improvements in the material conditions and consumption levels of Americans in the lowest income strata over the past four decades.

As we saw in chapter 1, Mollie Orshansky intended her original standard for counting the poor to designate an income level below which "everyday living implied choosing between an adequate diet of the most economical sort and some other necessity because there was not money enough to have both."[6] In subsequent writings, she would describe her original poverty thresholds as denoting "a stringent definition of poverty"; "a line below which deprivation is almost inevitable"; a standard "considered by some almost too niggardly to be called American."[7] The standard of living afforded by those original Orshansky poverty-line budgets may indeed look stringent— especially from our current national vantage point. At the risk of repetition, let us state once more: Those very same poverty thresholds (adjusted only for inflation) are being used to distinguish the official poverty population from the officially nonpoor today.

But the OPR's poverty thresholds seem to bear ever less correspondence to the actual consumption patterns of the poverty-level households supposedly defined by them. Though an absolute poverty measure should ordinarily be expected to establish, and track, a more or less fixed level of deprivation, the standard of living of those officially counted as poor has risen steadily over time. In purely material terms, today's American poverty population is incontestably better off than were Orshansky's poor back in 1965.

## The Principal Categories of Expenditures for Low-Income Consumers

To track the changing material circumstances of America's low-income population, we will follow trends in four areas: food and nutrition; housing; transportation; and health and medical care. From the early 1960s through the beginning of the twenty-first century, American consumers, poor and nonpoor alike, devoted the great majority of their personal expenditures to these categories of goods and services.

From 1960–61 to 2005, food, housing, transportation, and health and medical care together accounted for about 70–75 percent of mean U.S. household expenditures, and for a somewhat higher proportion (nearer 80 percent) of the expenditures of households in the lowest income quintile. And while the composition of these allocations by category shifted over these decades, their total claim within overall expenditures remained fairly stable. Let us examine in turn trends in these categories.

TABLE 6-1

PERCENTAGE COMPOSITION OF CONSUMER EXPENDITURES
FOR THE UNITED STATES, 1960/61 VS. 2005

|  | 1960/61 | 2005 |
| --- | --- | --- |
| Food (at home) | 24.5 (19.6) | 12.8 (7.1) |
| Housing | 28.9 | 32.7 |
| Transportation (public) | 15.3 (1.5a) | 18.1 (1.0) |
| Health and medical care | 6.7 | 5.7 |
| Other | 24.6 | 30.7 |

SOURCES: U.S. Department of Labor, Bureau of Labor Statistics, *Handbook of Labor Statistics 1975—Reference Edition*, BLS Bulletin 1865 (Washington, D.C.: U.S. Department of Labor, 1978), table 137; U.S. Bureau of Labor Statistics, "Consumer Expenditures in 2004," Report 992 (Washington, D.C.: U.S. Department of Labor, April 2006), http://www.bls.gov/cex/csxann04.pdf (accessed November 6, 2006).
NOTE: a. Non-automotive transportation.

TABLE 6-2

PERCENTAGE COMPOSITION OF CONSUMER EXPENDITURES
FOR LOW-INCOME AMERICANS, 1960/61–2005

|  | 1960/61 (families, lowest quartile) | 1972/73 (families, lowest quintile) | 2005 (consumer units, lowest quintile) |
| --- | --- | --- | --- |
| Food (at home) | 29.0 (24.5) | 24.2 (20.9) | 15.9 (10.4) |
| Housing | 33.7 | 37.7 | 39.4 |
| Transportation (public) | 9.1 (1.5a) | 14.5 (1.2) | 14.3 (0.7) |
| Health and medical care | 8.7 | 6.7 | 7.6 |
| Other | 19.5 | 16.9 | 22.8 |

SOURCES: U.S. Department of Labor, Bureau of Labor Statistics, *Handbook of Labor Statistics 1975—Reference Edition*, BLS Bulletin 1865 (Washington, D.C.: U.S. Department of Labor, 1978), table 137; *Consumer Expenditures Survey: Interview Survey 1972–73*, BLS Bulletin 1997 (Washington, D.C.: U.S. Department of Labor, 1978), volume 1, table 10; U.S. Bureau of Labor Statistics, "Consumer Expenditures in 2005," Report 998 (Washington, D.C.: U.S. Department of Labor, April 2006), http://www.bls.gov/cex/csxann05.pdf (accessed November 1, 2006).
NOTE: a. Non-automotive transportation.

FIGURE 6-1

PERCENTAGE OF HOUSEHOLD SPENDING ALLOCATED TO FOOD
BY REPORTED ANNUAL INCOME, 1960/61

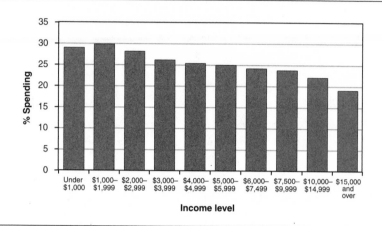

SOURCE: U.S. Department of Labor, Bureau of Labor Statistics, *Handbook of Labor Statistics 1975–Reference Edition*, BLS Bulletin 1865 (Washington, D.C.: U.S. Department of Labor, 1978), table 137.

**Food and Nutrition.** In the early 1960s—the years for which the poverty rate was first devised—undernutrition and hunger were unmistakably evident in the United States. Indeed, self-assessed food shortages were revealed by the expenditure patterns of American consumers. In the 1960–61 consumer expenditure survey, for example, the marginal propensity of consumers to spend income on food rose between the lowest and the next-lowest income grouping. With an income elasticity for food of more than 1.0, this poorest grouping—accounting for about 1 percent of the households surveyed—in effect defined a stratum within the population of the United States for which foodstuffs were "luxury goods." In no subsequent consumer expenditure surveys, however, is it possible to identify subcategories of the population with income elasticities of expenditure for foodstuffs in excess of 1.0.

Biometric assessments of nutritional status amplify and extend the evidence from consumer expenditure surveys. Health survey data collected by the National Center for Health Statistics (NCHS) of the U.S. Centers for Disease Control and Prevention (CDC) make the point. Between the early 1960s and the end of the century, for example, the proportion of the adult population

FIGURE 6-2
PERCENTAGE OF THE UNITED STATES POPULATION UNDERWEIGHT,
1960–62 TO 2001–4

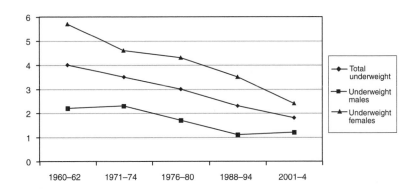

SOURCE: National Center for Health Statistics, *Health, United States, 2006* (Washington, D.C.: U.S. Government Printing Office, 2006), table 73, http://www.cdc.gov/nchs/hus.htm (accessed September 17, 2007).
NOTE: Body mass index of less than 18.5 defined as underweight. Data for U.S. adult population (20–74 years old).

twenty to seventy-four years of age diagnosed probabilistically as underweight from weight-for-height readings (that is, with a measured body mass index, or BMI, of under 18.5) dropped by half, from 4.0 percent to 1.9 percent.[8]

The main nutritional problem to emerge over those years in the anthropometric data was obesity (designated by a body mass index of 30 or greater), the prevalence of which—as predicted by weight-for-height data—soared from 13 percent in 1960–62 to 32 percent in 2001–4; at the turn of the new century, furthermore, the incidence of obesity was notably higher for the officially poor (35 percent) than for the general population.[9]

For purely biological reasons, a society's most nutritionally vulnerable groups are typically infants and children. Anthropometric and biometric data suggest that nutritional risk to American children has almost continuously declined over the past three decades. Even for low-income children—that is, those who qualify for means-tested public health benefits—nutritional risks look to have been declining progressively. According to the National Pediatric Surveillance System of the CDC, for example, the percentage of low-income children under five years of age categorized as underweight (in terms of BMI

FIGURE 6-3

**PERCENTAGE OF MEDICALLY EXAMINED LOW-INCOME CHILDREN SHORT OF STATURE OR UNDERWEIGHT, 1973–2005**

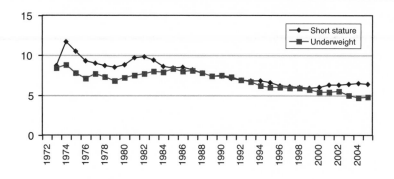

SOURCE: Centers for Disease Control and Prevention, "Summary of Trends in Growth and Anemia Indicators," 2005 Pediatric Nutrition Surveillance Report, table 12D, http://www.cdc.gov/pednss/pednss_tables/html/pednss_national_table12.htm (accessed September 17, 2007).

FIGURE 6-4

**PERCENTAGE OF MEDICALLY EXAMINED LOW-INCOME CHILDREN WITH LOW HEMOGLOBIN COUNT, 1973–2005**

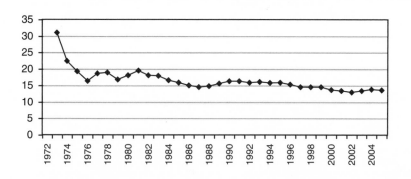

SOURCE: Centers for Disease Control and Prevention, "Summary of Trends in Growth and Anemia Indicators," 2005 Pediatric Nutrition Surveillance Report, table 12D, http://www.cdc.gov/pednss/pednss_tables/html/pednss_national_table12.htm (accessed September 17, 2007).

for age) dropped from 8 percent in 1973 to under 5 percent in 2005. Since the cutoff for "underweight" was defined probabilistically as the fifth percentile on standardized pediatric growth charts, the 2005 finding would be consistent with observations for a normalized population with an underweight prevalence of zero.

Similarly, the proportion of medically examined low-income children who presented height for age below the expected fifth percentile level on pediatric growth charts declined from 9 percent in 1973 to 6 percent in 2005. Blood work for these same children suggested a gradually declining risk of anemia, to judge by the drop in the proportion identified as having a low hemoglobin count. Note, paradoxically, that the OPR for children rose during the same period that broad improvements in childhood nutrition were being registered through the biometric and health data in figures 6-3 and 6-4: The official poverty rate for children was 14.4 percent in 1973, but 17.6 percent in 2005.

**Housing and Home Appliances.** Statistical information on U.S. housing conditions and home appurtenances is available today from three main sources: the decennial census of population and housing; the Census Bureau's American Housing Survey (AHS), conducted in 1984 and every few years thereafter; and the Department of Energy's Residential Energy Consumption Survey (RECS), initially conducted in 1978 and currently repeated every four years. Since 1970 the decennial census has cross-classified household housing conditions by official poverty status; the AHS and RECS also track poverty status and its correlates.

Basic trends in housing conditions for poor households and officially nonpoor households are highlighted in table 6-3. In terms of simple floor area, the homes of the officially poor were more spacious at the dawn of the twenty-first century than they had been three decades earlier. In 1970, about 14 percent of poverty-level households were officially considered "overcrowded" (the criterion being an average of more than one person per room). By 2001, according to the AHS, just 6 percent of poor households were overcrowded—a lower proportion than for nonpoor households as recently as 1970. Between 1980 and 2001, moreover, per-capita heated floor space in the homes of the officially poor appears to have increased substantially—to go by official data, by as much as 27 percent, or perhaps even more.[10] By 2001, the

TABLE 6-3
SELECTED UNITED STATES HOUSING CHARACTERISTICS:
POOR AND OTHER HOUSEHOLDS, 1970–2001

| | Non-poor households 1970 | Poor households 1970 |
|---|---|---|
| Homes with 1.0+ persons per room (%) | 7.0 | 13.6 |
| Homes lacking some or all plumbing facilities (%) | 3.4 | 17.5 |
| Homes without heating (%) | 0.6 | 0.9 |
| Mean heated square feet per home | N/A | N/A |
| Average heated square feet per household member | N/A | N/A |

SOURCES: U.S. Bureau of the Census, *1970 Census of Population: Subject Reports, Low-Income Population*, Final Report PC(2)-9A (Washington, D.C.: GPO, 1973), table 36; U.S. Bureau of the Census, *1980 Census of Housing: General Housing Characteristics*, part 1, HC 80-1a (Washington, D.C.: GPO, 1983), table 1; U.S. Department of Energy, *Residential Energy Consumption Survey: Housing Characteristics 1980* (Washington, D.C.: GPO, 1982), tables 9, 26; U.S. Department of Energy, *Residential Energy Consumption Survey: Housing Characteristics 1990* (Washington, D.C.: GPO, 1992), table 15; U.S. Department of Energy, *Residential Energy Consumption Survey: Housing Characteristics 1997* (Washington, D.C.: GPO, 1999), http://www.eia.doe.gov/emeu/recs/recs97/recs97.html#Household%20Characteristics, tables CE2-3c, HC2-4b; U.S. Bureau of the Census, *American Housing Survey of the United States: 2001*, Current Housing Reports H-150-01 (Washington, D.C.: GPO, 2002), tables 2-3, 2-4.
NOTE: a. 1997; N/A = not available.

fraction of poverty-level households lacking some plumbing facilities was reportedly down to 2.5 percent—a lower share than for nonpoor households in 1970.[11]

Trends in furnishings and appurtenances for American households are provided in table 6-4. These data record the steady spread of desirable consumer appliances to poor and nonpoor households alike.

There are, to be sure, some discrepancies between the AHS and RECS as to the availability of certain amenities in poverty-level households as of 2001, as noted above, and for a few items, such as dishwashers and central air conditioning systems, those discrepancies are nontrivial. Even so, poor households' access to or possession of modern conveniences has been increasing, and unmistakably so. For many of these items—including tele-

| All households 1980 | Poor households 1980 | Poor households 1990 | Poor households 2001 |
|:---:|:---:|:---:|:---:|
| 4.5 | N/A | N/A | 5.8 |
| 2.2 | N/A | N/A | 2.5 |
| 0.6 | 1.1 | N/A | 0.5 |
| 1,499 | 1,095 | 1,105 | 1,146[a] |
| 534 | 371 | 385 | 406[a] |

phones,television sets, central air conditioning, and microwave ovens—prevalence in poverty-level households as of 2001 exceeded availability in the typical 1980 U.S. household and in nonpoor 1970 households. By the same token, the proportion of households lacking air conditioning was lower among the officially poor in 2001 than among the general public in 1980. By 2001, over half of all poverty-level households had cable television and two or more television sets. Moreover, by 2001, one in four officially poor households had a personal computer, one in six had Internet access, and three in four had at least one VCR or DVD player—devices unavailable even to the affluent a generation earlier.

These data cannot tell us much about the quality of either the housing spaces that poverty-level households inhabit, or the quality of appurtenances furnished therein. They say nothing, furthermore, about nonphysical factors that bear directly on the quality of life in such housing units—the most obvious among these being crime. These data, however, strongly support the proposition that physical housing conditions are gradually improving, not only for the rest of America, but for the officially poor as well. In any given year, a gap in physical housing conditions separates the officially poor from the nonpoor—but the data for today's poor appear similar to those for the nonpoor a few decades earlier.

TABLE 6-4

PERCENTAGE OF POOR AND OTHER UNITED STATES HOUSEHOLDS
WITH SELECTED HOUSING APPLIANCES, 1970–2001

| | Non-poor households 1970 | Poor households 1970 |
|---|---|---|
| Telephone | 90.5 | 70.3 |
| TV | 96.8 | 88.4 |
| 2+ TVs | N/A | N/A |
| Washing machine | 74.1 | 55.8 |
| Dryer | 46.3 | 17.3 |
| Dishwasher | N/A | N/A · |
| No air conditioning | N/A | N/A |
| Central air conditioning | N/A | N/A |
| Refrigerator | N/A | N/A |
| 2+ Refrigerators | N/A | N/A |
| Outdoor gas grill | N/A | N/A |
| Microwave | N/A | N/A |
| Personal computer | N/A | N/A |
| Internet access | N/A | N/A |
| Cable TV | N/A | N/A |

SOURCES: 1970 Census of Population, loc. cit., table 36; RECS Housing Survey, loc. Cit., 1980 edition,
tables 26, 40; 1990 edition, tables 22, 38; U.S. Department of Energy, *Residential Energy Consumption
Survey: Housing Characteristics 2001* (Washington, D.C.: GPO, n.d.), http://www.eia.doe.gov/emeu/
recs/contents.html, tables HC5-3a, HC5-3b, HC 7-3a HC7-3b; U.S. Bureau of the Census, *Housing Survey for the United States in 1989,* Current Housing Reports H-150-89 (Washington, D.C.: GPO, 1991)
tables 2-4; 2001 edition, loc. Cit., tables 2-4, 2-7.
NOTES: 1. a. Color television; b. Automatic washing machine; c. Sum of values for "most used" and "second most used" household oven; N/A = not available; RECS = Residential Energy Consumption Survey.
2. Parenthetical data marked AHS come from the American Housing Survey.

**Transportation.** Trends in motor vehicle ownership or access from the
early 1970s are presented in table 6-5. At the time of the 1972–73 Consumer Expenditure Survey, almost three-fifths of the households in the lowest income quintile had no car. Since the OPR for families in those years was
only about 10 percent, we may suppose that the proportion of poverty-level
households without motor vehicles at that time was actually somewhat
higher than the numbers in table 6-5 suggest. By 2003, however, over

| All households 1980 | Poor households 1980 | Poor households 1990 | Poor households 2001 (RECS) |
|---|---|---|---|
| N/A | N/A | 81.5 (1989) | 94.5 |
| 82.0[a] | 60.6[a] | 90.2[a] | 97.5[a] |
| N/A | N/A | 28.8 | 54.7 |
| 71.6[b] | 53.7[b] | 57.3[b] | 55.7[b] |
| 61.3 | 34.6 | 37.6 | 43.5 (55.7 AHS) |
| 37.2 | 10.7 | 15.5 | 17.2 (34.0 AHS) |
| 42.8 | 58.8 | 51.7 | 36.1 |
| 26.8 | 14.7 | 16.9 | 29.8 (43.9 AHS) |
| 99.8 | 99.3 | 99.1 | 99.5 (99.0 AHS) |
| 14.0 | 6.7 | 6.1 | 5.8 |
| 8.6 | 1.9 | 8.0 | N/A |
| 14.3[c] | 2.3[c] | 55.8 | 73.5 |
| N/A | N/A | 4.9 | 24.4 |
| N/A | N/A | N/A | 18.3 |
| N/A | N/A | N/A | 77.9 |

three-fifths of U.S. poverty-level households had one or more car—and nearly three out of four had some sort of motor vehicle. (The distinction is pertinent, owing to the popularity and proliferation of SUVs, light trucks, and other forms of non-car motor vehicles from the late 1970s onward.) By 2003, quite a few poverty-level households had more than one motor vehicle: 14 percent had two or more cars, and 7 percent had two or more trucks. In 2003, to be sure, vehicle ownership was more limited among the officially poor than among the general public; for the country as a whole, fewer than 9 percent of households reported being without any motor transportation whatever.

The increase in motor vehicle ownership among officially poor households has followed the general rise for the American public—albeit with a very considerable lag. As of 2003, auto ownership rates for poverty-level

TABLE 6-5

MOTOR VEHICLE PATTERNS FOR LOW INCOME AMERICANS,
1972/73–2003

|  | 1972/73 (lowest income quintile, families) | 1985 (poverty households) | 1989 (poverty households) | 2003 (poverty households) |
|---|---|---|---|---|
| No car (%) | 56.5 | 44.0 | 41.9 | 37.9 |
| No vehicle (%) | N/A | 39.7 | 36.8 | 26.6 |
| 1 car (%) | N/A | 45.0 | 46.9 | 48.0 |
| 2+ cars (%) | N/A | 11.0 | 11.2 | 14.0 |

SOURCES: U.S. Department of Labor, Bureau of Labor Statistics, *Consumer Expenditure Survey: Interview Survey, 1972–73*, vol. 1, *U.S. Tables, Families Classified by Ten Family Characteristics* (Washington, D.C.: GPO, 1978), table 10; U.S. Bureau of the Census, *American Housing Survey for the United States in 1985*, Current Housing Reports H-150-85 (Washington, D.C.: GPO, 1988), table 2-7; U.S. Bureau of the Census, *American Housing Survey for the United States in 1989*, Current Housing Reports H-150-89 (Washington, D.C.: GPO, 1991), table 2-7; U.S. Bureau of the Census, *American Housing Survey for the United States in 2003*, Current Housing Reports H-150-03 (Washington, D.C.: GPO, 2004), table 2-7; U.S. Bureau of the Census, *Historical Statistics of the United States: Colonial Times to 1970*, part 2 (Washington, D.C.: GPO, 1975), http://www.census.gov/prod/www/abs/statab.html, 717.
NOTE: 1. N/A = not available. Totals may not add up to 100 due to rounding.
2. Share of U.S. families owning one or more cars in 1960: 77 percent; share owning two or more cars: 15 percent.

households mirrored those for U.S. families in general in the early 1950s; for all forms of motor transportation, they matched general levels from the early 1960s; and for two or more motor vehicles they paralleled the general public in the late 1950s or early 1960s.[12]

**Health and Medical Care.** Data from the National Center for Health Statistics can be used to illuminate two separate aspects of health status and medical care in modern America: outcomes and service utilization. Figures 6-5 to 6-10 highlight some selected facets of overall trends in each area.[13]

The most critical datum for health status is, arguably, mortality, as all other health indicators are subsidiary to survival. While the single most intuitively clear mortality indicator may be expectation of life, available data unfortunately do not permit the construction of "life tables" and attendant survival schedules by official poverty status.[14] Mortality data are, however,

FIGURE 6-5

AGE-ADJUSTED MORTALITY RATES:
UNITED STATES POPULATION AGES 25–64, 1950–2004

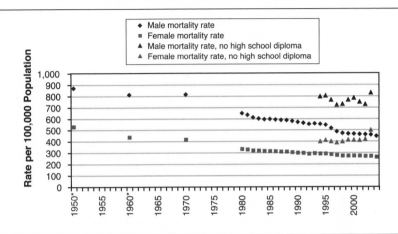

SOURCE: National Center for Health Statistics, *Health, United States, 2005*, tables 34 and 35 (Washington, D.C.: U.S. Government Printing Office, 2006), ftp://ftp.cdc.gov/pub/Health_Statistics/NCHS/Publications/Health_US/hus06tables/(accessed September 17, 2007).
NOTES: 1. Includes deaths of persons who were not residents of the 50 states and the District of Columbia.
2. In 2003, the series on age-standardized mortality by educational attainment underwent significant revisions.

available for adults by their educational attainment, and this proxy affords us a glimpse of some of the socioeconomic differences in death rates.

Perhaps not surprisingly, adults without high school diplomas had significantly higher age-standardized death rates than the general population; in 2003, the differential was over 50 percent among both men and women. Despite the relative magnitude of this disparity, however, in absolute terms death rates in 2003 for this educationally disadvantaged group were lower than they had been among the general public some years earlier. The overall age-standardized death rate for women twenty-five to sixty-four years of age in 1970, for example, was slightly higher than the 2003 rate for their counterparts who had not completed high school. Among adult men, death rates for the general public in 1970 were about 10 percent higher than among high school dropouts in 2003.[15]

For babies and infants, the single most important measure of health status is surely the infant mortality rate. Between 1970 and 2004, that rate fell

FIGURE 6-6

POVERTY RATES VS. INFANT MORTALITY RATES:
UNITED STATES, WHITE CHILDREN, 1959–2003

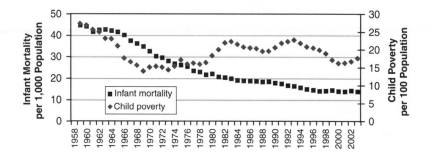

SOURCES: M.F. MacDorman and H.M. Rosenberg, "Trends in Infant Mortality by Cause of Death and Other Characteristics, 1960-1988," National Center for Health Statistics, *Vital and Health Statistics*, series 20, no. 20 (January 1993), table 2; Centers for Disease Control and Prevention, "Infant Mortality and Low Birth Weight Among Black and White Infants—United States, 1980–2000," *Morbidity and Mortality Weekly Report* 51, no. 27 (July 12, 2001): 589-592, table 1; Elizabeth Arias et al., "Deaths: Final Data for 2001," *National Vital Statistics Reports* 52, no. 3 (September 25, 2003), http://www.cdc.gov/nchs/pressroom/03facts/mortalitytrends.htm (accessed May 16, 2007); Kenneth D. Kochanek et al., "Deaths: Final Data for 2002," *National Vital Statistics Reports* 53, no. 5 (October 12, 2004), http://www.cdc.gov/nchs/data/nvsr/nvsr53/nvsr53_05.pdf (accessed May 16, 2007); Donna L. Hoyert et al., "Deaths: Final Data for 2003," *National Vital Statistics Reports* 54 no. 13 (April 19, 2006), http://www.cdc.gov/nchs/products/pubs/pubd/nvsr/54/54-20.htm (accessed November 6, 2006); Arialdi M. Miniño et al., "Deaths: Final Data for 2004," Health E-Stats, National Center for Health Statistics, table 2, http://www.cdc.gov/nchs/products/pubs/pubd/hestats/finaldeaths04/finaldeaths04.htm (accessed May 14, 2007); U.S. Bureau of the Census, "Poverty Status of People, by Age, Race, and Hispanic Origin," *Historical Poverty Tables*, table 3, http://www.census.gov/hhes/www/poverty/histpov/hstpov3.html (accessed November 6, 2006).

by nearly two-thirds in the United States, from 20 per 1,000 to 6.8 per 1,000 live births.[16] It continued its almost uninterrupted annual decline after 1973, when OPRs for U.S. children began to rise. The contradistinction is particularly striking for white babies. Between 1974 and 2004, their mortality rates fell by three-fifths, from 14.8 per 1,000 to 5.7 per 1,000; yet, over those same years, the official poverty rate for white children rose from 11.2 percent to 14.3 percent.[17]

These survival gains were achieved not only in the face of purportedly worsening poverty status, but also despite unfavorable trends in biological risk. In 2004, the proportion of white babies born at high-risk low birthweights

FIGURE 6-7

INFANT MORTALITY VS. LOW BIRTH WEIGHT:
UNITED STATES, WHITE CHILDREN, 1950–2004

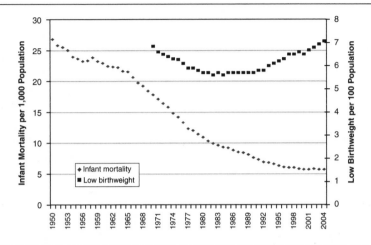

SOURCES: M.F. MacDorman and H.M. Rosenberg, "Trends in Infant Mortality by Cause of Death and Other Characteristics, 1960-1988," National Center for Health Statistics, *Vital and Health Statistics*, series 20, no. 20 (January 1993), table 2; Centers for Disease Control and Prevention, "Infant Mortality and Low Birth Weight Among Black and White Infants—United States, 1980–2000," *Morbidity and Mortality Weekly Report* 51, no. 27 (July 12, 2001): 589-592, table 1; Elizabeth Arias et al., "Deaths: Final Data for 2001," *National Vital Statistics Reports* 52, no. 3 (September 25, 2003), http://www.cdc.gov/nchs/pressroom/03facts/mortalitytrends.htm (accessed May 16, 2007); Kenneth D. Kochanek et al., "Deaths: Final Data for 2002," *National Vital Statistics Reports* 53, no. 5 (October 12, 2004), http://www.cdc.gov/nchs/data/nvsr/nvsr53/nvsr53_05.pdf (accessed May 16, 2007); Donna L. Hoyert et al., "Deaths: Final Data for 2003," *National Vital Statistics Reports* 54 no. 13 (April 19, 2006), http://www.cdc.gov/nchs/products/pubs/pubd/nvsr/54/54-20.htm (accessed November 6, 2006); Arialdi M. Miniño et al. "Deaths: Final Data for 2004," Health E-Stats, National Center for Health Statistics, table 2, http://www.cdc.gov/nchs/products/pubs/pubd/hestats/finaldeaths04/finaldeaths04.htm (accessed May 14, 2007); National Center for Health Statistics, *Health, United States, 2006*, table 13 (Washington, D.C.: U.S. Government Printing Office, 2006), http://www.cdc.gov/nchs/hus.htm (accessed May 14, 2007).

(below 2,500 grams) was actually somewhat higher than in 1973 (7.1 percent versus 6.4 percent). Yet despite this troubling trend in low–birth weight disposition, infant mortality rates had improved dramatically. Since the inherent biological disparities in mortality risk between low–birth weight and non-low–birth weight newborns did not diminish over this period,[18] the reasonable inference might be that medical and health-care interventions—changes in the quality and availability of services—accounted for most of the difference. And since low–birth weight infants are disproportionately born to

FIGURE 6-8

PROPORTION OF ADULT POPULATION WITH UNTREATED DENTAL CARIES,
1960–62 TO 1999–2002

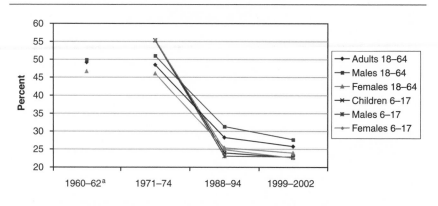

SOURCES: James E. Kelly, Lawrence E. Van Kirk, and Caroline C. Garst, "Decayed, Missing and Filled Teeth in Adults, 1960–1962," NCHS Series 11, no. 23 (February 1967), table 4; National Center for Health Statistics, *Health, United States, 2006* (Washington, D.C.: U.S. Government Printing Office, 2006).
NOTE: a. Adults ages 18–79.

mothers from disadvantaged socioeconomic backgrounds, a further reasonable inference is that these improvements in the quality and availability of medical care extended to America's poorer strata, not just the well-to-do.

One particularly revealing indicator of health status and health-care availability is dental health. Since at least the nineteenth century, with its pathbreaking reform-movement studies of the English working classes, the condition of a population's teeth has been recognized as a telling reflection of social well-being.[19] Dental health is also an informative proxy for health-care access, because dentistry is still widely regarded as an "optional" medical service. Between the early 1970s and the turn of the century (1999–2002), the share of the U.S. adult population with untreated caries (dental cavities) is estimated to have dropped by half, from 48 percent to 24 percent. Of the officially poor adults, fully two-fifths still had untreated cavities in the 1999–2002 NCHS survey—but since nearly two-thirds of poverty-level adults had untreated cavities in the 1971–74 surveys,[20] this represented a considerable advance over circumstances a generation earlier.

FIGURE 6-9

PROPORTION OF 65+ POPULATION WITH NO REMAINING NATURAL TEETH,
1960–62 TO 1999–2002

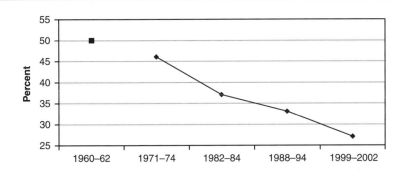

SOURCES: James E. Kelly, Lawrence E. Van Kirk, and Caroline Garst, "Total Loss of Teeth in Adults: United States, 1960–62," NCHS Series 11, no 27 (October 1967); National Center for Health Statistics, *Health, United States, 2006* (Washington, D.C.: U.S. Government Printing Office, 2006).
NOTE: 1960–62 value is for seniors 65 to 74 years old.

For older Americans, the loss of all natural teeth was always a likely outcome in later life, but a majority of those sixty-five years of age and older can now expect to avoid that fate. According to NCHS health examination surveys, the fraction of "edentulous" senior citizens declined from about 47 percent in the early 1970s to about 27 percent around the turn of the century. (No specific data are available here on trends for poverty-level seniors, but one study on overall trends in the prevalence of "edentulism" for the U.S. population twenty-five to seventy-four years of age noted substantial and continuing decreases between 1972 and 2001 for Americans of higher and lower socioeconomic standing alike.)[21]

Such improvements in dental conditions are suggestive of improved dental care. Time-series data on dental visits are not immediately available, but data for recent years could be consistent with increased use of dentistry by the official poverty-level population. By 2004, nearly half of poor adults ages eighteen to sixty-four and nearly two-thirds of poor children ages two to seventeen were reportedly making at least one dental visit a year.[22] Such rates would look comparable to those reported for the general population in the early 1960s.[23]

FIGURE 6-10

PERCENT OF CHILDREN UNDER 18 YEARS WITHOUT A REPORTED HEALTH
CARE VISIT IN THE PAST YEAR, BY PERCENT OF POVERTY THRESHOLD,
1982–2005

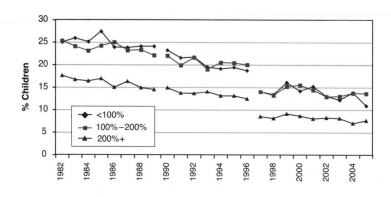

SOURCES: Jennifer Madans, Kimberly Lochner, and Diane Makuc, "Poverty and Health," (PowerPoint presentation, Reconsidering the Poverty Measure Seminar, Welfare Academy, University of Maryland, College Park, MD, March 8, 2005), http://welfareacademy.org/pubs/poverty/cdc.ppt (accessed September 19, 2007); National Center for Health Statistics, "Summary Health Statistics for U.S. Children: National Health Interview Survey, 2004," *Vital and Health Statistics*, Series 10, number 227 (Washington, D.C.: GPO, 2006); National Center for Health Statistics, "Summary Health Statistics for U.S. Children: National Health Interview Survey, 2005," *Vital and Health Statistics*, Series 10, number 231 (Washington, D.C.: GPO, 2006).

Trends in utilization of health care for the poor are further illustrated by the circumstances of children under eighteen—more particularly, by the proportion reporting no medical visits over the year preceding their health interview surveys. While the percentage of children without an annual medical visit has always been higher among the poor than the nonpoor, steady declines were reported for both groups—and the declines were substantial. The proportion of children without a reported visit was, in fact, significantly lower for the poor population in 2004 (12.0 percent) than it had been for the nonpoor population twenty-two years earlier (17.6 percent). Figure 6-10 cannot address the question of preexisting health needs, and it could be that pediatric medical problems were on the rise during this period; these data, thus, do not conclusively demonstrate that "access" or "availability" of health and medical care have been improving. But they are strongly suggestive of this possibility—all the more so in conjunction with the salutary trends in health-status outcomes.

## Living Standards for America's Poor:
## Constant Progress under a "Constant" Measure

To summarize the evidence from physical and biometric indicators, low-income and poverty-level households today are better-fed and less threatened by undernutrition than they were a generation ago. Their homes are larger, better-equipped with plumbing and kitchen facilities, and more capaciously furnished with modern conveniences. They are much more likely to own a car (or a light truck or other type of motor vehicle) now than thirty years earlier. By almost every indicator apart from obesity, their health-care status is considerably more favorable today than at the start of the War on Poverty. Their utilization of health and medical services has increased steadily over recent decades.

All of this is, in one sense, highly reassuring. These data underscore the basic fact that low-income Americans *have* been participating in what Orshansky termed "America's parade of progress." Orshansky had worried that the poor might be watching that parade and "wait[ing] for their turn— a turn that does not come."[24] Fortunately, that apprehension has proved to be unfounded.

To state that much is not to assert that material progress for America's "poverty population" has been satisfactory, much less optimal. Nor is it to deny the importance of relative as opposed to absolute deprivation in the phenomenon of poverty as the poor themselves experience it. Those are serious questions that merit serious discussion in their own right; but they are questions distinct and separate from the focus of this study—namely, the reliability of the OPR per se as an indicator of poverty and want.

As we have seen, the OPR is premised on the assumption that official poverty thresholds provide an *absolute* poverty standard—a fixed intertemporal resource constraint. Such a standard should mean that general material conditions for the "poverty population" will remain more or less invariant over time. Yet, quite clearly, the material condition of the poor population in the United States has *not* been invariant over time—it has been steadily improving. The OPR thus fails—one is tempted to say that it fails spectacularly—to measure what it purports to be tracking over time. As an indicator of a condition originally defined in 1965, the OPR seems to have become a less faithful and reliable measure with each passing year.

What explains this failure? The crux of the problem would appear to lie in the limitations of the type of indicator that was initially selected for tracking changes in material deprivation over time. The OPR, to repeat, relies upon annual reported money income to make its calculations about the prevalence of poverty. But since inflation-adjusted money incomes have scarcely increased for the lowest quintile of American households since 1973, an income-based metric would be hard pressed to explain the steady and almost continuous improvements in living standards for lower-income Americans that are evident throughout this period.[25] It is even less suited to explaining improvements in the living standards of the poor population, since the U.S. poverty thresholds are, by design, intended to be fixed at the same inflation-adjusted income levels from one year to the next, throughout the decades.

Some superficially plausible explanations for the contradiction between stagnant measured money incomes and increasing material living standards have been tendered, but, for the most part, they are unconvincing. Take, for example, the notion that living standards for the poor seem to have been rising due to changes in "relative prices." It is true, as some commentators have pointed out, that the relative price of food has somewhat declined over the years since the OPR was devised. Relative prices for other items in the household budgets of lower-income Americans have also declined over the decades, sometimes dramatically—think of consumer electronics, personal computers, mobile phones, and the like. But, as a theoretical proposition, it is impossible for the relative prices of *all* goods and services to fall simultaneously; and, as an arithmetic proposition, it is impossible to elicit major increases in consumption in food, housing, transportation, *and* health care, simultaneously and under a fixed-income constraint, through the device of changing relative prices—not if those four baskets of goods and services account for roughly 80 percent of (low-income) consumer outlays today, and likewise accounted for the vast majority of consumer outlays throughout the previous generation or two.

Public antipoverty programs offer another superficially plausible, but ultimately less than fully persuasive, explanation for the steady measured rise in living standards for the official poverty population. Official poverty status is determined by a family's reported pretax money income; noncash, means-tested benefits have always been excluded from this calculus.[26] Since in-kind social welfare outlays have soared since the launch of the War on Poverty, living standards of the poor have been subsidized in ways that the OPR, perforce, cannot track. The vast expansion of means-tested health benefits, for example, surely helps explain the steady improvements in health status for lower-income households. Subsidized nutrition programs may partly explain the increased food availability for poorer families, but only to a degree; real spending on means-tested food programs is, after all, scarcely higher today than it was in the early 1990s,[27] whereas the share of the poverty population's spending allocated to food has kept on declining— and the estimated prevalence of overweight and obesity among the poor has kept on rising. Government programs cannot directly explain the surge in ownership of motor vehicles and consumer durables among the officially poor over the past four decades—in these realms, no means-tested benefit programs exist. And, of course, in-kind benefit programs cannot explain the robust, long-term growth of cash outlays among lower-income households that we documented in previous chapters.

The poor performance of an income-based construct as a predictor of trends in material living standards for lower-income Americans (to say nothing of those officially in poverty) over the past three-plus decades provides still further proof that the problems with the OPR look to be systemic in nature. That is to say, annual money income may simply be the wrong tool for measuring living standards for lower-income households in modern America. Consumption-based indices promise to provide a more serviceable, consistent proxy for material well-being, and to bring to the account of how the poor have fared an empirical coherence that simply cannot be gleaned from any narrative dependent upon the current OPR.

# Conclusion:
# Wanted—New Poverty Measure(s)
# for Modern America

Let us briefly summarize and review the findings, and recapitulate the arguments, of the preceding chapters.

## The Case against the Official Poverty Rate

America's now official poverty rate was initially unveiled in 1965 and very rapidly became the primary statistical index used for measuring the country's performance against poverty, both at the national and more local levels. For over four decades, the OPR has been a central reference point— arguably, *the* central reference point—for all U.S. discourse about domestic poverty, whether among policymakers, in academic circles, or by concerned members of the general public.

Unfortunately, this "indispensable" indicator of progress in our national struggle against poverty appears to be incapable of accurately tracking trends in material well-being for lower-income groups within the population. Over time, the flaws and biases in the OPR's calculated results have become increasingly evident. Today, the contradiction between the numbers generated by the OPR, on the one hand, and an enormous mass of data from other U.S. statistical sources bearing upon domestic poverty and material well-being, on the other, is glaring—and all but impossible to ignore.

According to the official poverty rate, the early 1970s were the "golden age" of America's struggle against poverty. The OPR reached its historical low point in 1973. The incidence of officially measured poverty is higher today than it was nearly three and a half decades earlier, back in the Watergate era of the Nixon administration.

On its own, this would surely be taken as an ominous—even alarming—sounding. But many other social and economic trends bearing directly on domestic poverty have actually registered significant progress over those very same years. Real per-capita income in America, for example, is up sharply since 1973; the educational attainment of the working-age population (by the metric of high school degrees) has steadily improved; antipoverty spending has soared. And although unemployment has fluctuated dramatically between 1973 and the present, the country's civilian unemployment rate was actually lower in 2006 (4.6 percent) than it was back in 1973 (4.9 percent).[1] Despite all these signs of improvement, the OPR stubbornly—and improbably—reports that the incidence of poverty was higher in 2006 (12.3 percent) than in 1973 (11.1 percent).

As we have demonstrated, this anomalous and counterintuitive contraposition of the OPR and other major indicators bearing upon domestic material deprivation is not an aberration, nor an atypical statistical artifact for a single "odd year." To the contrary: Simple statistical analysis underscores the telling fact that changes in the OPR no longer correspond to changes in per-capita income, median family income, unemployment, educational attainment, or antipoverty spending through the sort of commonsense relationships one would ordinarily expect. Instead, in the years since 1973, the OPR has increasingly come to behave as a perverse and contrary arbiter of well-being, stubbornly in opposition to other—more transparent and perhaps self-evident—measures of material progress and material need.

As we saw in probing these relationships statistically through a variety of regression relationships, if per-capita income rises, the OPR will also oftentimes rise—and rise systematically—in tandem with increased income levels. A drop in unemployment should leave the poor better off, but reductions in the U.S. unemployment rate can be statistically associated with systematic *increases* in the official poverty rate. And although the spread of education in any country should abet the quest to contain or eliminate poverty, the steady improvements in educational attainment in the adult population in America over the past three-plus decades have been strongly and systematically associated with *increases* in the official poverty rate.

The official poverty rate, in fact, has taken to describing a United States fundamentally different from the one depicted by the other major statistical indicators of material progress and poverty. It is not too much to say that the OPR over the past three decades has undergone a progressive and systematic divorce from the economic and social realities of life in modern America, as reflected by the other main statistical indicators charged with similar service.

The OPR fails to match up with reality in other, less econometrically exacting ways as well. As initially constructed, and as it still operates to this day, the OPR assumes implicitly that a household's reported annual pretax money income establishes its spending power for that same year; more than that, it presumes that these two quantities are identical. But reported annual pretax money income is *not* a reliable predictor of expenditure levels for lower-income households today; in fact, income has become an ever less faithful indicator of actual spending patterns for poorer Americans over time.

As we have seen, spending already exceeded income for the poorest fourth of the American public in the early 1960s, when the now official poverty rate was being constructed. Today, however, reported annual expenditures exceed reported income for a third or more of all households in any given year—and, within the lowest fifth of households, reported spending is nearly twice as high as annual reported income.

Some part of this reported disparity may be a statistical artifact. Yet the great (and possibly still growing) discrepancy between reported incomes and reported expenditure patterns among our bottom quintile also appears to reflect genuine and important changes in the American economy, most notably the secular rise in year-to-year volatility in household income since 1973.

All other things being equal, greater "transitory variance" in household incomes will mean a greater disproportion between annual spending and annual income for households at the lower end of the annual income spectrum. The material well-being of lower-income households is, of course, directly tied to their spending power—that is to say, to their expenditure patterns—but the OPR, by its very design, is incapable of tracking those same spending patterns.

One additional and signal failure of the official poverty rate must be flagged in any empirical discussion of poverty and material well-being in America today. This is its manifest inability to provide an accurate reading of absolute poverty in the United States—the charge that the indicator was expressly assigned from the 1960s on.

The OPR is, by explicit official designation, meant to monitor absolute poverty—that is to say, to measure poverty in relation to a set income threshold, rather than in relation to the current incomes reported by families or some other relative, and thus perennially changing, standard. Ever since the OPR's original poverty thresholds were established back in 1965, they have been annually revised solely to take account of changes in the Consumer Price Index. In principle, this should mean that a fixed and unchanging income criterion is being used for determining the poverty status of families. Further, since the inflation-adjusted income threshold of those counted officially poor is supposed to remain constant over time, the material condition of those below the poverty line should similarly be more or less consistent from one decade to the next.

Yet, as we saw, this supposition is completely refuted by biometric and other physical data on the living conditions of the U.S. poverty population. With regard to food and nutrition, anthropometric data demonstrate that our poor are incontestably better off today than in 1965; ironically, in fact, overweight and obesity are the prime problems that have emerged over this interim as major nutritional concerns with regard to this population. With respect to housing, the poor today live in decidedly less crowded, more spacious, and better-furnished dwellings than they did four decades ago—and those housing standards appear to have improved steadily, decade by decade. By a number of benchmarks, indeed, the officially poor today enjoy better housing conditions than the nonpoor in 1970, or the American population as a whole as recently as 1980. With respect to transportation, a steadily increasing proportion (by now, the vast majority) of officially poor households own cars, trucks, or other sorts of motor vehicles, and a significant and rising minority of officially poor families have two or more motor vehicles. Finally, utilization of medical and health-care services by the officially poor has progressively expanded over the decades—so much so that children in families below the poverty line in 2004 were more likely to have at least one annual doctor's visit than were children in families with incomes well above the official poverty line only two decades earlier.

If the OPR were actually measuring what it presumes to track, such a steady and pervasive improvement in living standards for the poor population would be impossible to explain. Long-term increases in the consumption of *certain types* of goods or services could, of course, take place under a fixed-budget constraint; evolving tastes or fashions, technical innovations, and/or movements in relative prices are some of the factors that could account for such changes. But such changes would, perforce, be limited. In the jargon of modern welfare economics, under a genuinely fixed and constant budget constraint, we could see "substitution effects," but not overall "income effects."

On the basis of "substitution effects" alone, however, there is simply no way to account for the changing consumer patterns of officially poor households over the past four decades—patterns that have recorded simultaneous, steady, and significant increases in consumption of food, housing, transportation, and health. Taken together, those categories of consumer expenditures make up the overwhelming majority (around 80 percent) of items in the market basket of the poverty-level population. To make the point even more sharply, we can suggest that examination of the remaining categories within the market basket of the low-income consumer—clothing, entertainment, personal care, and so on—would reveal additional and analogous improvements in material circumstances over the past four decades. In virtually every budget category one might consider, the population below the official poverty line in the United States is not just consuming more today than in 1965; it is consuming dramatically more.

The patent inability of the OPR to maintain and measure a consistent standard of absolute poverty over time attests to a central, and ultimately irresolvable, defect in its design: The OPR is an income-based measure, but material living standards are instead determined by trends in consumption. While there is plenty of scope for improving the particular money measure employed in the OPR for reasons we have already seen, a better money measure in and of itself cannot hope to square the circle (or, perhaps more properly, to span the chasm) between income and consumption for the lower strata of the American income distribution in any given calendar year.

## Don't "Mend" It—End It

In sum, the U.S. official poverty rate is incapable of representing what it was devised to portray, and what the public and policymakers alike have been assured for decades that it does portray—namely, a constant level of absolute need in American society. The biases and flaws in the OPR are so severe that it has depicted a period of general (if uneven) and dramatic improvements in living standards—the decades from 1973 onward—as a time of increasing prevalence of absolute poverty. Unwittingly, for over a generation, we in the United States have been guiding our national antipoverty policies using a broken compass.

We would discard a statistical measure that claimed life expectancy was falling during a time of ever-increasing longevity, or one that asserted our national finances were balanced in a period of rising budget deficits. As central as the OPR has become to antipoverty policy—or, more precisely, especially because of its central role in such policies—the OPR should likewise be discarded in favor of a more accurate index, or set of indices, for describing material deprivation in modern America.

If heeded, the call to discard the OPR altogether in favor of other more accurate measures of want and need would, without question, take public policy into new and presently unfamiliar territory. I recognize that such a recommendation, by its somewhat novel and unfamiliar nature, may be prone to misinterpretation. Therefore, in the interest of clarity, it seems worthwhile to dwell on what this study does *not* imply, and on what it does not suggest.

First and foremost: The preceding analysis does *not* hold that all is well for America's poor—or even that their general plight is markedly better today than in 1965, when the War on Poverty was ramping up. To the contrary, I readily acknowledge that, in many tragic respects, the misery and degradation suffered by the country's most disadvantaged elements may arguably be even more acute today than forty years ago.

No matter what metric one cares to use, for example, family structure in contemporary America is far more frayed nowadays than it was in 1965. While the human consequences of family breakdown are seldom auspicious, they tend to be most severe and unforgiving for the poor. By the same token, despite the past decade and a half of trending downward, crime rates, for both violent and property crime, remain far higher today than in 1965. It is no secret that the greatest burden of crime also falls hardest on the very poor. (The corollary of that crime explosion—today's historically unprecedented levels of prison incarceration for young men—not only reflects on misery in modern America, but perhaps also further contributes to it.) Clearly, all is *not* well in our commonweal, especially for our most vulnerable citizens.

This study, however, does not presume to measure misery, degradation, or other essentially *noneconomic aspects of the quality of life* in modern America, important as these may be to any overall assessment of the plight of our poor. The focus of this study is more limited—namely, to the issue of the *economic resource constraints* faced by our poor. Very clearly, those economic resource constraints have been appreciably relaxed over the past generation, making possible the significant improvement in material living standards that we have detailed in the preceding pages. Just as clearly, the official poverty rate completely missed those improvements in the decades past. If and when further such improvements occur, the OPR will just as surely continue to miss those as well.

Second, and scarcely less important, this study does *not* render a verdict on the success or failure of America's postwar antipoverty policies— much less venture recommendations for "reform" or "improvement" of those same policies. It does not even attempt an overall assessment of the material impact of those policies.

Why not?[2] Because its aperture is too narrow for such an undertaking. The objective of this study, once again, is to evaluate the reliability of our country's chosen statistical measure for tracking trends in domestic poverty and material want. As we have seen, the OPR grossly misreads those trends. Whereas the OPR reports that we have made no progress in reducing the prevalence of absolute poverty over the past three and a half decades, practically every other available statistical indicator points to major improvements in material living standards for the country's poorest strata over those same years.

Accommodating such empirical findings will require a fairly major recasting of the conventionally delivered narrative about long-term progress against poverty in the United States. Yet rewriting that part of the narrative about poverty and material progress will hardly draw us—as interested and concerned citizens—to cloture and consensus on "welfare reform." More than we may perhaps at times recognize, our ongoing and contentious national debate about the adequacy and efficacy of public guarantees and social safety nets is, at heart, really a dispute over first principles and underlying premises rather than a wrangle over the brute facts at hand.

Consequently, this particular study will not—it cannot—settle the question of whether or not America's War on Poverty has "failed." What it does establish—I hope conclusively—is that the index we use for measuring results in that "war" is a failure, and an unmitigated one at that.

Third, this study does *not* insist that an absolute measure of poverty is the *only* criterion appropriate for assessing material deprivation. In any society or polity there will of course be a relative aspect to poverty as well. This basic truth, indispensable to a humane understanding of the human condition, was discussed by Adam Smith over two centuries ago:

> Consumable commodities are either necessaries or luxuries. By necessaries I understand, not only the commodities which are indispensably necessary for the support of life, but whatever the custom of the country renders it indecent for creditable people, even of the lowest order, to be without. A linen shirt, for example, is, strictly speaking, not a necessary of life. The Greeks and Romans lived, I suppose, very comfortably, though they had no linen. But in the present times, through the greater part of Europe, a creditable day-labourer would be ashamed to appear in public without a linen shirt, the want of which would be supposed to denote that disgraceful degree of poverty, which, it is presumed, nobody can well fall into without extreme bad conduct. Custom, in the same manner, has rendered leather shoes a necessary of life in England. The poorest creditable person, of either sex, would be ashamed to appear in public without them . . . Under necessaries, therefore, I comprehend, not only those things which nature, but those things which the established rules of decency have rendered necessary to the lowest rank of people.[3]

Though "shame," "disgrace," and stigma may play less of a role in demarcating "necessaries" today than in Adam Smith's own era, the list of "necessaries" themselves can be expected to evolve over time, especially as income levels and technological possibilities change. In the four-plus decades since the OPR was established in 1965, per-capita income in the United States has more than doubled.[4] It would not be unreasonable to expect social norms and notions about the minimum acceptable market basket for impoverished Americans to rise with this tide, as well. Indeed, quiet, spontaneous, and important changes in such norms may already be taking place, even in the absence of an explicit national conversation about new "necessaries" for our day and age.[5]

But, once again, such issues take us far beyond the purview of this particular study. Indeed, they amount to changing the subject at hand altogether. The determination of an acceptable minimum consumption level, guaranteed and supported through social policy and public funds, is, in essence, a political decision, conditioned by the subjective and possibly changing preferences and precepts of the American electorate. Even voters who wish to raise the level of assistance that public guarantees provide may want reliable information on America's performance against absolute want. The official poverty rate promises precisely such information, but cannot actually provide it.[6]

Fourth, while this analysis does indicate that reported annual income is an increasingly unreliable indicator of material deprivation and living standards in modern America, it does *not* follow that income metrics should be discarded altogether in the determination of need in all social policy. Let us be very clear here: Today and in the foreseeable future, the eligibility criterion for public welfare benefits will surely continue to be an income benchmark. But this is essentially an administrative consideration, not an analytical one. The bureaucratic and programmatic response to existing need will not necessarily involve the same tools required for evaluating performance against material poverty—nor should it. Though this might seem to go without saying, it may nonetheless be well to state as much explicitly.

Finally, this study does *not* propose to replace the OPR with some specific, alternative "poverty rate" or "poverty line." Our inquiry, to the contrary, offers scant encouragement to any who would hope that a "new and improved" version of the official poverty rate (that is to say, a measure based on matching some given poverty threshold against some given definition of annual family income) might somehow be free of the basic biases and defects we have described in the real, existing OPR.

The problem is this: A family's material circumstances will directly reflect its annual consumption, but will relate to its annual income only indirectly. In modern America, moreover, the link between annual income and annual consumption seems to have become markedly weaker, and the correspondence distinctly more distant, especially in recent decades. No income-based poverty measure can hope to square this circle, no matter how accurate its measurement—or comprehensive its definition—of annual income might happen to be.

This is not a brief against income data, of course. Timely and accurate information on annual trends in reported income should be of interest to policymakers and concerned citizens for a great many reasons. My point is simply that the desire for income-based estimates on the prevalence of absolute poverty in our country should not be one of them.

## New Directions

The findings in this study *do* point to some perhaps promising directions for inquiry in the years ahead. Consumption is, without doubt, a more faithful measure of material deprivation than income. Further, the complex (and, for our purposes, crucial) interplay between consumption and income can be much better captured by longitudinal surveys that track given households or persons over time than by "snapshot" measures that report on family circumstances for a single point in time. Not so incidentally, longitudinal data are necessary for any examination of the year-to-year changes in the incomes of families and individuals—and, as we have seen, such variability, or "instability," in incomes appears to have increased very substantially over the past generation. Detailed longitudinal financial data—on assets, liabilities, and net worth—for American households could provide much greater detail to the picture of material deprivation and economic insecurity, and the relationship between these two phenomena.

In addition, physical and biometric data—on food and nutrition, housing conditions, transportation, and health and medical care, among other things—can cast light on important aspects of actual living conditions (and material want) which might not be illuminated simply by dollar-denominated measures of consumption and income. Detailed, reliable, and regular data on all these dimensions of deprivation would consequently seem all but indispensable to any in-depth look at the problem of want and poverty in the United States today.

At the moment, however, we as a nation lack the statistical capability to describe annual consumption patterns by income level and locality (or by, say, ethnicity) with any great accuracy. Our statistical capacity to follow the long-term dynamics of household income and consumption—or wealth accumulation and depletion—is scarcely less limited. Additionally, while it is possible to assemble some physical and biometric data bearing on living conditions for lower-income Americans, many of these statistics are episodically collected, otherwise lacking in comparability, or unsuitable for analyses at much below the national level—and none of these data series is regularly compiled and presented for assessing our nation's performance against poverty. These are curious oversights for an information-rich society—all the more so, considering that we are approaching the half-century mark in our publicly declared War on Poverty.

If the public wants a better sense of living conditions facing the poor, it will have to develop a better (that is, more comprehensive, more accurate, and more timely) set of statistical indices for measuring the same—and it must also be willing to pay for that additional information. Compared to our public outlays for antipoverty programs—or other costs we bear for poverty in America—the price of better information will be a pittance.

At the end of the day, there is no single, "obvious" answer to the question of what indicator, or indicators, should be used to replace the OPR. It may be that the public good would be served by the simplicity of a single indicator of absolute poverty for our country. There is an alternative argument for a multiplicity of measures of material want—as there is for including measures of misery along with measures of material deprivation in our national conversation about poverty. And there is a case for a still broader array of social indicators, of the sort briefly produced by our government in the early 1970s,[7] so as to approach the problem of domestic poverty from the context of overall social well-being.

Whether one single indicator or, alternatively, an array of diverse indicators would be more appropriate for describing deprivation in modern America is a question that scholars, concerned citizens, and political leaders would be well advised to consider as they ponder the changing, but enduring, problem of poverty in modern America. What we have attempted to demonstrate here is that the OPR is a treacherous and untrustworthy yardstick, wholly unsuitable for informing public policy on poverty issues. Unburdening public discourse of this false counsel to policy will only be a single step toward a better approach to poverty reduction. But it will be an important step, nonetheless.

Insofar as the official poverty rate is a federal statistical measure, it would seem both advantageous and fitting for the federal government to take the initiative in the effort to replace the OPR with a more useful and reliable gauge of want and deprivation. To date, unfortunately, the federal government has devoted no sustained or continued attention to a reconsideration of its official poverty measure. But a lack of federal interest in, or effort toward, reexamining and ultimately replacing our country's broken official poverty indicator need not prevent government action in this realm altogether. Nor, in fact, is it doing so today. At this writing, the City of New York has announced its own initiative to develop an alternative poverty metric. According to the *New York Times*, the current city administration,

> frustrated by the federal government's Great Society method of determining who is poor, is developing its own measure, which city officials say will offer a more modern and accurate picture of poverty . . . About a year ago [Mayor Michael Bloomberg] announced that the city would put $150 million in public and private money toward new antipoverty programs. In developing the new programs, however, the city discovered a serious obstacle: the federal poverty standard was all but useless in assessing whether the efforts were having an effect . . . So the city began drafting a new measure.[8]

The New York City poverty measure is expected to debut in midyear 2008. The *Times* article adds that "city officials . . . hope the new measure will set off a nationwide re-examination of the current federal standard, and prompt other cities and states to adopt the city's method."[9] Regardless of whether other localities eventually choose to endorse New York City's as yet unveiled poverty measure, a state- and city-driven "nationwide reexamination" of the current federal poverty measure would be all for the good. Indeed, it could be precisely through this sort of local experimentation (or, if you will, "competitive federalism") that we might actually find ourselves able to build the knowledge base, and the political consensus, for a wholly revised and substantially improved method of measuring poverty in our country.

In some quarters, criticism of the various shortcomings of the official poverty rate will still be taken as indifference to the plight of our disadvantaged and poor. Such an inference is illogical at best. Guided by a biased and increasingly unreliable statistical measure, the resources of our antipoverty programs are likely to be targeted in an increasingly inefficient (and, arguably, in an increasingly inequitable) manner as well. At this juncture, as readers by now will understand, any reasonably efficient targeting of antipoverty monies through recourse to the OPR could only be expected to occur by sheer providence. Proponents of more effective antipoverty policies should therefore be in the very front ranks of those advocating more accurate information on America's poverty problem. Without such information, effective policy action will be impeded; under the influence of misleading information, policies will be needlessly costly—and ineffective.

The task of devising a better statistical lodestar for our nation's antipoverty efforts is by now far overdue. Properly pursued, an initiative would rightly tax both our formidable government statistical apparatus and our finest specialists in the relevant disciplines. But such exertions would also stand to benefit the commonweal in as yet incalculable ways.

# Appendix

This section extends (and sharpens the focus of) this study's earlier discussion regarding the statistical relationships between the official poverty rate and other macroeconomic indicators broadly bearing upon material deprivation. In previous pages we saw that such indicators as per-capita income, the unemployment rate, educational attainment for the adult population, and per-capita antipoverty spending do not regularly generate robust and commonsense correlations with the OPR for the period since 1973 (the year when the OPR hit its lowest readings to date for proportion of families below the poverty line and percentage of the national population in poverty). In this section we will try to examine this paradox more closely.

In each of the regressions in question, our specifications examined relationships for "log-log transformed data"—that is to say, the natural logarithm of the independent variables compared with the natural logarithm of the dependent variable (always the OPR). Although there were arguments for selecting other specifications—a linear relationship or a log-linear relationship—the virtue of the log-log specification is that it would reveal the elasticities between the variables under consideration. In the log-log specification, in other words, a calculated coefficient of 0.5 would signify a .5 percent increase in the dependent variable for every 1 percent increase in the independent variable, while a coefficient of –2.0 would mean a 2 percent decline in the dependent variable for every 1 percent increase in the independent variable. The log-log specification thus not only offers intrinsically valuable information on the relationship between any given dependent and independent variable, but also provides a basis for a standard comparison of the responsiveness or "elasticity" of a given dependent variable to a number of separate independent variables. (The transformation of the original data into natural logarithmic variants, incidentally, would not in itself account for any of the peculiar relationships that were revealed in the regressions in chapter 3 of this study.)

From an econometric standpoint, two possibilities are initially obvious as explanations for anomalous correspondences (that is, unexpected positive or negative signs for regression coefficient) and weak relationships (that is, low statistical significance) between the OPR and other selected variables under consideration. These are small sample size and high correlation among those independent variables (collinearity). With a time series extending only from 1973 to 2004 (and with data missing for one variable—antipoverty spending—for the year 1974) we have just thirty-one years of data to work with. This means we have relatively few degrees of freedom for testing multivariate relationships, and we thereby risk low calculated levels of statistical significance even when the underlying relationships are, in fact, meaningful. The problem of collinearity, for its part, threatens not only to reduce the statistical significance for the relationships we wish to examine, but also to bias the calculated correspondences between the OPR and the other variables that we attempt to explore here.

One possible solution to the problem of small sample size would be to follow a "panel data" approach to probing the OPR relationship—that is to say, we might attempt to pursue our regressions at a more local level, taking results from the state level as additional "experimental observations" for testing the correspondence between the OPR and, respectively, per-capita income, unemployment, educational attainment, and antipoverty spending over time.

In principle, this is an excellent scheme; in practice, it cannot be executed. Why not? Quite simply, because the data do not exist for all the regressions we would need to replicate. Data are available for the OPR at the state level since 1973 (albeit sometimes with high standard errors). State-level data are also available for per-capita income and unemployment rates from 1973 onward. But data on adult educational attainment by state are not as readily available. The Census Bureau's continuously published annual estimates of adult educational attainment by state only extend back to the 1990s[1]—and while it would, in principle, be possible to reconstruct earlier state-level trends on the basis of the Census Bureau's Current Population Survey, the undertaking would be laborious and expensive, well beyond the scope of the present study. Furthermore, with regard to time

TABLE A-1

SIMPLE CORRELATIONS AMONG THE POVERTY REGRESSION
VARIABLES FROM TABLE 3-2

| | PCI | Unemploy- ment rate | Antipov spending | % 25+ HS degree | Poverty rate |
|---|---|---|---|---|---|
| PCI | 1 | | | | |
| Unemployment rate | −0.6349 | 1 | | | |
| Antipov spending | 0.8952 | −0.5235 | 1 | | |
| % 25+ HS degree | 0.9572 | −0.4504 | 0.8981 | 1 | |
| Poverty rate | −0.0058 | 0.5583 | −0.0039 | 0.2699 | 1 |

SOURCES: U.S. Bureau of the Census, "Poverty Status of People by Family Relationship, Race, and Hispanic Origin: 1959 to 2006," *Historical Poverty Tables*, table 2, available at http://www.census.gov/hhes/www/poverty/histpov/hstpov2.html (accessed August 29, 2007); U.S. Bureau of the Census, "CPS Population and Per Capita Money Income, All Races: 1967 to 2004," *Historical Income Tables—People*, table P-1, available at http://www.census.gov/hhes/www/income/histinc/p01ar.html (accessed August 31, 2006); U.S. Department of Labor, Bureau of Labor Statistics, "Unemployment Rate—Civilian Labor Force," Labor Force Statistics from the Current Population Survey, available at http://www.bls.gov/data/home.htm (accessed September 21, 2006); U.S. Bureau of the Census, "Percent of People 25 Years and Over Who Have Completed High School or College, by Race, Hispanic Origin and Sex: Selected Years 1940 to 2006," *Historical Tables: Current Population Survey*, table A-2, available at http://www.census.gov/population/www/socdemo/educ-attn.html (accessed September 21, 2006); Congressional Research Service, "Cash and Noncash Benefits for Persons with Limited Income: Eligibility Rules, Recipient and Expenditure Data, FY2002-FY2004," CRS Report RL33340, March 27, 2006.
NOTE: PCI = U.S. per capita money income in thousand U.S. $; % 25+ HS degree = percent of the U.S. population age 25 or older with a high school degree.

series estimates of means-tested public benefits, no data whatever are available on a comprehensive, internally consistent basis for antipoverty spending for the states and the District of Columbia.

As to the collinearity problem, it is quite real in our particular exercise. Its contours are illustrated in table A-1, which reports the first-order correlations between our selected independent variables and the OPR. We *do* see extremely high correlations, for example, between per-capita income and antipoverty spending, per-capita income and adult educational attainment, and antipoverty spending and educational attainment; in each of these two-way relationships, the correlation coefficient approaches or exceeds 0.9. All other things being equal, this would make for biased and unstable estimates of regression coefficients in the sorts of multivariate analyses undertaken in this study.

But table A-1 reveals other aspects of the respective relationships between the OPR and the independent variables that also merit comment. We see a plausible and commonsensical correspondence between the OPR and the unemployment rate—but there appears to be virtually no association whatever (that is, an "r" of less than 0.01) between either the OPR and per-capita income or the OPR and antipoverty spending for the period since 1973 in our dataset—a curious result, to say the least.[2] No less curious, the first-order correlation between adult educational attainment and the OPR is positive—meaning that higher rates of high school graduation among the adult population track with higher OPRs! Further, there is a high degree of statistical significance in this association. As we will recall from equation 5 in table 3-2, even when all of our other independent variables were included in a regression against the OPR, the education variable retained an extremely high t-value (over 11.0!) indicating that the odds of the coefficients derived being a consequence of pure chance were infinitesimal. Clearly, the perverse results we encountered in the regression work earlier in this study were not entirely due to collinearity.

The adult educational attainment variable clearly deserved closer examination. Given the steady and regular (essentially demographic) nature of increases in the proportion of the adult population with high school diplomas, we initially suspected that our education variable was acting as a proxy for a "time variable," with predictable attendant biases. Therefore, we reran out regressions from table 3-2, introducing a new time variable to cover the calendar years 1973–2004. The results are presented in table A-2.

As may be seen, introduction of the time variable has a deep and immediate impact on many of our regression equations. Whereas heretofore, for example, a regression of per-capita income and antipoverty spending had essentially no explanatory power with respect to the OPR, adding the time variable to that same regression raises the overall association between the respective independent variables and the dependent variable from 0 to nearly 60 percent (r-squared of 0.58). While the relationship between antipoverty spending and the OPR remains less than meaningful in terms of statistical significance, the relationship between the OPR and per-capita income at last assumes not only the plausible negative sign, but also a very high level of statistical significance (t-value of over 9.0). Perhaps most interesting, the time variable itself carries a positive coefficient and a

TABLE A-2

REGRESSIONS AMONG VARIABLES FROM TABLE 3-2,
INTRODUCING A TIME-SERIES VARIABLE

| | Equation 1 | Equation 2 | Equation 3 | Equation 4 | Equation 5 |
|---|---|---|---|---|---|
| N | 31 | 31 | 31 | 31 | 31 |
| Adjusted RSq. | 0.58 | 0.62 | 0.61 | 0.72 | 0.92 |
| Ln PCI | –0.98 | –0.54 | –0.38 | | –1.86 |
| | (9.26) | (–1.58) | (–1.00) | | (–8.20) |
| Ln UNEM | | 0.18 | 0.20 | 0.39 | 0.02 |
| | | (1.62) | (1.77) | (7.08) | (0.43) |
| Ln HS25+ | | | | 1.82 | 3.80 |
| | | | | (3.37) | (10.13) |
| Ln ANTIPV | –0.05 | | –0.09 | –0.26 | –0.17 |
| | (–0.47) | | (–0.87) | (–3.07) | (–3.75) |
| Ln TimeSeries | 0.22 | 0.15 | 0.15 | –0.08 | –0.06 |
| | (6.58) | (2.92) | (2.89) | (–1.31) | (–1.88) |

SOURCES: U.S. Bureau of the Census, "Poverty Status of People by Family Relationship, Race, and His-panic Origin: 1959 to 2006," *Historical Poverty Tables*, table 2, available at http://www.census.gov/hhes/www/poverty/histpov/hstpov2.html (accessed August 29, 2007); U.S. Bureau of the Census, "CPS Population and Per Capita Money Income, All Races: 1967 to 2004," *Historical Income Tables—People*, table P-1, available at http://www.census.gov/hhes/www/income/histinc/p01ar.html (accessed August 31, 2006); U.S. Department of Labor, Bureau of Labor Statistics, "Unemployment Rate—Civilian Labor Force," Labor Force Statistics from the Current Population Survey, available at http://www.bls.gov/data/home.htm (accessed September 21, 2006); U.S. Bureau of the Census, "Percent of People 25 Years and Over Who Have Completed High School or College, by Race, Hispanic Origin and Sex: Selected Years 1940 to 2006," *Historical Tables: Current Population Survey*, table A-2, available at http://www.census.gov/population/www/socdemo/educ-attn.html (accessed September 21, 2006); Congressional Research Service, "Cash and Noncash Benefits for Persons with Limited Income: Eligibility Rules, Recipient and Expenditure Data, FY2002-FY2004," CRS Report RL33340, March 27, 2006.
NOTES: PCI = U.S. per capita money income in thousand U.S. $; UNEM = civilian unemployment rate; HS25+ = percentage of U.S. population 25 and older with at least a high school education; ANTIPV = per capita U.S. means-tested spending in thousand constant 2000 U.S. $; ANTIPV data for fiscal year, not calendar year; parenthetical numbers are "t-statistics," year 1974 excluded (lack of ANTIPV data). The dependent variable is the poverty rate for the total civilian noninstitutional popu-lation (transformed into natural logarithm).

high degree of statistical significance (t-value of over 6.5). In other words: after controlling for changes in per-capita income and antipoverty spend-ing, there appears to be a strong and very steady upward drift in reported OPRs for the period since 1973.

The situation is similar with former equation 2 (which regressed the OPR against per-capita income and unemployment). Adding the time variable to equation 2 finally produces commonsensical signs for the coefficients for both per-capita income and unemployment—but, in both cases, the variables fail to reach the 5 percent level of statistical significance. The time variable, on the other hand, achieves statistical significance at the 0.1 percent level of significance, with a clear positive coefficient once more—again implying a strong annual upward drift in the OPR, even if per-capita income and unemployment were unchanging or held constant.

With the time variable added to former equation 3 (the OPR regressed against per-capita income, unemployment, and antipoverty spending), the three original independent variables finally all assume their expected signs—but none of them remains statistically significant. The time variable, by contrast, remains statistically significant at the 1 percent level of probability, once again reporting a strong positive coefficient. Unlike its relationships with per-capita income, the unemployment rate, or per-capita antipoverty spending, the relationship between the OPR and our time variable appears to be highly robust. When per-capita income, the unemployment rate, and antipoverty spending are used together in various permutations to predict the official poverty rate for the period since 1973, the calculated results seem to exhibit a clear and statistically meaningful upward bias, such that even if per-capita income, unemployment, and antipoverty spending levels were completely static, according to these first three revised equations, the reported OPR would tend to register steadily higher results with each successive year.

Adding the time variable to former equation 4 (the OPR regressed against unemployment, educational attainment, and antipoverty spending) has virtually no impact on the explanatory power of the regression. This strongly suggests serious collinearity between our time variable and our education variable. Such collinearity is further indicated by the failure now of the time variable to achieve statistical significance at the 5 percent level of probability. With the time variable inserted, the relationship between the unemployment rate and the OPR at last gains its expected positive sign, retaining a high degree of statistical significance. The relationship between antipoverty spending and the poverty rate at last attains both a commonsensical (i.e., negative) sign on its coefficient and statistical significance, although the actual relationship indicated may seem surprisingly weak. (To go by the coefficients from this equation, a mere one-percentage-point drop in the poverty rate for 2004 would have required an additional $216 billion, which is to say a 37 percent hike, in antipoverty spending!) But the relationship between educational attainment and the OPR remains perverse and statistically significant: According to these numbers, a four-point increase in high school graduation rates for adults ages twenty-five and over would imply a rise in the poverty rate of roughly one point.

Adding the time variable to the former equation 5 (which regresses the OPR against all four of our independent variables) adds virtually no explanatory power to the regression; here again, the time variable is reduced to statistical insignificance, both features attesting to the collinearity of the time variable and our educational attainment variable. In this regression, per-capita income now has a strong and statistically significant negative association with the OPR. Given the increasing dispersion of income distribution in the United States in the post-1973 period, and the attendant modest or marginal increases in measured incomes in the lower reaches of the income distribution, some scholars have hypothesized that a strong association between the OPR and mean per-capita income might no longer exist.[3] Equation 5 suggests that, to the contrary, a commonsensical, fairly strong, and statistically significant relationship between the OPR and per-capita income can be established, under the appropriate specifications.

Continuing through equation 5, we see that the relationship between unemployment and the OPR is not statistically significant, and that the relationship between antipoverty spending and the OPR is statistically meaningful, but very weak. To go by this equation, reducing the official poverty rate by just one point in 2004 would require a 62 percent antipoverty spending hike. Yet even when controlled with an independent time variable, educational attainment is linked to the OPR through a relationship that is strong, statistically meaningful—and utterly perverse. The statistical significance of this relationship (with a t-value of over 10.0) is such that the calculated odds of witnessing this relationship purely by chance appear infinitesimal; the elasticity of the relationship is such that each 1 percent change in the adult population's high school graduation rate is associated with a change of nearly 4 percent in the OPR. But the association is a positive correlation: The regression suggests that, for the period since 1973, every improvement in the educational attainment of the adult U.S. population has brought a steep increase in the incidence of officially measured poverty.[4]

TABLE A-3

CORRELATIONS OF POVERTY REGRESSION VARIABLES FROM TABLE A-2

| | PCI | Unemploy-ment rate | Antipov spending | % 25+ HS degree | Poverty rate | Time series |
|---|---|---|---|---|---|---|
| PCI | 1 | | | | | |
| Unemployment rate | -0.6349 | 1 | | | | |
| Antipov spending | 0.8952 | -0.5235 | 1 | | | |
| % 25+ HS degree | 0.9572 | -0.4504 | 0.8981 | 1 | | |
| Poverty rate | -0.0058 | 0.5583 | -0.0039 | 0.2699 | 1 | |
| Time series | 0.9796 | -0.5146 | 0.9424 | 0.9826 | 0.1312 | 1 |

SOURCES: U.S. Bureau of the Census, "Poverty Status of People by Family Relationship, Race, and Hispanic Origin: 1959 to 2006," *Historical Poverty Tables*, table 2, http://www.census.gov/hhes/www/poverty/histpov/hstpov2.html (accessed August 29, 2007); U.S. Bureau of the Census, "CPS Population and Per Capita Money Income, All Races: 1967 to 2004," *Historical Income Tables—People*, table P-1, http://www.census.gov/hhes/www/income/histinc/p01ar.html (accessed August 31, 2006); U.S. Department of Labor, Bureau of Labor Statistics, "Unemployment Rate—Civilian Labor Force," Labor Force Statistics from the Current Population Survey, http://www.bls.gov/data/home.htm (accessed September 21, 2006); U.S. Bureau of the Census, "Percent of People 25 Years and Over Who Have Completed High School or College, by Race, Hispanic Origin and Sex: Selected Years 1940 to 2006," *Historical Tables: Current Population Survey*, table A-2, http://www.census.gov/population/www/socdemo/educ-attn.html (accessed September 21, 2006); Congressional Research Service, "Cash and Noncash Benefits for Persons with Limited Income: Eligibility Rules, Recipient and Expenditure Data, FY2002-FY2004," CRS Report RL33340, March 27, 2006.
NOTE: PCI = U.S. per capita money income in thousand U.S. $; % 25+ HS degree = percent of the U.S. population age 25 or older with a high school degree.

It is true that the time variable and educational attainment as measured in this study with our educational variable are extremely collinear ($r > 0.98$). The correlations of the time variable with our variables for per-capita income and antipoverty spending are also remarkably tight (simple r's in both cases are in excess of 0.94). Yet, as a practical matter, this extreme collinearity does not seem to have a strong impact on our calculated regression results. This may be seen by comparing the results from equation 5 in table 3-2 (no time variable) with equation 5 in table A-1 (where the time variable is introduced). For per-capita income, antipoverty spending, and educational attainment, introducing the time variable does not alter the sign of the coefficient—nor does it appreciably affect either the magnitude of the coefficient calculated or the (high) estimated level of statistical significance.

Is it possible to make intellectual sense of such an econometrically robust finding? Some economic research has, indeed, suggested that the public return on several decades of investment in education may have approximated zero in some particularly troubled parts of the world (such as sub-Saharan Africa).[5] But this work also suggests that the very same institutional and macroeconomic conditions that accounted for long-term economic decline in sub-Sahara were also responsible for low rates of return on human capital; and this argument is surely not pertinent to overall expenditures for education in the highly productive and steadily growing U.S. economy. Some economists have persuasively argued that expenditures on specific facets of secondary education in the United States have low or nonexistent returns; the Graduate Equivalence Degree (GED) in particular has been identified as a low- or zero-return educational investment.[6] But even low- or zero-return public expenditures on education would not ordinarily be expected to *raise* a country's poverty rate. For an accurately measured national poverty rate to rise in conjunction with increasing general educational attainment as indicated by high school graduation rates under conditions of general and orderly material advance, overall expenditures on education through the secondary level would have to generate overall social returns that were at once high and negative. As yet, not even the most trenchant critics of American education have accused the nation's school systems of immiserating their graduates.

Shifting to another issue, we will recall that the OPR is calculated by comparing a poverty threshold against a particular definition of family income (pretax income including government cash transfers, but excluding capital gains, the value of noncash transfers, and imputed income from home equity). Some analysts seem to believe that a more careful and comprehensive measure of income might, indeed, reduce or resolve some of the apparent discrepancies that currently attend measured poverty in modern America.[7] Would a more plausible association between the calculated U.S. poverty rate and our independent variables emerge if a different definition of income were utilized?

We can begin to pursue this line of inquiry with the help of work already undertaken by the Census Bureau. Over the past decade, the Census Bureau has computed a number of "alternative" or "experimental" and unofficial estimates of the incidence of poverty in the United States, altering such parameters of the OPR as the income deflator, the treatment of in-kind benefits (including health and medical care), the imputation of rental income from home ownership, and adjustments for tax payments and tax credits.[8] Perhaps

TABLE A-4

CENSUS BUREAU ESTIMATES OF POVERTY RATE
ACCORDING TO ALTERNATIVE INCOME DEFINITIONS

1. Excluding capital gains (current official measure)
2. Definition 1: less government transfers
3. Definition 2: plus capital gains (losses)
4. Definition 3: plus health insurance supplements to wage or salary income
5. Definition 4: less social security payroll taxes
6. Definition 5: less federal income taxes
7. Definition 6: plus EITC (earned income tax credit)
8. Definition 7: less state income taxes
9. Definition 8: plus non–means-tested government cash transfers
10. Definition 9: plus Medicare
11. Definition 10: plus regular-price school lunches
12. Definition 11: plus means-tested government cash transfers
13. Definition 12: plus Medicaid
14. Definition 13: plus non-cash transfers
15. Definition 14: plus net imputed return on equity in own home

SOURCE: Joe Dalaker, "Alternative Poverty Estimates in the United States: 2003," *Current Population Reports*, P60-227 (Washington, D.C.: U.S. Bureau of the Census, June 2005), http://www.census.gov/prod/2005pubs/p60-227.pdf (accessed August 31, 2007).
NOTE: Poverty thresholds are based on CPI-U.

the most comprehensive of these exercises to date was one released in 2005. That report calculated fourteen alternative unofficial poverty rates for the U.S. population for the period 1980–2003, each defined differently from the official poverty rate in terms of what was included in income for determination of poverty status against existing poverty thresholds.[9] The time series here offers only twenty-four observations—far from ideal as a sample size, but at least a start for testing the sensitivity of correlations between the poverty rate and our four dependent variables to varying definitions of income.

Table A-4 presents the fourteen definitions for income used by the Census Bureau in computing alternative poverty rates for the United States for the years 1980–2003 (along with the long-standing official definition of money income from the OPR, for a total of fifteen calculated poverty rates).

How do these various time series correspond with one another? With fif-teen separate definitions of income, and thus fifteen separate time-series estimates of poverty rates, there will be 105 different simple correlations; table A-5 presents those calculated for the period 1980–2003.

For the most part, the correlations between these alternative poverty-rate calculations were fairly strong. Of these 105 simple correlations, over half (fifty-four cases) offered an "r" value above 0.9—meaning that in these one-to-one match-ups, movements of one poverty rate corresponded with over 80 percent of the others. For another third of the match-ups (thirty-six cases), the "r" was above 0.8—meaning, in practice, that in over five-sixths of the overall match-ups, movement in one poverty rate time series tracked with two-thirds or more of the movement in the other. For the remainder of the match-ups, the "r" was under 0.8, with nine cases regis-tering an "r" of 0.71 or lower—these signifying cases where there was barely a 50 percent association between the two series, or less. (For what it is worth, all of those lowest-correlation associations involved the relationship between income measures that excluded all government transfers and the other calculated poverty rates.)

The alternative poverty-rate series permit us to replicate our regression runs from table 3-2 with fourteen different versions of the income measure, albeit over a different and briefer time span (1980–2003, rather than 1973–2004). Do these alternatives—any of these alternatives—track more closely with per-capita income, unemployment, educational attainment, and antipoverty spending than the OPR?

Table A-6 presents the results that might answer the question. With fourteen alternative poverty measures and the original five equations from table 3-2, we ended up running a total of seventy regressions. In fifty-three of the seventy cases, one or more variable not only failed the test of statis-tical significance, but also exhibited a relationship "pointing in the wrong direction"—that is, with signs on one or more coefficients that were implausible in view of the expected underlying relationships. In nine of these seventy cases, all variables passed the test of statistical significance—but one or more demonstrated a perverse and implausible relationship with the alternative poverty rate in question.

In just eight of the seventy cases did all the variables under considera-tion report the appropriate positive or negative sign, all of these occurring

TABLE A-5

CORRELATIONS AMONG ALTERNATIVE POVERTY MEASURES FOR TABLE A-4,
1980–2003

| 1 | 2 | 3 | 4 | 5 | 6 | 7 | 8 |
|---|---|---|---|---|---|---|---|
| 1 | | | | | | | |
| 0.7492 | 1 | | | | | | |
| 0.9511 | 0.7471 | 1 | | | | | |
| 0.9601 | 0.7467 | 0.9987 | 1 | | | | |
| 0.9462 | 0.7322 | 0.9956 | 0.9967 | 1 | | | |
| 0.9622 | 0.7241 | 0.9957 | 0.9975 | 0.9954 | 1 | | |
| 0.9743 | 0.7139 | 0.9336 | 0.9439 | 0.9254 | 0.9496 | 1 | |
| 0.9738 | 0.7115 | 0.9303 | 0.9414 | 0.9226 | 0.9472 | 0.9993 | 1 |
| 0.9579 | 0.6866 | 0.866 | 0.8838 | 0.8607 | 0.8901 | 0.9792 | 0.9825 |
| 0.9615 | 0.6827 | 0.8739 | 0.8906 | 0.8675 | 0.897 | 0.9816 | 0.9849 |
| 0.9619 | 0.6819 | 0.8719 | 0.8888 | 0.866 | 0.8956 | 0.9811 | 0.9843 |
| 0.9583 | 0.6704 | 0.8543 | 0.8715 | 0.8483 | 0.8794 | 0.9753 | 0.9776 |
| 0.9402 | 0.6413 | 0.8172 | 0.8349 | 0.808 | 0.8445 | 0.9593 | 0.9614 |
| 0.9398 | 0.6447 | 0.8172 | 0.8345 | 0.8111 | 0.8447 | 0.9522 | 0.9531 |
| 0.8709 | 0.6231 | 0.7844 | 0.8026 | 0.8037 | 0.8002 | 0.8076 | 0.8111 |

SOURCE: Joe Dalaker, "Alternative Poverty Estimates in the United States: 2003," *Current Population Reports*, P60-227 (Washington, D.C.: U.S. Bureau of the Census, June 2005), http://www.census.gov/prod/2005pubs/p60-227.pdf (accessed August 31, 2007).
NOTE: R > 0.9 = 54 cases; R between 0.9 and 0.8 = 36 cases; R between 0.8 and 0.7 = 8 cases; R < 0.7 = 7 cases.

when per-capita income and unemployment were tracked in tandem against the two broader alternative definitions for family income. In seven of those eight cases, none of the dependent variables in question met the 5 percent confidence level (the very lowest criterion ordinarily extended for acceptance of a statistical result in the social sciences).

Of these seventy regressions, only one managed to achieve both plausible signs and statistically significant coefficients for all dependent variables. This was the equation regressing per-capita income and unemployment against one particular income measure: the measure that encompassed pretax money income plus capital gains minus federal, state, and local taxes,

| 9 | 10 | 11 | 12 | 13 | 14 | 15 |
|---|---|---|---|---|---|---|
| 1 | | | | | | |
| 0.999 | 1 | | | | | |
| 0.9991 | 0.9998 | 1 | | | | |
| 0.9949 | 0.9952 | 0.9962 | 1 | | | |
| 0.984 | 0.9838 | 0.9852 | 0.9949 | 1 | | |
| 0.972 | 0.9722 | 0.9748 | 0.9891 | 0.9946 | 1 | |
| 0. 8351 | 0.8375 | 0.8399 | 0.8486 | 0.8306 | 0.8543 | 1 |

while including the value of the following governments transfers: Social Security, Medicare, school lunches, means-tested cash benefits, and Medicaid—but excluding the value of noncash transfers and the net imputed return on equity in one's own home.

Does this final, singular result (equation 2 regressed against alternative poverty-rate income definition 13) suggest that further econometric research may detect a meaningful underlying relationship between the existing poverty rate (if calculated against some broader and more reliable measure of family income than is currently in official use) and other macroeconomic indicators bearing upon material deprivation in modern America? Additional research here is incontestably desirable. As already underscored, today's alternative poverty-rate calculations provide a highly limited data series for statistical analysis. With the promise of new computer software

TABLE A-6

## Do "Alternative Poverty Rates" Perform Better?

### Results for 70 Regression Equations for the 1980–2003 Period

| Sign of coefficients plausible, p-values not significant (p<.05) [-,+] | Sign of coefficients plausible, p-values significant (p<.05) [+,+] |
|---|---|
| **Seven (Eq. 2, Alt. Pov. Rate 7, 8, 9, 10, 11, 12, 14)** | **One (Eq. 2, Alt. Pov. Rate 13)** |
| P-values not all significant (p<.05), not all coefficients with plausible sign [-,-] | P-values significant (p<.05), not all coefficients with plausible sign [+,-] |
| **Fifty-three** | **Nine** |

SOURCES: U.S. Bureau of the Census, "Poverty Status of People by Family Relationship, Race, and Hispanic Origin: 1959 to 2006," *Historical Poverty Tables*, table 2, http://www.census.gov/hhes/www/poverty/histpov/hstpov2.html (accessed August 29, 2007); U.S. Bureau of the Census, "CPS Population and Per Capita Money Income, All Races: 1967 to 2004," *Historical Income Tables—People*, table P-1, http://www.census.gov/hhes/www/income/histinc/p01ar.html (accessed August 31, 2006); U.S. Department of Labor, Bureau of Labor Statistics, "Unemployment Rate—Civilian Labor Force," Labor Force Statistics from the Current Population Survey, http://www.bls.gov/data/home.htm (accessed September 21, 2006); U.S. Bureau of the Census, "Percent of People 25 Years and Over Who Have Completed High School or College, by Race, Hispanic Origin and Sex: Selected Years 1940 to 2006," *Historical Tables: Current Population Survey*, table A-2, http://www.census.gov/population/www/socdemo/educ-attn.html (accessed September 21, 2006); Congressional Research Service, "Cash and Noncash Benefits for Persons with Limited Income: Eligibility Rules, Recipient and Expenditure Data, FY2002–FY2004," CRS Report RL33340, March 27, 2006; Joe Dalaker, "Alternative Poverty Estimates in the United States: 2003," *Current Population Reports* P60–227 (Washington, D.C.: U.S. Bureau of the Census, June 2005), http://www.census.gov/hhes/www/poverty/altpovest03/altpovestrpt.html (accessed November 6, 2006).
NOTE: This table presents results for the five equations presented in Table 3-2 for the years 1980–2003, regressed against the 14 "alternative poverty rates" proposed by the U.S. Bureau of the Census as described in Table A-4.

that will permit the user to estimate time series poverty rates for the country under the existing poverty threshold approach, but utilizing a wide variety of alternative definitions for "income," the sensitivity analysis that we have begun in this appendix can be more rigorously pursued.[10]

For now, one may note that the regressions harvesting statistically significant coefficients from calculated alternative poverty rates weigh very heavily on the side of implausible results (that is, in only one equation did all coefficients seem plausible, while in nine, one or more coefficients was significant but not plausible)—and none of the regressions could generate an inherently plausible relationship between poverty rates and educational attainment. Suffice it to say that there is no self-evident reason why this specific measure of income should appear preferable to all others in table A-4. Rather, we may be veering toward a classic "Type I error" in statistical analysis by the very dint of running such a large number of regression equations. With enough alternative specifications and a sufficiently forgiving threshold for establishing statistical significance, even a completely random real-life association can appear on occasion to be econometrically meaningful.

# Notes

## Introduction

1. Joseph P. Goldberg and William T. Moye, *The First Hundred Years of the Bureau of Labor Statistics* (Washington, D.C.: U.S. Government Printing Office, September 1985).

2. For informative background on the origin and evolution of the "poverty rate," see U.S. Bureau of the Census, "The Development of the Orshansky Poverty Thresholds and Their Subsequent History as the Official U.S. Poverty Measure," by Gordon M. Fisher, Poverty Measurement Studies and Alternative Measures (working paper, May 1992, partially revised September 1997), http://www.census.gov/hhes/www/povmeas/papers/orshansky.html (accessed May 14, 2007), and U.S. Bureau of the Census, "From Hunter to Orshansky: An Overview of (Unofficial) Poverty Lines in the United States from 1904 to 1965," by Gordon M. Fisher, Poverty Measurement Studies and Alternative Measures (paper presented at the Fifteenth Annual Research Conference of the Association for Public Policy Analysis and Management, October 28, 1993, revised August 1997), http://www.census.gov/hhes/www/povmeas/papers/hstorsp4.html (accessed November 1, 2007). I am grateful to Mr. Fisher for generously and patiently explaining some of the finer points of this history to me.

3. Cf. U.S. Bureau of the Census, "Small Area Income and Poverty Estimate (SAIPE) Main Page," http://www.census.gov/hhes/www/saipe/saipe.html (accessed May 14, 2007).

4. Douglas J. Besharov and Peter Germanis, "Reconsidering the Federal Poverty Measure: Project Description" (paper presented at Reconsidering the Poverty Measure Seminar, Welfare Academy, University of Maryland, College Park, Md., June 14, 2004), http://welfareacademy.org/pubs/poverty/povmeasure.pdf (accessed November 28, 2005). "Poverty guidelines" are a simplified version of the poverty thresholds. Unlike the thresholds, the guidelines do not have separate figures for aged and non-aged one- and two-person households, and do not distinguish between adult and child family members. The guidelines have a simple, constant-increment-per-person equivalence scale rather than the irregular equivalence scale implicit in the weighted-average poverty thresholds. Note also that eligibility for many contemporary

means-tested benefit programs is set not directly at the poverty threshold, but instead at some multiple of that level. For example, a family with income up to 130 percent of the poverty level qualifies for food stamps, up to 150 percent for home energy assistance, up to 185 percent for the Women, Infant, and Children (WIC) supplemental nutrition program, up to 250 percent for Medicaid, and so forth.

5. Katherine K. Wallman (chief statistician, United States Office of Management and Budget), communication with the author, September 16, 2005.

6. Derived from Congressional Research Service, "Cash and Noncash Benefits for Persons with Limited Income: Eligibility Rules, Recipient and Expenditure Data, FY2002–FY2004," by Karen Spar et al., CRS Report RL33340, March 27, 2006, 20–27, 233–46. To go by the estimates in this report, roughly two-thirds (65.4 percent) of all means-tested public spending in America in FY 2004 was allocated using the official poverty rate.

7. Milestones in this literature would include U.S. Department of Health, Education and Welfare, Office of the Assistant Secretary for Planning and Evaluation, *The Measure of Poverty: A Report to Congress as Mandated by the Education Amendments of 1974* (April 1976), and the eighteen technical reports that accompanied this paper, http://www.census.gov/hhes/www/povmeas/measureofpov75.html (accessed October 11, 2007); Patricia Ruggles, *Drawing The Line: Alternative Poverty Measures and Their Implications for Public Policy* (Washington, D.C.: Urban Institute, 1990); Daniel T. Slesnick, "Gaining Ground: Poverty in the Postwar United States," *Journal of Political Economy* 101, no. 1 (February 1993): 1–38; Constance F. Citro and Robert T. Michael, eds., *Measuring Poverty: A New Approach* (Washington, D.C.: National Academy Press, 1995); Dale W. Jorgenson, "Did We Lose the War on Poverty?" *Journal of Economic Perspectives* 12, no. 1 (Winter 1998): 79–96; U.S. Bureau of the Census, "Experimental Poverty Measures: 1990 to 1997," by Kathleen Short, Thesia Garner, David Johnson, and Patricia Doyle, *Current Population Reports*, P60-205 (June 1999), http://www.census.gov/prod/99pubs/p60-205.pdf (accessed October 11, 2007); U.S. Bureau of the Census, "Alternative Poverty Estimates in the United States: 2003," by Joe Dalaker, *Current Population Reports*, P60-227 (June 2005), http://www.census.gov/prod/2005pubs/ p60-227.pdf (accessed August 31, 2007); and John Iceland, rapporteur, *Experimental Poverty Measures: A Summary of a Workshop* (Washington, D.C.: National Academy Press, 2005).

8. For a now classic study on the impact of family size and composition on patterns of expenditure (and the implications for "equivalence scales"), see Edward P. Lazear and Robert T. Michael, *Allocation of Income within the Household* (Chicago: University of Chicago Press, 1988). Lazear and Michael, however, did not specifically examine the question of equivalence scales in relation to poverty thresholds. For an exploration of the sensitivity of poverty thresholds to alternative equivalence scales, see David M. Betson, "Poverty Equivalence Scales: Adjustment for Demographic Differences across Families" (paper presented to the National Academy of Sciences Workshop on Experimental Poverty Measures, Washington, D.C., June

15, 2004), http://www7.nationalacademies.org/cnstat/Poverty_Equivalence_Scales_Betson_Paper_PDF.pdf (accessed March 31, 2008).

9. Harvard University's Christopher Jencks is one of the few social scientists who has pursued this question in a sustained fashion. See, *inter alia*, Christopher Jencks, "The Hidden Prosperity of the 1970s," *Public Interest*, no. 77 (Fall 1984): 37–61; Susan E. Mayer and Christopher Jencks, "Poverty and the Distribution of Material Hardship," *Journal of Human Resources* 24, no. 1 (Winter 1989): 88–114; and Christopher Jencks, Susan E. Mayer, and Joseph Swingle, "Can We Fix the Federal Poverty Measure So It Provides Reliable Information about Changes in Children's Living Conditions?" (unpublished paper, September 7, 2004), http://www.welfareacademy.org/pubs/poverty/povmeas_canwefix.pdf (accessed October 11, 2007). Further light was peripherally cast on this issue by David M. Cutler and Lawrence F. Katz in "Rising Inequality? Changes in the Distribution of Income and Consumption in the 1980's," *American Economic Review* 82, no. 2 (May 1992): 546–51. Two official inquiries into the area are also worth noting: U.S. Bureau of the Census, "Supplementary Measures of Material Well-Being: Expenditures, Consumption, and Poverty, 1998 and 2001," *CPS Special Studies*, P23-201 (September 2003), http://www.census.gov/prod/2003pubs/p23-201.pdf (accessed October 11, 2007), and U.S. Bureau of the Census, "Supplemental Measures of Material Well-Being: Basic Needs, Consumer Durables, Energy and Poverty, 2001 and 2002," *CPS Special Reports*, P23-202 (December 2005), http://www.census.gov/prod/2005pubs/p23-202.pdf (accessed October 11, 2007).

## Chapter 1: What Is the Official Poverty Rate, and What Does It Actually Measure?

1. Mollie Orshansky, "Counting the Poor: Another Look at the Poverty Profile," *Social Security Bulletin* 28, no. 1 (January 1965): 3–29.

2. Alice O'Connor, *Poverty Knowledge: Social Science, Social Policy and the Poor in Twentieth-Century America* (Princeton, N.J.: Princeton University Press, 2001), 166.

3. President's Council of Economic Advisers, "The Problem of Poverty in America," in *Economic Report of the President Transmitted to the Congress January 1964 Together With the Annual Report of the Council of Economic Advisers* (Washington, D.C.: U.S. Government Printing Office, 1964), 55–84.

4. Mollie Orshansky, "How Poverty Is Measured," *Monthly Labor Review* 92, no. 2 (February 1969): 37. Quoted in O'Connor, *Poverty Knowledge*, 183–84.

5. Mollie Orshansky, "Children of the Poor," *Social Security Bulletin* 26, no. 7 (July 1963): 3–13.

6. Orshansky, "Counting the Poor," 4.

7. Ibid., 7. Actually, Orshansky developed two sets of poverty thresholds, the second being scaled against the somewhat less stringent USDA Low-Cost Food

Plan, but these other thresholds were never officially used for calculating American poverty rates. It was the U.S. government and not Orshansky that chose to use the more modest Economy Food Plan as the basic reference point for poverty thresholds. For background on the Economy Food Plan (now known as the Thrifty Food Plan), see U.S. Department of Agriculture, Center for Nutrition Policy and Promotion, *Thrifty Food Plan, 2006,* by Andrea Carlson, Mark Lino, WenYen Juan, Kenneth Hanson, and P. Peter Basiotis (Report CNPP-19, April 2007), http://www.cnpp.usda.gov/Publications/FoodPlans/MiscPubs/TFP2006Report.pdf (accessed November 26, 2007).

8. H. S. Houthakker, "An International Comparison of Household Expenditure Patterns, Commemorating the Centenary of Engel's Law," *Econometrica* 25 (July 1957): 532–51. See also Rajiv Chaudri and C. Peter Timmer, "The Impact of Changing Affluence on Diet and Demand Patterns for Agricultural Commodities" (Working Paper 785, World Bank, 1986).

9. As she cautioned at the outset of her study, "There is not, and indeed in a rapidly changing pluralistic society there cannot be, one standard universally accepted and uniformly applicable by which it can be decided who is poor." Orshanksy, "Counting the Poor," 3.

10. Orshansky assigned one-person units a poverty threshold set at 80 percent of the level for two-person families with comparable demographics, even though a scaling purely in accordance with Economy Food Plan budgets per se would have meant setting those levels at 56 percent of the apposite two-person level. Cf. Eloise Cofer, Evelyn Grossman, and Faith Clark, "Family Food Plans and Food Costs," *USDA Home Economics Research Report,* no. 20 (November 1962): 53–54, http://aspe.hhs.gov/poverty/familyfoodplan.pdf (accessed October 11, 2007), and U.S. Department of Health, Education, and Welfare, "Food Plans for Poverty Measurement," by Betty Peterkin (Technical Paper XII [supporting data for *The Measure of Poverty: A Report to Congress as Mandated by the Education Amendments of 1974*], November 1976), http://www.census.gov/hhes/www/povmeas/pdf/tp_xii.pdf (accessed October 11, 2007).

11. "At the economy level incomes are so low that for most families of more than two persons and for aged unrelated individuals no tax would be required." Orshansky, "Counting the Poor," 10.

12. In 1980, the government began to index poverty thresholds against the CPI-U, a CPI variant for urban areas reflecting expenditure levels of about 87 percent of the U.S. population; it continues to use this particular deflator to this writing.

13. Orshansky, "Counting the Poor," 2.

14. See the discussion of consumption theory in chapter 4.

15. Alice O'Connor points to an additional factor favoring the use of the already existing P-60 series for fashioning a poverty measure. This was "the decision, favored by the economists who dominated early [War on Poverty] task force discussions, to define the poverty problem as a lack of income, reflecting their

assumption not only that income offered a universalistic and straightforward measure of need, but also their confidence that they had the means—through an economic growth-centered strategy—to win a war against poverty so defined."
O'Connor, *Poverty Knowledge*, 182–83.

16. Orshansky, "How Poverty Is Measured," 38.

17. For an exposition on the theoretical considerations in defining and measuring
poverty, see Martin Ravallion, *Poverty Comparisons* (Philadelphia: Harwood Publishers, 1994). For background on current approaches to poverty measurement in
developed and low-income countries, see United Nations Statistical Office, "Handbook on Poverty Statistics: Concepts, Methods, and Policy Use," http://unstats.
un.org/unsd/methods/poverty/Chapters.htm (accessed May 15, 2007). As draft
chapter 4 of the handbook reveals, no other country compiling poverty statistics has
ever embraced the U.S. technique for estimating the prevalence of poverty.

## Chapter 2: Poverty Trends in Modern America, according to the Official Poverty Rate

1. U.S. Bureau of the Census, "People in Poverty by Nativity: 1993 to 2006,"
*Historical Poverty Tables*, table 23, http://www.census.gov/hhes/www/poverty/
histpov/hstpov23.html (accessed October 20, 2005). The Census Bureau did not
begin reporting poverty by nativity until 1993, so long-term trends are unavailable.
Interestingly enough, however, between 1993 and 2006, the official poverty rate
was consistently higher for the foreign-born than the native-born, but also consistently lower for naturalized citizens than for native-born Americans.

2. Data in this discussion are drawn from U.S. Bureau of the Census, *Historical
Poverty Tables—People*, http://www.census.gov/hhes/www/poverty/histpov/perindex.
html (accessed October 20, 2005), and U.S. Bureau of the Census, "Income, Poverty,
and Health Insurance Coverage in the United States: 2005," by Carmen DeNavas-
Walt, Bernadette D. Proctor, and Cheryl Hill Lee, *Current Population Reports*, P60-231
(Washington, D.C.: U.S. Government Printing Office, 2006). We should note that
official poverty data seem to suggest some favorable trends for both Asian-Pacific
Americans and foreign-born Americans, but since data in these series are only available for the years since 1987 and 1993, respectively, they are not comparable with
the longer-term data in our figure 2-2.

3. Mollie Orshansky, "Counting the Poor: Another Look at the Poverty Profile,"
*Social Security Bulletin* 28, no. 1 (January 1965): 4.

4. Cf. Samir Amin, *Accumulation on a World Scale: A Critique of the Theory of
Underdevelopment* (New York: Monthly Review Press, 1972); Arghiri Emmanuel,
*Unequal Exchange: A Study of Imperialism* (New York: Monthly Review Press, 1974);
Andre Gunder Frank, *Dependent Accumulation and Underdevelopment* (London:
Macmillan, 1978).

5. Cf. M. Panič, "Does Europe Need Neoliberal Reforms?" *Cambridge Journal of Economics* 31, no. 1 (January 2005): 145–69.

## Chapter 3: The Official Poverty Rate versus Other Statistical Indicators Bearing on Material Deprivation in America: Growing Discrepancies and Contradictions

1. David T. Ellwood and Lawrence H. Summers, "Poverty in America: Is Welfare the Answer or the Problem?" (Working Paper 1711, National Bureau of Economic Research, October 1985), http://www.nber.org/papers/w1711 (accessed March 17, 2008), 1.

2. David T. Ellwood and Lawrence H. Summers, "Is Welfare Really The Problem?" *Public Interest* 83 (Spring 1986): 60.

3. Ibid.

4. In figure 3-1 we compare the OPR with the poverty rate for the nonelderly population, as Ellwood and Summers did in their studies. A more conventional comparison might show median family income against the OPR for the total population. That correlation is only slightly stronger, registering an "r-squared" of less than 0.03—meaning that changes in real median family income can predict less than 3 percent of the corresponding changes in the OPR for the total population for the years 1973–2005. The striking lack of association between median family income and OPR in figure 3-1, in other words, cannot be explained away as a quirk due to some particular choice of population coverage.

5. Real per-capita GDP estimates are derived from U.S. Department of Commerce, Bureau of Economic Analysis, "Frequently Requested NIPA Tables," *National Economic Accounts*, http://www.bea.doc.gov/bea/dn/nipaweb/SelectTable.asp? Popular=Y (accessed May 15, 2007), and midyear population for 1973 and 2001 are as reported in U.S. Bureau of the Census, *Statistical Abstract of the United States: 2004–2005* (2005), table 2, http://www.census.gov/prod/2004pubs/04statab/pop.pdf (accessed May 15, 2007).

6. Data derived from U.S. Bureau of the Census, *Statistical Abstract of the United States: 2002* (2002), tables 560 and 561, http://www.census.gov/compendia/statab/past_years.html (accessed May 15, 2007); U.S. Bureau of the Census, *Statistical Abstract of the United States: 1976* (1976), tables 569 and 570, http://www.census.gov/compendia/statab/past_years.html (accessed May 15, 2007).

7. U.S. Bureau of the Census, *Statistical Abstract of the United States: 2003* (2003), table HS-20, http://www.census.gov/statab/hist/HS-20.pdf (accessed October 21, 2005).

8. Derived from Congressional Research Service, "Cash and Noncash Benefits for Persons with Limited Income: Eligibility Rules, Recipient and Expenditure Data, FY2002–FY2004," by Karen Spar et al., CRS Report RL33340, March 27, 2006,

tables 2 and 3, and U.S. Bureau of the Census, *Statistical Abstract of the United States: 2004–2005*, table 2.

9. Derived from U.S. Bureau of the Census, *Statistical Abstract of the United States: 1976*, table 510, and U.S. Bureau of the Census, *Statistical Abstract of the United States: 2004–2005*, tables 2, 563, and 697.

10. Derived from Congressional Research Service, "Cash and Noncash Benefits," tables 2 and 3, and U.S. Bureau of the Census, *Statistical Abstract of the United States: 2004–2005*, table 2. Note that a major source of means-tested cash aid in America today is the Earned Income Tax Credit (EITC), a refund available to low-income workers since 1975. In FY 2004, the federal government dispensed an estimated $34 billion to 19 million households or earners filing for the EITC in their tax returns. The EITC thus accounts for the greatest part by far of the total rise in means-tested public cash outlays between 1973 and the present. The EITC is significant here in another respect. Because it is a *tax refund* rather than an *income transfer*, it is not included as "income" from the standpoint of poverty-rate calculations, unlike, say, Supplementary Security Income (SSI), Temporary Aid for Needy Families (TANF), or other government-provided, means-tested aid. This exclusion has a direct and, given the steady rise in EITC refunds over the past several decades, increasing bearing on the reliability of the calculated U.S. poverty rate.

11. Actually, the "adjusted r-squared" for equation 1 in table 3-2 is slightly negative—that is, slightly below zero; without getting into the arcana, suffice it to say that this result is tantamount to a zero correlation.

12. See, for example, Rebecca M. Blank and Alan Blinder, "Macroeconomics, Income Distribution and Poverty," in *Fighting Poverty: What Works and What Doesn't?* ed. Sheldon H. Danziger and Daniel H. Weinberg, 180–208 (Cambridge, Mass.: Harvard University Press, 1986); David M. Cutler and Lawrence F. Katz, "Rising Inequality? Changes in the Distribution of Income and Consumption in the 1980's," *American Economic Review* 82, no. 2 (May 1992): 546–51; Elizabeth T. Powers, "Growth and Poverty Revisited," *Economic Commentary*, Federal Bank of Cleveland, April 15, 1995; James Tobin, "Poverty in Relation to Macroeconomic Trends Cycles and Policies," in *Confronting Poverty: Prescriptions for Change*, ed. Sheldon H. Danzinger, Gary E. Sandefur, and Daniel H. Weinberg, 147–67 (Cambridge, Mass.: Harvard University Press, 1994); Rebecca M. Blank, "Fighting Poverty: Lessons from Recent U.S. History," *Journal of Economic Perspectives* 14, no. 2 (Spring 2000): 3–19; and Robert Haveman and Jonathan Schwabish, "Has Macroeconomic Performance Regained Its Antipoverty Bite?" *Contemporary Economic Policy* 18, no. 4 (October 2000): 415–27.

13. Haveman and Schwabish, "Has Macroeconomic Performance Regained Its Antipoverty Bite?"

## Chapter 4: Systematic Differences between Income and Expenditures among Poorer Households in Modern America: A Blind Spot for the Official Poverty Rate

1. *New York Times,* "Shriver Announces New Yardstick to Determine the Standard of Poverty," May 3, 1965. The study in question would subsequently appear as U.S. Chamber of Commerce, Task Force on Economic Growth and Opportunity, *The Concept of Poverty* (Washington, D.C.: U.S. Government Printing Office, 1965).

2. A number of contentious issues relating to the present OPR construct remain, as yet, unresolved, however, despite considerable research and debate. Prime among these is the assertion that poverty thresholds should be raised across the board to reflect the rise in living standards in the United States since 1965. This is an enduring objection to the OPR and, on its face, a serious one. It should be immediately apparent, however, that this particular objection is at heart normative in nature. The proper venue—indeed the only feasible venue—for answering this objection lies within the political process, not within the realm of technical or expert review. We will have more to say about this objection, however, in the concluding chapter of this study.

3. CPI-U and CPI-U-RS are two slightly different variants of the Consumer Price Index (CPI) regularly calculated and released by the U.S. Bureau of Labor Statistics (BLS) to track changes in the price levels (the "cost of living") faced by American consumers. "CPI-U" stands for "Consumer Price Index-All Urban Consumers," "CPI-U-RS" for "Consumer Price Index-All Urban Consumers-Research Series." The CPI has been published continuously since 1921, but CPI-U, which superseded CPI-W (Consumer Price Index-Urban Wage Earners and Clerical Workers), is meant to measure the entire urban population (around 87 percent of the national population), not just wage earners and clerical employees (who today account for less than a third of the total U.S. population). CPI-U-RS, first unveiled in 1999, also covers cost-of-living changes for the entire urban population from 1978 onward, but uses updated and improved techniques for tracking such phenomena as quality improvements and technical innovation. For more information, see Kenneth J. Stewart and Stephen B. Reed, "Consumer Price Index research series using current methods, 1978–98," *Monthly Labor Review,* vol. 122, no. 6 (June 1999): 29–38, http://www.bls.gov/opub/mlr/1999/06/art4full.pdf (accessed July 3, 2008).

4. Cf. U.S. Bureau of the Census, "Alternative Poverty Estimates in the United States: 2003," by Joe Dalaker, *Current Population Reports,* P60-227 (June 2005), http://www.census.gov/prod/2005pubs/p60-227.pdf (accessed May 15, 2007).

5. Cf. U.S. Bureau of the Census, Wealth and Asset Ownership website on Publications, Reports, Research and Analysis, http://www.census.gov/hhes/www/wealth/publications.html. Curiously, although these studies do provide information on the distribution of and trends in wealth and asset holdings for lower-income families, they make no regular attempt to estimate assets and wealth for families below the federal poverty threshold.

6. See, for example, U.S. Bureau of the Census, "The Effects of Taxes and Transfers on Income and Poverty in the United States: 2005," *Current Population Reports*, P60-232 (March 2007), http://www.census.gov/prod/2007pubs/p60-232.pdf (accessed November 2, 2007).

7. See, for example, U.S. Bureau of the Census, "Cohabitation and the Measurement of Child Poverty," by Marcia Carlson and Sheldon Danziger (Poverty Measurement Working Paper Series, February 1998), http://www.census.gov/hhes/www/povmeas/papers/cohabit.html (accessed April 3, 2008); see also Kurt J. Bauman, "Shifting Family Definitions: The Effect of Cohabitation and Other Nonfamily Household Relationships on Measures of Poverty," *Demography* 36, no. 3 (August 1999): 315–25.

8. See. for example, U.S. Bureau of the Census, "Experimental Poverty Measures: 1999," by Kathleen Short, *Current Population Reports* P60-216 (October 2001), http://www.census.gov/prod/2001pubs/p60-216.pdf (accessed April 3, 2008); and U.S. Bureau of the Census, "The Distributional Implications of Geographic Adjustments of Poverty Thresholds," by Charles Nelson and Kathleen Short (unpublished paper, December 8, 2003), http://www.census.gov/hhes/www/povmeas/papers/geopaper.pdf (accessed April 3, 2008).

9. Simply making this arithmetical calculation by no means settles the underlying question of whether, or to what degree, children in cohabiting households are actually supported by the incomes of the adults not related to them.

10. Mollie Orshansky, "Counting the Poor: Another Look at the Poverty Profile," *Social Security Bulletin* 28, no. 1 (January 1965), 4.

11. Classics in this literature include, but are not limited to, James S. Duesenberry, *Money, Income and the Theory of Consumer Behavior* (Cambridge, Mass.: Harvard University Press, 1949); Franco Modigliani and Richard H. Brumberg, "Utility Analysis and the Consumption Function: An Interpretation of Cross-Section Data," in *Post-Keynesian Economics*, ed. Kenneth K. Kurihara, 388–436 (New Brunswick, N.J.: Rutgers University Press, 1954), 388–436; Milton Friedman, *A Theory of the Consumption Function* (Princeton, N.J.: Princeton University Press, 1957); and Hendrik S. Houthakker and Lester D. Taylor, *Consumer Demand in the United States: Analyses and Projections* (Cambridge, Mass.: Harvard University Press, 1970).

12. The concept of "transitory income" can be traced back at least as far as Milton Friedman and Simon S. Kuznets, *Income from Independent Professional Practice* (New York: National Bureau of Economic Research, 1945), where the term itself was perhaps coined.

13. Current students of economic theory may find much of the following discussion obvious or unnecessary: as a matter of course, after all, today's economists are taught that they can proxy permanent income through household expenditures. To the trained economist nowadays, it may therefore seem self-evident that a consumption measure should be used as the starting point for any poverty metric. But this study is an empirical investigation rather than a theoretical treatise.

Therefore, we will be describing, documenting, and attempting to explain the actual (and gradually changing) relationship between income and spending for lower-income households in modern America in considerable detail, if only to underscore the declining reliability in practice of income as a predictor of poverty in the United States.

14. For further discussion of the distinctions among expenditures, outlays, and consumption as they relate to the BLS Consumer Expenditure Survey, see David S. Johnson, "Measuring Consumption and Consumption Poverty: Possibilities and Issues" (paper prepared for Reconsidering the Federal Poverty Measure, American Enterprise Institute, November 18, 2004), http://www.welfareacademy.org/pubs/poverty/Johnson.pdf (accessed October 25, 2007), and U.S. Bureau of the Census, "Supplementary Measures of Material Well-Being: Expenditures, Consumption, and Poverty, 1998 and 2001," *CPS Special Studies*, P23-201 (September 2003), especially 28, http://www.census.gov/prod/2003pubs/p23-201.pdf (accessed October 11, 2007).

15. Economists would note, *inter alia*, that a comprehensive treatment of "consumption" should include a household's "home production" of goods and services (such as food preparation and cleaning), none of which is included in expenditures and outlays. And an economic measure of consumption would, properly, value household leisure—a quantity only touched upon through expenditures and outlays when vacation or holiday or entertainment spending are involved. For some empirical research on the distinction between expenditures and consumption, especially as these relate to household food usage, see Mark Aguiar and Erik Hurst, "Consumption versus Expenditure," *Journal of Political Economy* 113, no. 5 (October 2005): 919–48, and Thomas DeLeire and Helen Levy, "How Well Can We Measure the Well-Being of the Poor Using Food Expenditure?" (Working Paper 06-29, National Poverty Center, Gerald R. Ford School of Public Policy, University of Michigan, August 2006), http://www.npc.umich.edu/publications/workingpaper06/paper29/working_paper06-29.pdf (accessed October 25, 2007). For some quantitative research on leisure time in America and its bearing on well-being and consumption, see Mark Aguiar and Erik Hurst, "Measuring Trends in Leisure: The Allocation of Time over Five Decades," *Quarterly Journal of Economics* 122, no. 3 (August 2007): 969–1006.

16. Other major data sources for tracking spending patterns in America would include the Survey of Consumer Finance (SCF), which is produced by the Federal Reserve Board, and the Panel Study of Income Dynamics (PSID), which, though largely government-funded, is produced by researchers and scholars in the U.S. academic community. We will be using SCF and PSID data as well as CE data in this study, but for separate purposes. SCF data are best for examining the family balance sheet: assets, liabilities and net worth. PSID, as the survey's own title suggests, is most appropriate for looking at long-term family or household income dynamics. The CE is most reliable and detailed for the breakdown of consumer expenditures and consumer outlays. One may note that the Census Bureau's Survey of Income

and Program Participation (SIPP) also contains information on spending and spending patterns, but of a more limited and episodic variety than can be found in the other three data sources.

17. Four CE surveys were conducted from 1945 to 1980, for the years 1950, 1960–61, 1972–73, and 1980, respectively.

18. One slight difference between the CPS and the CE income measures is that the latter includes the value of food stamps, while the former excludes them, since they are a noncash benefit.

19. This difference in basic reference units between the Census Bureau's CPS and the BLS's Consumer Expenditure Survey should be highlighted. The CPS money income series reports results for families and unrelated individuals, whereas the CE reports results for "consumer units." Families count as "consumer units" in the BLS taxonomy, as do most unrelated individuals, but some additional household arrangements also qualify. As the Bureau of Labor Statistics explains, consumer units comprise "members of a household consisting of (a) occupants related by blood, marriage, adoption, or some other legal arrangement; (b) a single person living alone or sharing a household with others, but who is financially independent; or (c) two or more persons living together who share responsibility for at least 2 out of 3 major types of expenses—food, housing, and other expenses. Students living in university-sponsored housing are also included in the sample as separate consumer units." U.S. Department of Labor, Bureau of Labor Statistics, "Consumer Expenditures in 2005" (report 998, February 2007), 6, http://www.bls.gov/cex/csxann05.pdf (accessed October 11, 2007). In practical terms, this means there will be some differences in comparability between quintiles of families and quintiles of "consumer units" in our analysis—although those differences will, for the most part, be rather small. We will have to keep this distinction in mind when we compare CPS and CE data for the lowest quintile of the U.S. population.

20. Cf. Kerwin Kofi Charles, Geng Li, and Robert Schoeni, "Overspending—Who, Why and How?" (unpublished paper, National Poverty Center, Gerald R. Ford School of Public Policy, University of Michigan, May 2006), table 2, http://www.npc.umich.edu/news/events/consumption06_agenda/charles-li-schoeni.pdf (accessed October 25, 2007).

21. The CE's reported trends on what Charles et al. term "overspending"—in aggregate, and by income quartile—are corroborated by data from the PSID. Ibid., table 3. The PSID data, for their part, suggested that an average of about 35 percent of American households ("families") were spending more than their reported after-tax income for the years 1999 and 2001—64 percent of those in the lowest quartile, and 13 percent of those in the highest. Charles and his colleagues describe the patterns in the CE data and the PSID data as "strikingly similar," given the differing methodologies of the two surveys. Ibid., 11.

22. We use unweighted per-capita consumption here rather than a weighted adjustment (that is, an "equivalence scale") because the former measure is more

straightforward. There are good arguments for the latter, insofar as we might expect consumption "needs" of children and the elderly to be lower than those of "working-age" adults. But since there is no single and universally accepted gradient of differentials for such weightings (notwithstanding the OPR's own implicit use of "equivalence scale," as embedded in the federal poverty measure's poverty thresholds for families of different size and demographic composition), we opt here for transparency over sophistication.

23. And note that table 4-3 is comparing the lowest *25 percent* of households from 1960–61 with the poorest *20 percent* of households in 2005—a contraposition that necessarily understates the true increase in spending for lower-income households over the decades in question.

24. Cf. U.S. Department of Commerce, Bureau of Economic Analysis, *National Economic Accounts*, http://www.bea.gov/bea/dn/nipaweb/index.asp (accessed November 1, 2007).

25. Kevin Hassett and Aparna Mathur, "An Empirical Analysis of Middle Class Welfare: Testing Alternative Approaches" (Working Paper 134, American Enterprise Institute, January 17, 2007), http://www.aei.org/publications/pubID.25484/pub_detail.asp (accessed October 25, 2007).

26. Nor, of course, should we presume that the PCE series is perfectly flawless in its depiction of trends in personal consumption for the U.S. macroeconomy.

27. Thesia I. Garner, George Janini, William Passero, Laura Paszkiewicz, and Mark Vendemia, "The CE and the PCE: A Comparison," *Monthly Labor Review* 129, no. 9 (September 2006): 20–46.

28. E. Raphael Branch, "The Consumer Expenditure Survey: A Comparative Analysis," *Monthly Labor Review* 117, no. 12 (December 1994): 47–55.

29. Derived from Congressional Research Service, "Cash and Noncash Benefits for Persons with Limited Income: Eligibility Rules, Recipient and Expenditure Data, FY2002–FY2004," by Karen Spar et al., CRS Report RL33340, March 27, 2006, table 5. Calculations for in-kind, means-tested benefits subtract cash benefits from total benefits.

30. For an outline of some of the issues in question, see Gary Burtless and Sarah Siegel, "Medical Spending, Health Insurance and Measurement of American Poverty" (unpublished paper, Brookings Institution, August 21, 2001), http://www.brookings.edu/~/media/Files/rc/reports/2001/08useconomics_burtless/poverty.pdf (accessed October 25, 2007), and Jessica S. Banthin, "Where Do We Stand in Measuring Medical Care Needs for Poverty Definitions? A Summary of Issues Raised in Recent Papers" (unpublished paper, Agency for Healthcare Research and Quality, Center for Financing Access and Cost Trends, June 2004).

31. In the interests of transparency and replicability, we should perhaps describe exactly how we attempted to estimate public spending for nonhealth, in-kind, means-tested benefits (minus food stamps). We started with total (federal plus state and local) spending on means-tested programs, and subtracted both medical

benefits and cash aid. From this subtotal we then further subtracted the calculated real cost of the food stamp program. Real FY 2004 estimates were available from CRS for all of these numbers, save food stamps. The data on FY 2004 and FY 1973 benefits from the foods stamp program are available (in current dollars) from the 2005 edition of the Social Security Administration's *Annual Statistical Supplement.* To adjust reported FY 1973 food stamp program benefits for comparability with FY2004, we used the CPI-U-RS price index (for the period 1973–2004). Insofar as the U.S. federal fiscal year does not coincide with the calendar year, and we use full-calendar-year deflators, a slight error is introduced in our calculations; for practical purposes, however, this tiny bias does not affect the calculated results presented in the text. CRS-based estimates were derived from Congressional Research Service, "Cash and Noncash Benefits for Persons with Limited Income." Food stamp figures were derived from U.S. Social Security Administration, *Annual Statistical Supplement to the Social Security Bulletin, 2005,* table 9H, http://www.ssa.gov/policy/docs/statcomps/supplement/2005/9h.pdf (accessed March 17, 2008). For the CPI-U-RS, see U.S. Bureau of the Census, "Annual Average Consumer Price Index Research Series Using Current Methods (CPI-U-RS) All Items: 1947 to 2006," http://www.census.gov/hhes/www/income/income06/AA-CPI-U-RS.pdf (accessed August 29, 2007).

32. Moreover, given the lack of comparability between the CRS estimates of total expenditures on means-tested benefits, the Census Bureau estimates of program participation, and the Consumer Expenditure Survey, even a fairly extensive effort here could only produce a rough approximation of the incidence that interests us here.

33. Derived from Congressional Research Service, "Cash and Noncash Benefits for Persons with Limited Income," and U.S. Social Security Administration, *Annual Statistical Supplement to the Social Security Bulletin.*

34. In 2005, the weighted "poverty threshold" for a two-person family was $12,755—well above the top annual income for this grouping. Even for individuals living alone and under sixty-five years of age, the poverty threshold was over $10,000. For unrelated individuals ages sixty-five and over, the threshold in 2005 was slightly under $10,000 ($9,367). Cf. U.S. Census Bureau, "Poverty Thresholds in 2005," http://www.census.gov/hhes/www/poverty/threshld/thresh05.html (accessed March 17, 2008). Senior citizens living alone and reporting more than this amount of annual income, but less than $10,000, would have been counted as "nonpoor" in accordance with the federal poverty measure. In practice, such persons would have accounted for a very small share of the under-$10,000 group (not least because the under-$10,000 group has the very youngest mean age for head of household of any income grouping in America). Cf. U.S. Department of Labor, Bureau of Labor Statistics, "Consumer Expenditures in 2005."

35. This discrepancy has been noted in Bruce D. Meyer and James X. Sullivan, "Three Decades of Consumption and Income Poverty" (Working Paper Series 04.17, Harris School of Public Policy, University of Chicago, September 17, 2007),

http://harrisschool.uchicago.edu/About/publications/working-papers/pdf/wp_
04_16.pdf (accessed October 25, 2007).

    36. Orshansky, "Counting the Poor," 3.

## Chapter 5: Accounting for the Widening Reported Gap between Income and Consumption for Lower-Income Americans

    1. There are, to be sure, exceptions. To cite some of these precious few: David M. Cutler and Lawrence F. Katz, "Rising Inequality? Changes in the Distribution of Income and Consumption in the 1980s," *American Economic Review* 82, no. 2 (May 1992): 546–51; Dale W. Jorgenson, "Did We Lose the War on Poverty?" *Journal of Economic Perspectives* 12, no. 1 (Winter 1998): 79–96; Daniel T. Slesnick, *Consumption and Social Welfare: Living Standards and Their Distribution in the United States* (New York: Cambridge University Press, 2001); and Bruce D. Meyer and James X. Sullivan, "Three Decades of Consumption and Income Poverty" (Working Paper Series 04.17, Harris School of Public Policy, University of Chicago, September 17, 2007), http://harrisschool.uchicago.edu/About/publications/working-papers/pdf/wp_04_16.pdf (accessed October 25, 2007).

    2. Note that we are comparing ratios for the lowest *quartile* of the 1960–61 CE survey with the lowest *quintile* from the CE surveys of 1972–73 and 2005. Since we would expect the ratio of expenditure to income to be higher at lower income deciles, this contraposition of quartiles and quintiles tends to exaggerate the rise in the ratio of expenditures to income for the period between 1960–71 and 1972–73. Even so, there is no question that the reported ratio of expenditures to pretax income rose for lower-income households over this interim. As it happens, families with less than $5,000 in annual income accounted for very nearly a quarter (24.7 percent) of all households in the 1972–73 CE survey. Their ratio of spending to income was 131 percent—up from 112 percent for the bottom quartile in 1960–61. Derived from U.S. Department of Labor, Bureau of Labor Statistics, *Consumer Expenditure Survey: Interview Survey 1972–73, Volume 1: U.S. Tables, Families Classified by 10 Family Characteristics*, BLS Bulletin 1997 (Washington, D.C.: U.S. Government Printing Office, 1978), table 10, and U.S. Department of Labor, Bureau of Labor Statistics, *Handbook of Labor Statistics 1975—Reference Edition*, BLS Bulletin 1865 (Washington, D.C.: U.S. Government Printing Office, 1978), table 137.

    3. The concept of household overspending per se is not rigorously pursued in the literature on consumption economics (where this phenomenon would be framed in terms of "permanent" and "transitory" consumption). For some recent exploratory work on consumer "overspending," see Kerwin Kofi Charles, Geng Li, and Robert Schoeni, "Overspending—Who, Why and How?" (unpublished paper, National Poverty Center, Gerald R. Ford School of Public Policy, University of Michigan, May 2006), http://www.npc.umich.edu/news/events/consumption06_agenda/charles-li-

schoeni.pdf (accessed October 25, 2007), and David S. Johnson, "Measuring Consumption and Consumption Poverty: Possibilities and Issues" (paper prepared for Reconsidering the Federal Poverty Measure, American Enterprise Institute, November 18, 2004), http://www.welfareacademy.org/pubs/poverty/Johnson.pdf (accessed October 25, 2007).

4. The SCF appears to offer a more comprehensive inventory of the various components of household wealth. For a detailed comparison and evaluation, see John L. Czajka, Jonathan E. Jacobson, and Scott Cody, *Survey Estimates of Wealth: A Comparative Analysis and Review of the Survey of Income and Program Participation* (Washington D.C.: Mathematica Policy Research Inc., August 22, 2003). For reasons outlined in the work by Czajka and his colleagues, the SCF series on household wealth is probably somewhat more reliable than the SIPP data.

5. Between the first quarter of 1989 and the first quarter of 2004, housing prices in the United States rose by 89 percent, according to the U.S. Office of Federal Housing Enterprise Oversight, "U.S. Housing Prices Slow, OFHEO House Price Index Shows Smallest Quarterly Increase since 1994," press release, August 30, 2007, http://www.ofheo.gov/media/hpi/2q07hpi.pdf (accessed November 2, 2007).

6. Note further that our estimates above, which are the product of mean increases in per-household assets or net worth on the one hand and the total number of households in the bottom income quintile as of 2004 on the other, may be said to understate the upswing in aggregate assets and net wealth for this bottom income quintile, since these calculations entirely exclude the impact of population growth. In 1989, the bottom income quintile of the SCF encompassed 18.6 million American households, whereas by 2004 it comprised 22.4 million. If we were to compare assets and net wealth of the 1989 bottom quintile population to the 2004 bottom quintile population, including the demographic growth effect, the intervening increase in assets would be $1.15 trillion; the increase in nonhousing assets, $567 billion; the increase in net worth, $919 billion; and the proportional growth of net worth between 1989 and 2004, over 130 percent.

7. The following discussion draws especially upon Eva Jacobs and Stephanie Shipp, "A History of the U.S. Consumer Expenditure Survey: 1935–36 to 1988–89," *Journal of Economic and Social Measurement* 19, no. 1 (1993): 59–96; Constance F. Citro and Robert T. Michael, eds., *Measuring Poverty: A New Approach* (Washington, D.C.: National Academy Press, 1995), 391–95; Charles L. Schultze and Christopher Mackie, eds., *At What Price? Conceptualizing and Measuring Cost-of-Living and Price Indexes* (Washington, D.C.: National Academy Press, 2002): 253–63; Bruce D. Meyer and James X. Sullivan, "Measuring the Well-Being of the Poor Using Income and Consumption," *Journal of Human Resources* 38, supplement (September 2003): 1180–1220; and Bruce D. Meyer and James X. Sullivan, "Further Results on Measuring the Well-Being of the Poor Using Income and Consumption" (Working Paper 07.19, Harris School of Public Policy, University of Chicago, August 2007),

http://harrisschool.uchicago.edu/About/publications/working-papers/pdf/wp_07_19.pdf (accessed March 17, 2008).

8. In the 1972–73 Consumer Expenditure Survey and subsequent CE surveys, data from the interview survey have been supplemented with data from a diary survey. The diary survey is independent of the interview survey, and collects daily information from a much smaller sample of households on a revolving basis, typically for a two-week period. Results from the interview survey and the diary survey are integrated for the annual estimates of consumer expenditures.

9. U.S. Bureau of the Census, "The 1972–73 Consumer Expenditure Survey—A Preliminary Evaluation," by Robert B. Pearl, Technical Paper 45 (Washington, D.C.: U.S. Government Printing Office, 1978), 1.

10. Additionally, there is some evidence that incomplete responses may be on the rise on the Consumer Expenditure Survey. Using survey microdata, Meyer and Sullivan, in "Further Results on Measuring the Well-Being of the Poor," estimate that the rate of nonresponse rose from 16 percent in 1993 to 21 percent in 2003.

11. Slesnick, *Consumption and Social Welfare,* 140–42.

12. As reported in Douglas J. Besharov and Gordon Green, "Summary of Session #2: Measuring the Material Well-Being of Poor Children" (memorandum and comments on Second Seminar on Reconsidering the Federal Poverty Measure, October 18, 2004), 10, http://welfareacademy.org/pubs/poverty/PovertyMeasureSeminar. Summary.Session%202.pdf (accessed May 15, 2007).

13. U.S. Department of Labor, Bureau of Labor Statistics, Consumer Expenditure Survey, "Frequently Asked Questions," no. 20, http://www.bls.gov/cex/csxfaqs.htm#q20 (accessed November 8, 2005).

14. CE staff calculate that a weighted average of about 1.5 percent of households ("consumer units") reported zero or negative income in the 2005 CE survey. William Passero, Economist, U.S. Bureau of Labor Statistics, personal communication with the author, October 24, 2007. By way of comparison, according to author calculations of CPS data using Data Ferrett (a data-mining tool developed by the Census Bureau), the CPS survey for 2005 estimated that 1.4 million households had no income—1.3 percent of the national total. By way of further comparison, the 2000 census counted 690,000 families with no reported income in the year 1999—just 1 percent of the families tabulated in that population count. Cf. U.S. Bureau of the Census, "Areas with Concentrated Poverty: 1999," by Alameyehu Bishaw, *Census 2000 Special Reports,* CENSR-16 (July 2005), http://www.census.gov/prod/2005pubs/censr-16.pdf (accessed November 2, 2007).

15. The diagnostic was informed by long-standing reservations among students of consumption patterns regarding reported income. Thus, in 1970, for example, Houthakker and Taylor wrote of "the notorious unreliability of respondents' reports on their incomes" and warned that "the common practice, also followed by BLS, of tabulating survey results primarily by income needs reconsideration." Hendrik S. Houthakker and Lester D. Taylor, *Consumer Demand in the United States: Analyses*

*and Projections* (Cambridge, Mass.: Harvard University Press, 1970), 259.

16. John M. Rogers and Maureen B. Gray, "CE Data: Quintiles of Income versus Quintiles of Outlays," *Monthly Labor Review* 177, no. 12 (December 1994): 32–37. As defined by the BLS, "current outlays" is a slightly more comprehensive measure of spending than "total expenditures."

17. But some observers suggest just this. For analysis pointing to significant underreporting of income for poorer households in the CPS and other official data series, see Meyer and Sullivan, "Measuring the Well-Being of the Poor Using Income and Consumption."

18. Government officials and researchers responsible for preparing the CPS and the CE surveys commonly caution that the results for the bottom income quintile from the two studies are not fully comparable, owing to the differences in objectives, methods, and approaches for the surveys themselves—and, not incidentally, to the differences in the reference units under study. Both surveys present results for what we can term "households," but the CPS tracks families and unrelated individuals, whereas the CE follows "consumer units" (described in greater detail in note 31 in the previous chapter). Daniel H. Weinberg (Chief, Housing and Household Economic Statistics Division, U.S. Census Bureau), and David S. Johnson (Assistant Commissioner for Consumer Prices and Price Indexes, U.S. Bureau of Labor Statistics), personal communications with the author, 2006. As it happens, however, the demographic composition of the lowest quintile of "households" in question in these two surveys is reasonably similar today. For 2005, the lowest quintile of CE households ("consumer units") averaged a total of 1.7 persons; for CPS, the mean size of the lowest quintile's household ("families and unrelated individuals") was 1.85 persons. For CE, the average number of children under age eighteen was 0.4; for CPS, 0.48. For CE, the average number of persons ages sixty-five and over was 0.4; for CPS, 0.44. Perhaps most important for what it suggests about the comparability of income levels between the bottom CE and CPS quintiles, the average numbers of earners per household unit appear to be very close. For CE, this figure was 0.5; for CPS, 0.48. (Note that, unlike CPS online data, the CE online dataset does not readily allow estimation of household composition to the second decimal place.) Thus, as a practical matter, the lowest quintile "households" depicted in these two surveys appear to be quite similar, despite the surveys' differences in definition and technique of "household" coverage. On its face, this would hardly seem to discourage an initial tabular comparison of results for the bottom quintile of "households" from the two surveys—so long as the comparisons treat these data with care. Further, more precise comparisons of the characteristics of lowest quintile households must await analysis of the microdata from the CPS and CE data files—but, at first inspection, it is by no means obvious that differences in "household" definition between these two surveys can do much to help us explain the puzzle we are examining in this chapter. Data derived from U.S. Department of Labor, Bureau of Labor Statistics, "Consumer Expenditures in 2005"

(report 998, February 2007), 6, http://www.bls.gov/cex/csxann05.pdf (accessed October 11, 2007); U.S. Bureau of the Census, "Household Income Table of Contents: Table HINC-05. Percent Distribution of Households, by Selected Characteristics within Income Quintile and Top 5 Percent in 2005," http://pubdb3.census.gov/macro/032006/hhinc/new05_000.htm; and Current Population Survey data available through the Census Bureau's Data Ferret program.

19. Cf. Richard Bavier, "Income and Expenditure Data in Poverty Measurement" (unpublished paper, April 3, 2006).

20. U.S. Department of Labor, Bureau of Labor Statistics, "Consumer Expenditures in 2004" (report 992, April 2006), http://www.bls.gov/cex/csxann04.pdf (accessed November 1, 2007).

21. Congressional Research Service, "Cash and Noncash Benefits for Persons with Limited Income: Eligibility Rules, Recipient and Expenditure Data, FY2002–FY2004," by Karen Spar et al., CRS Report RL33340, March 27, 2006, 231.

22. U.S. Department of Labor, Bureau of Labor Statistics, Federal Economic Statistics Advisory Committee, "Alternative Measures of Household Income: BEA Personal Income, CPS Money Income, and Beyond," by John Ruser, Adrienne Pilot, and Charles Nelson, committee paper, December 14, 2004, http://www.bls.gov/bls/fesacp1061104.pdf (accessed October 25, 2007).

23. If we presumed that CE expenditures for the lowest quintile were underreported to the same extent as in the rest of the population, and accepted the ratio of 0.81 offered by Garner et al. as the current metric for discrepancies between the CE and the PCE, this would imply that an additional $97 billion in personal expenditures by the lowest quintile in 2004 were not included in our reckoning above—begging the question, to those entertaining the theory that annual income and expenditures should be in overall balance, of what additional unreported sources on annual income could be identified to offset them. Thesia I. Garner, George Janini, William Passero, Laura Paszkiewicz, and Mark Vendemia, "The CE and the PCE: A Comparison," *Monthly Labor Review* 129, no. 9 (September 2006): 20–46. Note that an underreporting of expenditures by 19 percent would imply a mean level of personal expenditures for the lowest CE quintile of approximately $22,000 in 2004. Those who believe that annual income, if measured accurately, would really match annual expenditures for this stratum of households would also implicitly be graduating the great majority of them out of official poverty status, since the income levels requisite in this theory would bring most of the bottom quintile above the official poverty thresholds.

24. In all, the median duration of officially defined poverty for those who experienced it at any point during 1996–99—and over 100 million Americans were "poor" for a month or more during those four years—was about four months. The median duration for poverty spells was very similar irrespective of ethnicity, age, sex, region, education, employment status, or family size.

25. The PSID is not a U.S. government survey—its base of operations is the University of Michigan—but it is a government project in the sense that its funding has always come mainly from U.S. public monies; its main sponsor is now the National Science Foundation.

26. Peter Gottschalk and Robert A. Moffitt, "The Growth of Earnings Instability in the U.S. Labor Market," *Brookings Papers on Economic Activity*, no. 2 (1994): 217–72; Robert A. Moffitt and Peter Gottschalk, "Trends in the Transitory Variance of Earnings in the United States," *Economic Journal* 112 (March 2002): C68–C73. Moffitt and Gottschalk determined empirically that the best "fit" for their model was a five-year time horizon for modeling the shocks implied by stochastic and, thus, transitory changes in annual household earnings.

27. Note that these calculations exclude single-person households.

28. Jacob S. Hacker, *The Great Risk Shift* (New York: Oxford University Press, 2006), 2, 22–32.

29. Peter G. Gosselin, "If America Is Richer, Why Are Its Families So Much Less Secure?" *Los Angeles Times*, October 10, 2004, http://www.latimes.com/business/la-newdeal-cover,0,6544446.special (accessed May 15, 2007).

30. Technically speaking, Moffitt's measure in figure 5-15 uses the statistical benchmark of a single standard deviation of variance to establish what the *Los Angeles Times* series referred to as the "maximum fluctuation in annual household income for 68 percent of U.S. families." That is to say, assuming the year-to-year variations in family income conform to the bell-shaped "normal distribution," this calculation delineates the mark at which just over two-thirds of observed stochastic variations in income for median-income families would be expected to fall.

31. Though not, perhaps as yet, absolutely conclusive. There are some recent studies, using other data sources, that question whether any long-term increase in year-to-year volatility in earnings has actually occurred over the past several decades. See, for example, Congressional Budget Office, *Trends in Earnings Variability Over the Past Twenty Years*, 2007, http://www.cbo.gov/ftpdocs/80xx/doc8007/04-17-EarningsVariability.pdf (accessed March 17, 2008).

32. For the official U.S. data on these trends, see U.S. Bureau of the Census, "The Changing Shape of the Nation's Income Distribution, 1947–1998," by Arthur F. Jones Jr. and Daniel H. Weinberg, *Current Population Reports*, P60-204 (June 2000), http://www.census.gov/prod/2000pubs/p60-204.pdf (accessed May 15, 2007); and, for some updated data for 1967–2006, see U.S. Bureau of the Census, *Historical Income Inequality Tables,* http://www.census.gov/hhes/www/income/histinc/p60no231_tablea3.pdf (accessed October 11, 2007).

33. Broadly speaking, the general mechanisms by which the nonpoor maintain consumption during periods of temporary income shortfalls are understood; they include the drawdown or liquidation of assets, the accumulation of liabilities or debt, and gifts or resource transfers from other sources both private (such as relatives) and public (such as social programs). Recent work has examined some of the

particulars of these mechanisms. See, for example, James X. Sullivan, "Borrowing During Unemployment: Unsecured Debt as a Safety Net," *Journal of Human Resources* 43, no. 2 (Spring 2008): 383–412. Note that some of the institutional instruments available to the long-term nonpoor for maintaining consumption are not available to the long-term poor. See also Dirk Krueger and Fabrizio Perri, "Does Income Inequality Lead to Consumption Inequality? Evidence and Theory," *Review of Economic Studies* 73, no. 1 (January 2006): 163–93, which offers some formal models for the role of credit in smoothing consumption for households in contemporary America.

34. Initial research relying upon other longitudinal data series, such as SIPP, also point to an increase in income volatility. For a PSID study that also summarizes these SIPP findings, see Karen E. Dynan, Douglas W. Elmendorf, and Daniel E. Sichel, "The Evolution of Household Income Volatility" (unpublished paper, Brookings Institution, June 2007), http://www3.brookings.edu/views/papers/elmendorf200706.pdf (accessed October 25, 2007).

35. Dirk Krueger and Fabrizio Perri, "Does Income Inequality Lead to Consumption Inequality?" By their calculations, the Gini coefficient for expenditures rose from 0.23 to 0.26 between 1980 and 2003, while the coefficient for income rose from 0.30 to 0.37.

## Chapter 6: Trends in Living Standards for Low-Income Americans: Indications from Physical and Biometric Data

1. The official determination that the original thresholds should be adjusted to reflect changes in the cost of living—retrospectively as far as 1959, and forward for each new calendar year—emerged as a recommendation from an interagency Poverty Level Review Committee in March 1969, subsequently authorized through a directive from the Bureau of the Budget in August 1969. For more details, see U.S. Bureau of the Census, "The Development of the Orshansky Poverty Thresholds and Their Subsequent History as the Official U.S. Poverty Measure," by Gordon M. Fisher, Poverty Measurement Studies and Alternative Measures (working paper, May 1992, partially revised September 1997), http://www.census.gov/hhes/www/povmeas/papers/orshansky.html (accessed May 14, 2007).

2. One slight caveat against this generalization needs to be noted now. In 2000, the Census Bureau began to use a different consumer price deflator for its adjustments to the poverty threshold and its adjustments for its household money income series, embracing the CPI-U for the former and the CPI-U-RS for the latter. The CPI-U-RS implies a somewhat slower pace of consumer price change from 1978 (its starting point) to the present than does the CPI-U. From January 1978 to December 2006, the CPI-U-RS rose by 196.4 percent, as against the CPI-U's 222.6 percent. In effect, a slight real increase in year-to-year poverty thresholds has been

implicitly introduced through the somewhat curious decision to use different price deflators for poverty thresholds and money income. For the CPI-U-RS, see U.S. Bureau of the Census, "Annual Average Consumer Price Index Research Series Using Current Methods (CPI-U-RS) All Items: 1947 to 2006," http://www. census.gov/hhes/www/income/income06/AA-CPI-U-RS.pdf (accessed August 29, 2007); for CPI-U, see U.S. Department of Labor, Bureau of Labor Statistics, "Consumer Price Index: All Urban Consumer (CPI-U)" (September 9, 2007), ftp://ftp.bls.gov/pub/special.requests/cpi/cpiai.txt (accessed November 2, 2007).

3. Mollie Orshansky, "Recounting the Poor—A Five Year Review," *Social Security Bulletin* 29, no. 4 (April 1966): 22. We note that Orshanshy did not advocate *exclusive* use of an absolute measure for assessing trends in poverty for the United States; from her writings, it is clear she also favored use of some sort of relative poverty measure. In her published work, for example, she repeatedly notes the desirability of raising society's definition of the minimum acceptable level of poverty as overall income levels and living standards improve. But the OPR was not fated to be a relative poverty measure, and, in fact, Orshanksy herself was involved in the aforementioned interagency process that finally formalized the OPR's enduring status as an absolute poverty measure in 1969. Cf. U.S. Bureau of the Census, "The Development of the Orshansky Poverty Thresholds."

4. Cf. David T. Ellwood and Lawrence H. Summers, "Poverty in America: Is Welfare the Answer or The Problem?" (Working Paper 1711, National Bureau of Economic Research, October 1985), 3, http://www.nber.org/papers/w1711 (accessed March 17, 2008).

5. David Leonhardt, "More Americans Were Uninsured and Poor in 2003, Census Finds," *New York Times*, August 27, 2004.

6. Mollie Orshansky, "Counting the Poor: Another Look at the Poverty Profile," *Social Security Bulletin* 28, no. 1 (January 1965): 4.

7. Orshansky, "Recounting the Poor"; Mollie Orshansky, "Who's Who Among the Poor: A Demographic View of Poverty," *Social Security Bulletin* 28, no. 7 (July 1965): 3–32; and Mollie Orshansky, "The Shape of Poverty in 1966," *Social Security Bulletin* 31, no. 3 (March 1968): 3–32.

8. The body mass index (BMI) is an anthropometric measure of weight to height, conventionally calculated by dividing a person's weight in kilograms by the square of his or her height in meters. The measure is currently often used as a presumed proxy for a subject's body fat composition. Weight-for-height designations of obesity should be regarded as probabilistic because they do not actually measure or estimate a given individual's proportion of body fat (as is done clinically through skin-fold tests, for example).

9. U.S. Department of Health and Human Services, Centers for Disease Control and Prevention, National Center for Health Statistics, *Health, United States, 2006* (2006), http://www.cdc.gov/nchs/data/ hus/hus06.pdf (accessed November 1, 2007).

10. The RECS 2001 (upon whose figures the above calculation was based) places the mean heated floor space per poor household at 472 square feet per person; the AHS 2001, for its part, indicates a median value of 739 square feet per person for poor households, although this total appears to include both heated and unheated floor space and pertains only to the 55 percent of poverty-level households in single, detached, and/or mobile or manufactured homes. U.S. Bureau of the Census, "Size of Unit and Lot—Occupied Units," *American Housing Survey 2001*, table 2-3, http://www.census.gov/hhes/www/housing/ahs/ahs01/ tab23.html (accessed May 15, 2007).

11. On the negative side of the ledger, the fraction of poverty-level homes without heating seems to have risen over time, from a reported 0.9 percent in 1970 to a reported 2.2 percent in 2001. Interpretation of these results, however, is a bit tricky. In the 1970 population census, the Census Bureau asked whether heating facilities were physically absent from the homes of the families questioned; in 2001, by contrast, the RECS queried households whether they "do not heat their home"; the 2.2 percent of poverty-level households that responded in the affirmative included 1.5 percent who said they "have heating equipment but do not use it." U.S. Bureau of the Census, *1970 Census of Population: Subject Reports, Low-Income Population,* Final Report PC(2)-9A (Washington, D.C.: GPO, 1973), table 36; U.S. Bureau of the Census, *American Housing Survey of the United States: 2001,* Current Housing Reports H-150-01 (Washington, D.C.: GPO, 2002), tables 2-3, 2-4; U.S. Department of Energy, *Residential Energy Consumption Survey: Housing Characteristics 1997* (Washington, D.C.: GPO, 1999), http://www.eia.doe.gov/emeu/recs/recs97/recs97.html#Household%20Characteristics, tables CE2-3c, HC2-4b.

12. U.S. Bureau of the Census, "Percent Distribution of Automobile Ownership, and Financing: 1940–1970," *Historical Statistics of the United States: Colonial Times to 1970,* part 2, (1975), Series Q 175–86, http://www2.census.gov/prod2/statcomp/documents/CT1970p2-01.pdf (accessed October 25, 2007). In 1962, 74 percent of U.S. families reportedly owned automobiles; by 1959, 15 percent of U.S. families owned two or more automobiles.

13. While data on nutritional conditions have an important bearing on health status, we will not review them here because the matter of food and diet has already been addressed.

14. The immediate practical problem here is that American health and economic statistics are administered by separate authorities, with very little integration between these two vast arrays of data. Birth certificates and death certificates, for example, provide no direct data on income level or poverty status. Even if this problem were resolved, there would remain the theoretical issue of how to compute life expectancy with respect to poverty status, since the latter is a temporary and highly transient characteristic, unlike age, gender, ethnicity, educational status, and so on.

15. The year 2003 marked a discontinuity in the U.S. data series on age-adjusted mortality by educational status, due to a revision in procedures for collection of educational attainment data. After this revision, combined age-standardized mortality

rates for adults ages twenty-five to sixty-four with less than twelve years of education were nearly 17 percent higher in 2003 than they had been in 2002—about 14 percent higher for males, and nearly 18 percent higher for females. U.S. Department of Health and Human Services, Centers for Disease Control and Prevention, National Center for Health Statistics, *Health, United States, 2006*, table 34.

16. Ibid., 7; preliminary data.

17. We cannot use our benchmark year, 1973, for this comparison because the Census Bureau only provides data on poverty rates for "all children" from 1974 onward. For white "children in families," however, the OPR rose from 9.6 percent in 1973 to 14.3 percent in 2004; over those same years, white infant mortality fell by almost two-thirds, from 15.8 per 1,000 to 5.7 per 1,000. Cf. U.S. Bureau of the Census, *Historical Poverty Tables*, table 3, http://www.census.gov/hhes/www/poverty/histpov/hstpov3.html (accessed October 25, 2007), and U.S. Department of Health and Human Services, Centers for Disease Control and Prevention, National Center for Health Statistics, "Deaths: Final Data for 2004," by Melanie P. Heron et al., Health E-Stats, table 2, http://www.cdc.gov/nchs/products/pubs/pubd/hestats/finaldeaths04/finaldeaths04.htm (accessed May 14, 2007).

18. In 2003, the U.S. infant mortality rate for newborns with birth weights below 2,500 grams was twenty-six times higher than that for newborns weighing 2,500 grams or more at birth. In 1983, that same disparity was twenty to one. U.S. Department of Health and Human Services, Centers for Disease Control and Prevention, National Center for Health Statistics, *Health, United States, 2006*, table 21. In 1974–75, the ratio was also twenty to one. Derived from U.S. Department of Health and Human Services, Centers for Disease Control and Prevention, National Center for Health Statistics, *Health, United States, 1981* (1981), 8, http://www.cdc.gov/nchs/data/hus/hus81acc.pdf (accessed October 11, 2007).

19. Cf. Alfred Hill, *The History of the Reform Movement in the Dental Profession in Great Britain During the Last Twenty Years* (London: Truebner and Co., 1877).

20. U.S. Department of Health and Human Services, Centers for Disease Control and Prevention, National Center for Health Statistics, *Health, United States, 2006*, table 75. Among children six to seventeen years of age, comparable, or even more dramatic, patterns of improvement were evident for both the general population and the "poverty population." Among children two to five years of age, however, little improvement was reported for the general population, and virtually no change in untreated cavities was reported for the poverty-level grouping. At 17 percent for the general population, older adults sixty-five to seventy-four years of age had the lowest prevalence of untreated dental caries of any group surveyed for 1999–2002—and those older adults in official poverty status likewise had a lower prevalence of untreated cavities (28 percent) than any younger poverty population.

21. J. Cunha-Cruz, P. P. Hujoel, and P. Nadanovsky, "Secular Trends in Socioeconomic disparities in Edentulism: USA, 1972–2001," *Journal of Dental Research*, vol. 86, no. 2 (February 2007):131–36.

22. Ibid., table 91.

23. In 2004, 64 percent of children two to seventeen years of age from poverty-level households had reportedly seen a dentist in the past year. By contrast, in 1963–64 only 54.9 percent of all U.S. children ages five to fourteen had had a reported dental visit during the previous year. Derived from U.S. Department of Health and Human Services, Centers for Disease Control and Prevention, National Center for Health Statistics, *Health, United States, 2006*, table 91; and U.S. Department of Health, Education, and Welfare, "Dental Visits: Time Interval Since Last Visit, July 1963–June 1964," by George S. Chulis, in *NCHS Vital and Health Statistics*, series 10, no. 29 (April 1966), http://www.cdc.gov/nchs/data/series/sr_10/sr10_076.pdf (accessed November 1, 2007). For adults, the corresponding figures were 44 percent for persons ages eighteen to sixty-four in poor households in 2004, and 47 percent for all adults fifteen to sixty-four in 1963–64.

24. Orshansky, "Counting the Poor," 3.

25. As we saw in chapter 4, between 1973 and 2005, according to Census Bureau calculations, the real pretax money income of the lowest quintile of American households rose by a mere 10 percent, from $9,663 to $10,665 (in 2005 constant dollars deflated by CPI-U-RS). See U.S. Bureau of the Census, *Historical Income Inequality Tables*, table IE-1.

26. As Ellwood and Summers put it, "It is also important to recognize that only cash payments are treated as part of income in the official poverty measure. In-kind benefits such as medical care, food stamps, or housing assistance are not counted at all." Ellwood and Summers, "Poverty in America," 3.

27. Cf. Congressional Research Service, "Cash and Noncash Benefits for Persons with Limited Income," table 5.

## Conclusion: Wanted—New Poverty Measure(s) for Modern America

1. U.S. Department of Labor, Bureau of Labor Statistics, "Access to Historical Data for the 'A' Tables of the Employment Situation News Release," table A-1, http://www.bls.gov/webapps/legacy/cpsatab1.htm (accessed November 2, 2007).

2. Certainly not because the author is without opinions on these matters. For some of my own perspectives on these questions, see Nicholas Eberstadt, *The Tyranny of Numbers: Mismeasurement and Misrule* (Washington, D.C.: American Enterprise Institute Press, 1995), and Nicholas Eberstadt, *Prosperous Paupers and Other Population Problems* (New Brunswick, N.J.: Transaction Publishers, 2000).

3. Adam Smith, *The Wealth of Nations*, book V, chapter 2, Project Gutenberg, http://www.gutenberg.org/ dirs/etext02/wltnt11.txt (accessed November 2, 2007).

4. In 1965, per-capita disposable income for the United States averaged $11,594 (in chained 2000 dollars); for 2005, the corresponding figure was $27,370, an

increase of 136 percent. Data drawn from U.S. Bureau of the Census, *Statistical Abstract of the United States: 2007*, table 655, http://www.census.gov/prod/www/statistical-abstract.html (accessed May 21, 2008).

5. As much is suggested by patterns and trends in means-tested public programs. In 2002 (the latest year for which such data are available), the overwhelming majority of U.S. households collecting one or more needs-based government benefits were *above* the poverty line; in fact, nearly twice as many recipient households were identified as being above the poverty line as below it. Twenty years earlier (1982), by contrast, the number of recipient households accepting at least one needs-based government benefit was split almost evenly between those below the poverty line and those above it. In 1982, just under 17 percent of households reportedly received at least one means-tested benefit; by 2002, the corresponding proportion was up to 20 percent. Note that this gradual expansion of needs-based welfare benefits well beyond the ranks of the officially poor took place despite the ostensible "end of welfare as we know it" in 1996, with the Temporary Assistance for Needy Families Act (TANF). Data derived from U.S. Bureau of the Census, *Statistical Abstract of the United States: 2007*, table 529, and U.S. Bureau of the Census, *Statistical Abstract of the United States: 1985*, table 595, http://www.census.gov/compendia/statab/ (accessed November 9, 2007)

6. Note that Americans seem to be much less concerned about the relative facet of poverty than their European counterparts. Europeans are much more likely to regard economic differences as fixed, and beyond individual control; Americans, by contrast, are more likely to regard society and economy as fluid and individuals as mobile, and capable of affecting their circumstances through their own efforts. See, for example, Alberto Alesina, Rafael di Tella, and Robert McCollough, "Inequality and Happiness: Are Europeans and Americans Different?" (Working Paper 8198, National Bureau of Economic Research, November 2001), http://www.nber.org/papers/w8198 (accessed March 17, 2008). This critical difference may help to explain why Western European countries have typically adopted some relative measure for evaluating domestic poverty, whereas the United States has instead opted for an absolute poverty measure. The absence of a prominent and readily available official indicator of relative poverty in the United States, in short, is not the result of some inexplicable bureaucratic oversight. In any case, irrespective of any arguments about the merit or desirability of relative poverty indicators, it would seem hard to argue with the proposition that the American public deserves accurate official information on absolute poverty in response to its own expressed political priorities and ethical concerns.

7. Cf. Office of Management and Budget, Statistical Policy Division, *Social Indicators 1973: Selected Statistics on Social Conditions and Trends in the United States* (Washington, D.C.: U.S. Government Printing Office, 1973).

8. Leslie Kaufman, "Bloomberg Seeks New Ways to Decide Who Is Poor," *New York Times*, December 31, 2007.

9. Ibid.

## Appendix

1. See U.S. Bureau of the Census, "Educational Attainment," http://www.census.gov/population/www/socdemo/educ-attn.html (accessed March 17, 2008).

2. We may also note that antipoverty spending is very strongly correlated with per-capita income—in a *positive* manner—for the years since 1973, while also being *negatively* associated with the unemployment rate. So much for countercyclical income-stabilization effects from our antipoverty policies as actually implemented!

3. Robert Haveman and Jonathan Schwabish, "Has Macroeconomic Performance Regained Its Antipoverty Bite?" *Contemporary Economic Policy* 18, no. 4 (October 2000): 415–27.

4. Note that we are discussing elasticities here—not absolute percentage points of change to the prevalence of high school diplomas among the adult population, or percentage points in the official poverty rate. As of 2004, the elasticity of the OPR with respect to our measure of educational attainment would have indicated an increase in the OPR of around half a point for every one-point rise in the percentage of adults twenty-five years of age and older with high school diplomas.

5. Lant Pritchett, "Where Has All the Education Gone?" *World Bank Economic Review* 15, no. 3 (2001): 367–91.

6. Cf. Stephen V. Cameron and James J. Heckman, "The Nonequivalence of High School Equivalents," *Journal of Labor Economics* 11, no. 1 (January 1993): 1–47; James J. Heckman and Paul A. LaFontaine, "Bias-Corrected Estimates of GED Returns," *Journal of Labor Economics* 24, no. 3 (July 2006): 661–700.

7. See, for example, Richard Bavier, "Income and Expenditure Data in Poverty Measurement" (unpublished paper, April 3, 2006).

8. See, for example, U.S. Bureau of the Census, "Experimental Poverty Measures: 1990 to 1997," by Kathleen Short, Thesia Garner, David Johnson, and Patricia Doyle, *Current Population Reports*, P60-205 (June 1999), http://www.census.gov/prod/99pubs/p60-205.pdf (accessed October 11, 2007); U.S. Bureau of the Census, "Alternative Poverty Estimates in the United States: 2003," by Joe Dalaker, *Current Population Reports*, P60-227 (June 2005), http://www.census.gov/prod/2005pubs/p60-227.pdf (accessed May 15, 2007); and U.S. Bureau of the Census, "The Effects of Taxes and Transfers on Income and Poverty in the United States: 2005," *Current Population Reports*, P60-232 (March 2007), http://www.census.gov/prod/2007pubs/p60-232.pdf (accessed November 2, 2007).

9. U.S. Bureau of the Census, "Alternative Poverty Estimates in the United States: 2003."

10. Cf. Poverty Analysis and Tabulation Tool (PATT) (University of Maryland/American Enterprise Institute), http://www.aeimirror.org/poverty (for analyzing data on poverty).

# Bibliography

Aguiar, Mark, and Erik Hurst. "Consumption versus Expenditure." *Journal of Political Economy* 113, no. 5 (October 2005): 919–48.

———. "Measuring Trends in Leisure: The Allocation of Time Over Five Decades." *Quarterly Journal of Economics* 122, no. 3 (August 2007): 969–1006.

Alesina, Alberto, Rafael di Tella, and Robert McCollough. "Inequality and Happiness: Are Europeans and Americans Different?" Working Paper 8198, National Bureau of Economic Research, November 2001. http://www.nber.org/papers/w8198 (accessed March 17, 2008).

Amin, Samir. *Accumulation on a World Scale: A Critique of the Theory of Underdevelopment.* New York: Monthly Review Press, 1972.

Banthin, Jessica S. "Where Do We Stand in Measuring Medical Care Needs for Poverty Definitions? A Summary of Issues Raised in Recent Papers." Unpublished paper, Agency for Healthcare Research and Quality, Center for Financing Access and Cost Trends, June 2004.

Bauman, Kurt J. "Shifting Family Definitions: The Effect of Cohabitation and Other Nonfamily Household Relationships on Measures of Poverty." *Demography* 36, no. 3 (August 1999): 315–25.

Bavier, Richard. "Income and Expenditure Data in Poverty Measurement." Unpublished paper, April 3, 2006.

Besharov, Douglas J., John Coder, and Gordon Green. *UMD/AEI Poverty Tabulator—User's Guide*, November 2007 (draft). http://www.welfareacademy.org/pubs/poverty/Poverty_Tabulator_Users_Guide.pdf (accessed March 17, 2008).

Besharov, Douglas J., and Peter Germanis. "Reconsidering the Federal Poverty Measure: Project Description." Paper presented at Reconsidering the Poverty Measure Seminar, Welfare Academy, University of Maryland, College Park, Md., June 14, 2004. http://welfareacademy.org/pubs/poverty/povmeasure.pdf (accessed November 28, 2005).

Besharov, Douglas J., and Gordon Green. "Summary of Session #2: Measuring the Material Well-Being of Poor Children." Memorandum and comments on Second Seminar on Reconsidering the Federal Poverty Measure, October 18, 2004, 10. http://welfareacademy.org/pubs/poverty/PovertyMeasureSeminar.Summary.Session%202.pdf (accessed May 15, 2007).

Betson, David M. "Poverty Equivalence Scales: Adjustment for Demographic Differences across Families." Paper presented to the National Academy of Sciences Workshop on Experimental Poverty Measures, Washington, D.C., June 15, 2004. http://www7.nationalacademies.org/cnstat/Poverty_Equivalence_Scales_Betson_Paper_PDF.pdf (accessed March 31, 2008).

Blank, Rebecca M. "Fighting Poverty: Lessons from Recent U.S. History." *Journal of Economic Perspectives* 14, no. 2 (Spring 2000): 3–19.

Blank, Rebecca M., and Alan Blinder. "Macroeconomics, Income Distribution and Poverty." In *Fighting Poverty: What Works and What Doesn't?* ed. Sheldon H. Danziger and Daniel H. Weinberg, 180–208. Cambridge, Mass.: Harvard University Press, 1986.

Branch, E. Raphael. "The Consumer Expenditure Survey: A Comparative Analysis." *Monthly Labor Review* 117, no. 12 (December 1994): 47–55.

Burtless, Gary, and Sarah Siegel. "Medical Spending, Health Insurance and Measurement of American Poverty." Unpublished paper, Brookings Institute, August 21, 2001. http://www.brookings.edu/~/media/Files/rc/reports/2001/08useconomics_burtless/poverty.pdf (accessed October 25, 2007).

Cameron, Stephen V., and James J. Heckman. "The Nonequivalence of High School Equivalents." *Journal of Labor Economics* 11, no. 1 (January 1993): 1–47.

Case, Karl E., and Robert J. Shiller. "Is There a Bubble in the Housing Market?" *Brookings Papers on Economic Activity* 2003-II: 299–362

Charles, Kerwin Kofi, Geng Li, and Robert Schoeni. "Overspending—Who, Why and How?" Unpublished paper, National Poverty Center, Gerald R. Ford School of Public Policy, University of Michigan, May 2006. http://www.npc.umich.edu/news/events/consumption06_agenda/charles-li-schoeni.pdf (accessed October 25, 2007).

Chaudri, Rajiv, and C. Peter Timmer. "The Impact of Changing Affluence on Diet and Demand Patterns for Agricultural Commodities." Working Paper No. 785, World Bank, 1986.

Citro, Constance F., and Robert T. Michael, eds. *Measuring Poverty: A New Approach.* Washington, D.C.: National Academy Press, 1995.

Cofer, Eloise, Evelyn Grossman, and Faith Clark. "Family Food Plans and Food Costs," *USDA Home Economics Research Report*, no. 20 (November 1962). http://aspe.hhs.gov/poverty/familyfoodplan.pdf (accessed October 11, 2007).

Congressional Budget Office. *Trends in Earnings Variability Over the Past Twenty Years.* Washington, D.C.: CBO, 2007. http://www.cbo.gov/ftpdocs/80xx/doc8007/04-17-EarningsVariability.pdf (accessed March 17, 2008).

Congressional Research Service. "Cash and Noncash Benefits for Persons with Limited Income: Eligibility Rules, Recipient and Expenditure Data, FY2002–FY2004," by Karen Spar et al. CRS Report RL33340, March 27, 2006.

Cunha-Cruz, J., P. P. Hujoel, P. Nadanovsky. "Secular Trends in Socio-economic Disparities in Edentulism: USA, 1972–2001," *Journal of Dental Research*, vol. 86, no. 2 (February 2007): 131–36.

Cutler, David M., and Lawrence F. Katz. "Rising Inequality? Changes in the Distribution of Income and Consumption in the 1980's." *American Economic Review* 82, no. 2 (May 1992): 546–51.

Czajka, John L., Jonathan E. Jacobson, and Scott Cody. *Survey Estimates of Wealth: A Comparative Analysis and Review of the Survey of Income and Program Participation*. Washington, D.C.: Mathematica Policy Research Inc., August 22, 2003.

DeLeire, Thomas, and Helen Levy. "How Well Can We Measure the Well-Being of the Poor Using Food Expenditure?" Working Paper 06-29, National Poverty Center, Gerald R. Ford School of Public Policy, University of Michigan, August 2006, http://www.npc.umich.edu/publications/workingpaper06/paper29/working_paper06-29.pdf (accessed October 25, 2007).

Duesenberry, James S. *Money, Income and the Theory of Consumer Behavior.* Cambridge, Mass.: Harvard University Press, 1949.

Dynan, Karen E., Douglas W. Elmendorf, and Daniel E. Sichel. "The Evolution of Household Income Volatility." Unpublished paper, Brookings Institution, June 2007. http://www3.brookings.edu/views/papers/elmendorf200706.pdf (accessed October 25, 2007).

Eberstadt, Nicholas. *Prosperous Paupers and Other Population Problems.* New Brunswick, N.J.: Transaction Publishers, 2000.

———. *The Tyranny of Numbers: Mismeasurement and Misrule.* Washington, D.C.: American Enterprise Institute Press, 1995.

Ellwood, David T., and Lawrence H. Summers. "Is Welfare Really the Problem?" *Public Interest* 83 (Spring 1986): 57–78.

———. "Poverty in America: Is Welfare the Answer or the Problem?" Working Paper 1711, National Bureau of Economic Research, October 1985. http://www.nber.org/papers/w1711 (accessed March 17, 2008).

———. "Poverty in America: Is Welfare the Answer or the Problem?" in *Fighting Poverty: What Works and What Doesn't*, ed. Sheldon H. Danziger and Daniel H. Weinberg. Cambridge, Mass.: Harvard University Press, 1986.

Emmanuel, Arghiri. *Unequal Exchange: A Study of Imperialism.* New York: Monthly Review Press, 1974.

Federal Reserve Board, Survey of Consumer Finances, various years, http://www.federalreserve.gov/Pubs/oss/oss2/scfindex.html (accessed September 19, 2007).

———. *2004 Survey on Consumer Finances Chartbook.* http://www.federalreserve.gov/pubs/oss/oss2/2004/scf2004home.html (accessed September 17, 2007).

Frank, Andre Gunder. *Dependent Accumulation and Underdevelopment.* London: Macmillan, 1978.

Friedman, Milton. *A Theory of the Consumption Function.* Princeton, N.J.: Princeton University Press, 1957.

Friedman, Milton, and Simon S. Kuznets. *Income from Independent Professional Practice*. New York: National Bureau of Economic Research, 1945.

Garner, Thesia I., George Janini, William Passero, Laura Paszkiewicz, and Mark Vendemia. "The CE and the PCE: A Comparison." *Monthly Labor Review* 129, no. 9 (September 2006): 20–46.

Goldberg, Joseph P., and William T. Moye. *The First Hundred Years of the Bureau of Labor Statistics*. Washington, D.C.: U.S. Government Printing Office, September 1985.

Gosselin, Peter G. "If America Is Richer, Why Are Its Families So Much Less Secure?" *Los Angeles Times*. October 10, 2004. http://www.latimes.com/business/la-newdeal-cover,0,6544446.special (accessed May 15, 2007).

Gottschalk, Peter, and Robert A. Moffitt. "The Growth of Earnings Instability in the U.S. Labor Market." *Brookings Papers on Economic Activity*, no. 2 (1994): 217–72.

Hacker, Jacob S. *The Great Risk Shift*. New York: Oxford University Press, 2006.

———. "Table 1: Permanent and Transitory Variances of Log Income, 1969–1998." http://pantheon.yale.edu/~jhacker/PSID_Data_NYT.htm (accessed May 16, 2007).

Hassett, Kevin, and Aparna Mathur. "An Empirical Analysis of Middle Class Welfare: Testing Alternative Approaches." Working Paper No. 134, American Enterprise Institute, January 17, 2007. http://www.aei.org/publications/pubID.25484,filter.all/pub_detail.asp (accessed October 25, 2007).

Haveman, Robert, and Jonathan Schwabish. "Has Macroeconomic Performance Regained Its Antipoverty Bite?" *Contemporary Economic Policy* 18, no. 4 (October 2000): 415–27.

Heckman, James J., and Paul A. LaFontaine. "Bias-Corrected Estimates of GED Returns." *Journal of Labor Economics* 24, no. 3 (July 2006): 661–700.

Hill, Alfred. *The History of the Reform Movement in the Dental Profession in Great Britain During the Last Twenty Years*. London: Truebner and Co., 1877.

Houthakker, Hendrik S. "An International Comparison of Household Expenditure Patterns, Commemorating the Centenary of Engel's Law." *Econometrica* 25 (July 1957): 532–51.

Houthakker, Hendrik S., and Lester D Taylor. *Consumer Demand in the United States: Analyses and Projections*. Cambridge, Mass.: Harvard University Press, 1970.

Iceland, John. *Experimental Poverty Measures: A Summary of a Workshop*. Washington, D.C.: National Academy Press, 2005.

Jacobs, Eva, and Stephanie Shipp. "A History of the U.S. Consumer Expenditure Survey: 1935–36 to 1988–89." *Journal of Economic and Social Measurement* 19, no. 1 (1993): 59–96.

Jencks, Christopher. "The Hidden Prosperity of the 1970s." *Public Interest*, no. 77 (Fall 1984): 37–61.

Jencks, Christopher, Susan E. Mayer, and Joseph Swingle. "Can We Fix the Federal Poverty Measure So It Provides Reliable Information about Changes in Children's

Living Conditions?" Unpublished paper, September 7, 2004. http://www.welfareacademy.org/pubs/poverty/povmeas_canwefix.pdf (accessed October 11, 2007).

Johnson, David S. "Measuring Consumption and Consumption Poverty: Possibilities and Issues." Paper prepared for Reconsidering the Federal Poverty Measure, American Enterprise Institute, November 18, 2004. http://www.welfareacademy.org/pubs/poverty/Johnson.pdf (accessed October 25, 2007).

Jorgenson, Dale W. "Did We Lose the War on Poverty?" *Journal of Economic Perspectives* 12, no. 1 (Winter 1998): 79–96.

Kaufman, Leslie. "Bloomberg Seeks New Ways to Decide Who Is Poor." *New York Times,* December 31, 2007.

Krueger, Dirk, and Fabrizio Perri. "Does Income Inequality Lead to Consumption Inequality? Evidence and Theory." *Review of Economic Studies* 73, no. 1 (January 2006): 163–93.

Lazear, Edward P., and Robert T. Michael. *Allocation of Income within the Household.* Chicago, Ill.: University of Chicago Press, 1988.

Leonhardt, David. "More Americans Were Uninsured and Poor in 2003, Census Finds." *New York Times,* August 27, 2004.

*Los Angeles Times.* "The Source of the Statistics and How They Were Analyzed." December 29, 2004. http://www.latimes.com/business/la-fi-riskshift3oct10-method,1,2775842.story (accessed May 17, 2007).

Madans, Jennifer, Kimberly Lochner, and Diane Makuc. "Poverty and Health." PowerPoint presentation for Reconsidering the Poverty Measure Seminar, Welfare Academy at the University of Maryland and the American Enterprise Institute, College Park, Md., March 8, 2005. http://welfareacademy.org/pubs/poverty/cdc.ppt (accessed September 19, 2007).

Mayer, Susan E., and Christopher Jencks. "Poverty and the Distribution of Material Hardship." *Journal of Human Resources* 24, no. 1 (Winter 1989): 88–114.

Bruce D. Meyer and James X. Sullivan. "Further Results on Measuring the Well-Being of the Poor Using Income and Consumption." Working Paper 07.19. Harris School of Public Policy, University of Chicago, August 2007.

———. "Three Decades of Consumption and Income Poverty." Working Paper Series 04.17, Harris School of Public Policy, University of Chicago, September 17, 2007. http://harrisschool.uchicago.edu/About/publications/working-papers/pdf/wp_04_16.pdf (accessed October 25, 2007).

Modigliani, Franco, and Richard H. Brumberg. "Utility Analysis and the Consumption Function: An Interpretation of Cross-Section Data." In *Post-Keynesian Economics,* ed. Kenneth K. Kurihara, 388–436. New Brunswick, N.J.: Rutgers University Press, 1954.

Moffitt, Robert A., and Peter Gottschalk. "Trends in the Transitory Variance of Earnings in the United States." *Economic Journal* 112 (March 2002): C68–C73.

*New York Times,* "Shriver Announces New Yardstick to Determine the Standard of Poverty," May 3, 1965.

O'Connor, Alice. *Poverty Knowledge: Social Science, Social Policy and the Poor in Twentieth-Century America.* Princeton, N.J.: Princeton University Press, 2001.

Office of Management and Budget. Statistical Policy Division. *Social Indicators 1973: Selected Statistics on Social Conditions and Trends in the United States.* Washington, D.C.: U.S. Government Printing Office, 1973.

Orshansky, Mollie. "Children of the Poor." *Social Security Bulletin* 26, no. 7 (July 1963): 3–13.

———. "Counting the Poor: Another Look at the Poverty Profile." *Social Security Bulletin* 28, no. 1 (January 1965): 3–29.

———. "How Poverty Is Measured." *Monthly Labor Review* 92, no. 2 (February 1969): 37–41.

———. "Recounting the Poor—A Five Year Review." *Social Security Bulletin* 29, no. 4 (April 1966).

———. "The Shape of Poverty in 1966," *Social Security Bulletin* 31, no. 3 (March 1968): 3–32.

———. "Who's Who Among the Poor: A Demographic View of Poverty," *Social Security Bulletin* 28, No. 7 (July 1965): 3–32.

Panić, M. "Does Europe Need Neoliberal Reforms?" *Cambridge Journal of Economics* 31, no. 1 (January 2005): 145–69.

Poverty Analysis and Tabulation Tool (PATT). University of Maryland/American Enterprise Institute. http://www.aeimirror.org/poverty.

Powers, Elizabeth T. "Growth and Poverty Revisited." *Economic Commentary*, Federal Bank of Cleveland, April 15, 1995.

President's Council of Economic Advisers. "The Problem of Poverty in America." In *Economic Report of the President Transmitted to the Congress January 1964 Together With the Annual Report of the Council of Economic Advisers.* Washington, D.C.: U.S. Government Printing Office, 1964, 55–84.

Pritchett, Lant. "Where Has All the Education Gone?" *World Bank Economic Review* 15, no. 3 (2001): 367–91.

Ravallion, Martin. *Poverty Comparisons.* Philadelphia: Harwood Publishers, 1994.

Rogers, John M., and Maureen B. Gray. "CE Data: Quintiles of Income versus Quintiles of Outlays." *Monthly Labor Review* 177, no. 12 (December 1994): 32–37.

Ruggles, Patricia. *Drawing the Line: Alternative Poverty Measures and Their Implications for Public Policy.* Washington, D.C.: Urban Institute, 1990.

Schultze, Charles L., and Christopher Mackie, eds. *At What Price? Conceptualizing and Measuring Cost-of-Living and Price Indexes.* Washington, D.C.: National Academy Press, 2002.

Slesnick, Daniel T. *Consumption and Social Welfare: Living Standards and Their Distribution in the United States.* New York: Cambridge University Press, 2001.

———. "Gaining Ground: Poverty in the Postwar United States." *Journal of Political Economy* 101, no. 1 (February 1993): 1–38.

Smith, Adam. *The Wealth of Nations*, book V, chapter 2. Project Gutenberg, http://www.gutenberg.org/dirs/etext02/wltnt11.txt (accessed November 2, 2007).

Stewart, Kenneth J., and Stephen B. Reed. "Consumer Price Index Research Series Using Current Methods, 1978–98." *Monthly Labor Review*, vol. 122, no. 6 (June 1999): 29–38. http://www.bls.gov/opub/mlr/1999/06/art4full.pdf (accessed July 3, 2008).

Sullivan, James X. "Borrowing During Unemployment: Unsecured Debt as a Safety Net." *Journal of Human Resources* 43, no. 2 (Spring 2008): 383–412.

Tobin, James. "Poverty in Relation to Macroeconomic Trends Cycles and Policies." In *Confronting Poverty: Prescriptions for Change*, ed. Sheldon H. Danzinger, Gary E. Sandefur, and Daniel H. Weinberg, 147–67. Cambridge, Mass.: Harvard University Press, 1994.

U.S. Bureau of the Census. "Alternative Poverty Estimates in the United States: 2003," by Joe Dalaker. *Current Population Reports*, P60-227. June 2005. http://www.census.gov/prod/2005pubs/p60-227.pdf (accessed August 31, 2007).

———. *American Housing Survey of the United States: 1985*. Current Housing Reports H-150-85. Washington, D.C.: U.S. Government Printing Office, 1988.

———. *American Housing Survey of the United States: 1989*. Current Housing Reports H-150-89. Washington, D.C.: U.S. Government Printing Office, 1991.

———. *American Housing Survey of the United States: 2001*. Current Housing Reports H-150-01. Washington, D.C.: U.S. Government Printing Office, 2002.

———. *American Housing Survey of the United States: 2003*. Current Housing Reports H-150-03. Washington, D.C.: U.S. Government Printing Office, 2004.

———. "Annual Average Consumer Price Index Research Series Using Current Methods (CPI-U-RS) All Items: 1947 to 2006." http://www.census.gov/hhes/www/income/income06/AA-CPI-U-RS.pdf (accessed August 29, 2007).

———. "Areas with Concentrated Poverty: 1999," by Alameyehu Bishaw. *Census 2000 Special Reports, CENSR-16*. July 2005. http://www.census.gov/prod/2005pubs/censr-16.pdf (accessed November 2, 2007).

———. "Asset Ownership of Households: 1993," by T. J. Eller and Wallace Fraser. *Current Population Reports*, P70-47. September 1995. http://www.sipp.census.gov/sipp/p70s/p70-47.pdf (accessed May 16, 2007).

———. "The Changing Shape of the Nation's Income Distribution, 1947–1998," by Arthur F. Jones Jr. and Daniel H. Weinberg. *Current Population Reports*, P60-204. June 2000. http://www.census.gov/prod/2000pubs/p60-204.pdf (accessed May 15, 2007).

———. "Cohabitation and the Measurement of Child Poverty," by Marcia Carlson and Sheldon Danziger. Poverty Measurement Working Paper Series. February 1998. http://www.census.gov/hhes/www/povmeas/papers/cohabit.html (accessed April 3, 2008).

———. "CPS Population and Per Capita Money Income, All Races: 1967 to 2004." *Historic Income Tables—People*, table P-1. http://www.census.gov/hhes/www/income/histinc/p01ar.html (accessed August 31, 2006).

————. "The Development of the Orshansky Poverty Thresholds and Their Sub-sequent History as the Official U.S. Poverty Measure," by Gordon M. Fisher, Poverty Measurement Studies and Alternative Measures, working paper, May 1992, partially revised September 1997. http://www.census.gov/hhes/www/povmeas/papers/orshansky.html (accessed May 14, 2007).

————. "The Distributional Implications of Geographic Adjustments of Poverty Thresholds," by Charles Nelson and Kathleen Short. Unpublished paper. December 8, 2003. http://www.census.gov/hhes/www/povmeas/papers/geopaper.pdf (accessed April 3, 2008).

————. "Dynamics of Economic Well-Being: Poverty 1996–1999," by John Iceland. *Current Population Reports*, P70-91. July 2003. http://www.census.gov/prod/2003pubs/p70-91.pdf (accessed May 16, 2007).

————. "Educational Attainment." http://www.census.gov/population/www/socdemo/educ-attn.html (accessed March 17, 2008).

————. "The Effects of Taxes and Transfers on Income and Poverty in the United States: 2005." *Current Population Reports*, P60-232. March 2007. http://www.census.gov/prod/2007pubs/p60-232.pdf (accessed November 2, 2007).

————. "Experimental Poverty Measures: 1990 to 1997," by Kathleen Short, Thesia Garner, David Johnson, and Patricia Doyle. *Current Population Reports*, P60-205. June 1999. http://www.census.gov/prod/99pubs/p60-205.pdf (accessed October 11, 2007).

————. "Experimental Poverty Measures: 1999," by Kathleen Short. *Current Population Reports*, P60-216. October 2001. http://www.census.gov/prod/2001pubs/p60-216.pdf (accessed April 3, 2008).

————. "From Hunter to Orshansky: An Overview of (Unofficial) Poverty Lines in the United States from 1904 to 1965," by Gordon M. Fisher. Poverty Measurement Studies and Alternative Measures. Paper presented at the Fif-teenth Annual Research Conference of the Association for Public Policy Analy-sis and Management. October 28, 1993, revised August 1997. http://www.census.gov/hhes/www/povmeas/papers/hstorsp4.html (accessed November 1, 2007).

————. *Historical Income Inequality Tables*. http://www.census.gov/hhes/www/income/histinc/p60no231_tablea3.pdf (accessed October 11, 2007).

————. *Historical Poverty Tables,* table 3, http://www.census.gov/hhes/www/poverty/histpov/hstpov3.html (accessed October 25, 2007).

————. *Historical Poverty Tables—People.* http://www.census.gov/hhes/www/poverty/histpov/perindex.html (accessed October 20, 2005).

————. *Historical Statistics of the United States: Colonial Times to 1970*, part 2. 1975. http://www2.census.gov/prod2/statcomp/documents/CT1970p2-01.pdf (accessed October 25, 2007).

————. "Household Income Table of Contents: Table HINC-05. Percent Distri-bution of Households, by Selected Characteristics within Income Quintile and

Top 5 Percent in 2005," http://pubdb3.census.gov/macro/032006/ hhinc/ new05_000.htm (accessed November 9, 2007).

———. "Household Wealth and Asset Ownership: 1984." *Current Population Reports*, P70-7. 1986. http://www.sipp.census.gov/sipp/p70-7.pdf (accessed May 17, 2007).

———. "Household Wealth and Asset Ownership: 1988," by Judith Eargle. *Current Population Reports*, P70-22. December 1990. http://www.sipp.census.gov/ sipp/p70-22.pdf (accessed May 17, 2007).

———. "Household Wealth and Asset Ownership: 1991," by T. J. Eller. *Current Population Reports*, P70-34. January 1994. www.sipp.census.gov/sipp/ sb94_02.pdf (accessed November 9, 2007).

———. "Household Net Worth and Asset Ownership: 1995," by Michael Davern and Patricia Fisher. *Current Population Reports*, P70-71. February 2001. http://www.sipp.census.gov/sipp/p70s/p70-71.pdf (accessed May 16, 2007).

———. "Income, Poverty, and Health Insurance Coverage in the United States: 2005," by Carmen DeNavas-Walt, Bernadette D. Proctor, and Cheryl Hill Lee. *Current Population Reports*, P60-231. Washington, D.C.: U.S. Government Printing Office, 2006.

———. "Income, Poverty, and Health Insurance Coverage in the United States: 2006," by Carmen DeNavas-Walt, Bernadette D. Proctor, and Cheryl Hill Lee. *Current Population Reports*, P60-233. Washington, D.C.: U.S. Government Printing Office, 2007.

———. "Mean Household Income Received by Each Fifth and Top 5 Percent, All Races: 1967 to 2005." *Historical Income Tables—Households*, table H-3. http://www. census.gov/hhes/www/income/histinc/h03ar.html (accessed August 22, 2007).

———. "Net Worth and Asset Ownership of Households," by Shawna Orzechowski and Peter Sepielli. *Current Population Reports*, P70–88. May 2003. http://www.census.gov/prod/2003pubs/p70-88.pdf (accessed May 16, 2007).

———. *1980 Census of Housing: General Housing Characteristics*, part I, HC-80-1a. Washington, D.C.: U.S. Government Printing Office, 1983.

———. *1970 Census of Population: Subject Reports, Low-Income Population*, Final Report PC(2)-9A. Washington, D.C.: U.S. Government Printing Office, 1973.

———. "The 1972–73 Consumer Expenditure Survey—A Preliminary Evaluation," by Robert B. Pearl. Technical Paper 45. Washington, D.C.: U.S Government Printing Office, 1978.

———. "People in Poverty by Nativity: 1993 to 2006," *Historical Poverty Tables*, table 23, http://www.census.gov/hhes/www/poverty/histpov/hstpov23.html (accessed October 20, 2005).

———. "Percent Distribution of Automobile Ownership and Financing: 1940–1970." *Historical Statistics of the United States: Colonial Times to 1970*. Part 2. 1975. Series Q 175-86, http://www2.census.gov/prod2/statcomp/documents/ CTI1970p2-01.pdf (accessed October 25, 2007).

————. "Percent of People 25 Years and Over Who Have Completed High School or College, by Race, Hispanic Origin and Sex: Selected Years 1940 to 2006." *Historical Tables: Current Population Survey*, table A-2. http://www. census.gov/population/www/socdemo/educ-attn.html (accessed September 21, 2006).

————. "Poverty Status of Families, by Type of Family, Presence of Related Children, Race, and Hispanic Origin: 1959 to 2006." *Historical Poverty Tables*, table 4. http://www.census.gov/hhes/www/poverty/histpov/hstpov4.html (accessed August 27, 2007).

————. "Poverty Status of People, by Age, Race, and Hispanic Origin: 1959 to 2006." *Historical Poverty Tables*, table 3. http://www.census.gov/hhes/www/ poverty/histpov/hstpov3.html (accessed August 29, 2007).

————. "Poverty Status of People by Family Relationship, Race, and Hispanic Origin: 1959 to 2006." *Historical Poverty Tables*, table 2. http://www.census. gov/hhes/www/poverty/histpov/hstpov2.html (accessed August 29, 2007).

————. "Poverty Thresholds in 2005." http://www.census.gov/hhes/www/ poverty/threshld/thresh05.html (accessed March 17, 2008).

————. "Race and Hispanic Origin of Householder—Households by Median and Mean Income: 1967 to 2006." Historical Income Tables—Households, table H-5. http://www.census.gov/hhes/www/income/histinc/h05.html (accessed March 17, 2008).

————. "Size of Unit and Lot—Occupied Units." *American Housing Survey 2001*, table 2-3. http://www.census.gov/hhes/www/housing/ahs/ahs01/tab23.html (accessed May 15, 2007).

————. "Small Area Income and Poverty Estimate (SAIPE) Main Page." http:// www.census.gov/hhes/www/saipe/saipe.html (accessed May 14, 2007).

————. "Spells of Poverty for Persons Who Became Poor During the 1996 SIPP Panel, by Selected Characteristics: 1996–1999." *Poverty—Poverty Dynamics 1996–9*, table 4. http://www.census.gov/hhes/www/poverty/sipp96/table04.html (accessed May 16, 2007).

————. *Statistical Abstract of the United States: 1976*, tables 510, 569, and 570. http:// www.census.gov/compendia/statab/past_years.html (accessed May 15, 2007).

————. *Statistical Abstract of the United States: 1985*, table 595. http://www2.census. gov/prod2/statcomp/documents/1985-06.pdf (accessed January 9, 2008).

————. *Statistical Abstract of the United States: 2002*, tables 560 and 561. http:// www.census.gov/compendia/statab/past_years.html (accessed May 15, 2007).

————. *Statistical Abstract of the United States: 2003*. Washington, D.C.: U.S. Government Printing Office, 2003.

————. *Statistical Abstract of the United States: 2004–2005*, tables 2, 563, and 697. http://www.census.gov/prod/2004pubs/04statab/pop.pdf (accessed May 15, 2007).

————. *Statistical Abstract of the United States: 2007*, tables 529 and 655. http:// www.census.gov/prod/www/statistical-abstract.html (accessed May 21, 2008).

————. "Supplemental Measures of Material Well-Being: Basic Needs, Consumer Durables, Energy and Poverty, 2001 and 2002." CPS *Special Reports*, P23-202. December 2005. http://www.census.gov/prod/2005pubs/p23-202.pdf (accessed October 11, 2007).

————. "Supplementary Measures of Material Well-Being: Expenditures, Consumption, and Poverty, 1998 and 2001." CPS *Special Studies*, P23-201. September 2003. http://www.census.gov/prod/2003pubs/p23-201.pdf (accessed October 11, 2007).

————. Wealth and Asset Ownership website on Publications, Reports, Research, and Analysis, http://www.census.gov/hhres/www/wealth/publications.html.

U.S. Chamber of Commerce. Task Force on Economic Growth and Opportunity. *The Concept of Poverty*. Washington, D.C.: U.S. Government Printing Office, 1965.

U.S. Department of Agriculture. Center for Nutrition Policy and Promotion. *Thrifty Food Plan, 2006*, by Andrea Carlson, Mark Lino, WenYen Juan, Kenneth Hanson, and P. Peter Basiotis. Report CNPP-19. April 2007. http://www.cnpp.usda.gov/Publications/FoodPlans/MiscPubs/TFP2006Report.pdf (accessed November 26, 2007).

U.S. Department of Commerce. Bureau of Economic Analysis. "Frequently Requested NIPA Tables." *National Economic Accounts*. http://www.bea.doc.gov/bea/dn/nipaweb/SelectTable.asp?Popular=Y (accessed May 15, 2007).

U.S. Department of Energy. *Residential Energy Consumption Survey: Housing Characteristics 1980*. Washington, D.C.: U.S. Government Printing Office, 1982.

————. *Residential Energy Consumption Survey: Housing Characteristics 1990*. Washington, D.C.: U.S. Government Printing Office, 1992.

————. *Residential Energy Consumption Survey: Housing Characteristics 1997*. 1999. http://www.eia.doe.gov/emeu/recs/recs97/recs97.html#Household%20Characteristics (accessed July 27, 2007).

————. *Residential Energy Consumption Survey: Housing Characteristics 2001*. n.d. http://www.eia.doe.gov/emeu/recs/contents.html (accessed October 25, 2007).

U.S. Department of Health and Human Services. Centers for Disease Control and Prevention. National Center for Health Statistics. "Deaths: Final Data for 2001," by Robert N. Anderson, Elizabeth Arias, Kenneth D. Kochanek, Hsiang-Ching Kung, and Sherry L. Murphy. *National Vital Statistics Reports* 52, no. 3 (September 25, 2003). http://www.cdc.gov/nchs/pressroom/03facts/mortalitytrends.htm (accessed May 16, 2007).

————. "Deaths: Final Data for 2002," by Robert N. Anderson, Kenneth D. Kochanek, Sherry L. Murphy, and Chester Scott. *National Vital Statistics Reports* 53, no. 5 (October 12, 2004). http://www.cdc.gov/nchs/data/nvsr/nvsr53/nvsr53_05.pdf (accessed May 16, 2007).

————. "Deaths: Final Data for 2003," by Melonie P. Heron, Donna L. Hoyert, Hsiang-Ching Kung, and Sherry L. Murphy. *National Vital Statistics Reports* 54, no. 13 (April 19, 2006). http://www.cdc.gov/nchs/products/pubs/pubd/nvsr/54/54-20.htm (accessed November 6, 2006).

————. "Deaths: Final Data for 2004," by Melonie P. Heron, Kenneth D. Kochanek, Arialdi M. Miniño, and Sherry L. Murphy. Health E-Stats, table 2. http://www.cdc. gov/nchs/products/pubs/pubd/hestats/finaldeaths04/finaldeaths04.htm (accessed May 14, 2007).

————. "Decayed, Missing and Filled Teeth in Adults, 1960–1962," by James E. Kelly, Lawrence E. Van Kirk, and Caroline C. Garst. NCHS Series 11, no. 23, February 1967.

————. Health, United States, 1981. 1981. http://www.cdc.gov/nchs/data/hus/ hus81acc.pdf (accessed October 11, 2007).

————. Health, United States, 2004. 2004. http://www.cdc.gov/nchs/data/hus/ hus04.pdf (accessed November 1, 2007).

————. Health, United States, 2005. 2005. http://www.cdc.gov/nchs/data/hus/ hus05.pdf (accessed November 1, 2007).

————. Health, United States, 2006. 2006. http://www.cdc.gov/nchs/data/hus/ hus06.pdf (accessed November 1, 2007).

————. "Infant Mortality and Low Birth Weight Among Black and White Infants—United States, 1980–2000." Morbidity and Mortality Weekly Report 51, no. 27 (July 12, 2001): 589–92.

————. "Summary Health Statistics for U.S. Children: National Health Interview Survey, 2004." Vital and Health Statistics, series 10, no. 227. Washington, D.C.: U.S. Government Printing Office, 2006.

————. "Summary Health Statistics for U.S. Children: National Health Interview Survey, 2005." Vital and Health Statistics, series 10, no. 231. Washington, D.C.: U.S. Government Printing Office, 2006.

————. "Summary of Trends in Growth and Anemia Indicators." 2005 Pediatric Nutrition Surveillance Report, table 12D. http://www.cdc.gov/pednss/pednss_ tables/html/pednss_national_table12.htm (accessed September 17, 2007).

————. "Total Loss of Teeth in Adults: United States, 1960–62," by James E. Kelly, Lawrence E. Van Kirk, and Caroline Garst. NCHS Series 11, no 27 (October 1967).

————. "Trends in Infant Mortality by Cause of Death and Other Characteristics, 1960–1988," by M. F. MacDorman and H. M. Rosenberg. Vital and Health Statistics, series 20, no. 20 (January 1993).

U.S. Department of Health, Education, and Welfare. "Dental Visits: Time Interval Since Last Visit, July 1963–June 1964," by George S. Chulis. NCHS Vital and Health Statistics, series 10, no. 29 (April 1966). http://www.cdc.gov/nchs/data/ series/sr_10/sr10_076.pdf (accessed November 1, 2007).

————. "Food Plans for Poverty Measurement," by Betty Peterkin. Technical Paper XII (supporting data for The Measure of Poverty: A Report to Congress as Mandated by the Education Amendments of 1974). November 1976. http://www.census.gov/hhes/www/povmeas/pdf/tp_xii.pdf (accessed October 11, 2007).

———. *The Measure of Poverty: A Report to Congress as Mandated by the Education Amendments of 1974.* April 1976. http://www.census.gov/hhes/www/povmeas/measureofpov75.html (accessed October 11, 2007).

U.S. Department of Labor. Bureau of Labor Statistics. "Access to Historical Data for the 'A' Tables of the Employment Situation News Release," table A-1. http://www.bls.gov/webapps/legacy/cpsatab1.htm (accessed November 2, 2007).

———. "Consumer Expenditures in 2004." Report 992. April 2006. http://www.bls.gov/cex/csxann04.pdf (accessed November 6, 2006).

———. "Consumer Expenditures in 2005." Report 998. February 2007. http://www.bls.gov/cex/csxann05.pdf (accessed October 11, 2007).

———. "Frequently Asked Questions," no. 20. *Consumer Expenditure Survey.* http://www.bls.gov/cex/csxfaqs.htm#q20 (accessed November 8, 2005).

———. *Consumer Expenditure Survey: Interview Survey 1972–73, Volume 1: U.S. Tables, Families Classified by 10 Family Characteristics.* BLS Bulletin 1997. Washington, D.C.: U.S. Government Printing Office, 1978.

———. "Consumer Price Index: All Urban Consumers (CPI-U)." September 9, 2007. ftp://ftp.bls.gov/pub/special.requests/cpi/cpiai.txt (accessed November 2, 2007).

———. *Handbook of Labor Statistics 1975—Reference Edition.* BLS Bulletin 1865. Washington, D.C.: U.S. Government Printing Office, 1978.

———. "Quintiles of Income Before Taxes: Average Annual Expenditures and Characteristics." Consumer Expenditure Survey standard tables, 1984–2004. http://www.bls.gov/cex/csxstnd.htm (accessed August 22, 2007).

———. "Unemployment Rate—Civilian Labor Force." Labor Force Statistics from the Current Population Survey. http://www.bls.gov/data/home.htm (accessed September 21, 2006).

U.S. Department of Labor. Federal Economic Statistics Advisory Committee. "Alternative Measures of Household Income: BEA Personal Income, CPS Money Income, and Beyond," by John Ruser, Adrienne Pilot, and Charles Nelson. Committee paper, December 14, 2004.http://www.bls.gov/bls/fesacp1061104.pdf (accessed October 25, 2007).

U.S. Office of Federal Housing Enterprise Oversight. "U.S. Housing Prices Slow, OFHEO House Price Index Shows Smallest Quarterly Increase since 1994." Press release, August 30, 2007. http://www.ofheo.gov/media/hpi/2q07hpi.pdf (accessed November 2, 2007).

U.S. Social Security Administration. *Annual Statistical Supplement to the Social Security Bulletin, 2005.* http://www.ssa.gov/policy/docs/statcomps/supplement/2005/9h.pdf (accessed March 17, 2008).

United Nations Statistical Office. "Handbook on Poverty Statistics: Concepts, Methods, and Policy Use." http://unstats.un.org/unsd/methods/poverty/Chapters.htm (accessed May 15, 2007).

# Index

absolute vs. proportional income
  variability, 68–70
absolute vs. relative poverty
  OPR's measurement of, 10, 76–77,
    95–96, 100–101, 147n3
  relative poverty's importance,
    105–106, 147n3
  U.S. vs. European attitudes, 151n6
affluent vs. poor households
  and expenditures in excess of
    income, 37, 38
  transitory income variance, 69–70,
    145–146n33
African Americans, 12, 14, 64
Agriculture Department, U.S. (USDA),
  food plan data and OPR, 7, 8
alternative poverty metrics (income),
    29–30, 31–33, 106, 109,
    119–125
American Housing Survey (AHS), 83
antipoverty policies and programs
  importance of accurate data for
    effective, 110
  increase in spending for, 21–22, 99
  OPR-based indictment of, 15
  and per-capita income, 152n2
  reliance upon OPR, 2–3
  and restrictions on study's conclusions,
    104–105
  and rise in living standards for
    poor, 97

spending vs. OPR, 18, 21, 23–26,
    114, 116–118
transitory income variability effects
  on, 73
and unemployment rate, 152n2
See also means-tested public benefits
assets, 30, 32, 49–57, 141n6

biometric data for living standards
  food and nutrition, 80–83
  health and medical care, 88–95
  value of, 107, 108
Bureau of Economic Analysis (BEA), 20
Bureau of Labor Statistics (BLS), 8, 35,
    36, 59
  See also Consumer Expenditure
    (CE) Survey

capital gains, inclusion in alternative
    income measure, 30, 31, 122–123
capitalism, OPR-based trends as
    indictment of, 15
cash benefits, publicly funded
  OPR's inclusion of only, 30, 31, 43,
    44, 62, 97
  welfare reform's reduction in, 22
CE (Consumer Expenditure) Survey,
    see Consumer Expenditure (CE)
    Survey
CEA (Council of Economic Advisers),
    6

Census Bureau
    AHS, 83
    alternative income measures, 31–33,
        119–125
    CPS, 20, 36–37, 59–61, 137n19,
        143–144n18
    and pretax money income measure
        for OPR, 9, 10
    SIPP, 50, 63–64, 72
Centers for Disease Control and
    Prevention (CDC), 80–81
children
    medical health services usage,
        94–95
    nutritional status of, 81–83
    OPR-based trends in poverty, 12, 14
chronic vs. episodic poverty, 63–66
cohabitation, OPR's failure to account
    for, 31, 32
collinearity of OPR with other
    indicators, 112–114
Community Development Block
    Grants, 2
Consumer Expenditure (CE) Survey
    vs. CPS, 36–37, 59–61, 137n19,
        143–144n18
    and income vs. expenditures for
        lower-income households, 36–40
    method changes in, 57–59, 62, 73
    vs. PCE data, 41–44
    as primary data source for
        expenditures, 35
consumer expenditures
    categories for lower-income
        households, 78
    vs. consumption levels, 40–44
    CPS vs. CE survey, 36–37, 59–61,
        137n19, 143–144n18
    as in excess of income, 34–35,
        37–40, 46–47
    and food budget as cost measure
        for OPR, 6–8

vs. outlays, 35–36
overall patterns, 40
underreporting in CE survey, 62
See also Consumer Price Index
    (CPI); expenditures vs. income;
    living standards
consumer outlays vs. expenditures,
    35–36
Consumer Price Index (CPI)
    and changes in absolute poverty, 101
    CPI-U (urban) as source for, 130n12
    CPI-U vs. CPI-U-RS, 31, 134n3,
        146–147n2
    and inflation adjustments to OPR,
        9–10, 76
consumption levels
    actual increase in, 45
    vs. consumer expenditures, 40–44
    definitional issues, 35–36
    establishing minimum acceptable, 106
    as in excess of income, 34, 37,
        46–47
    and home production of goods and
        services, 136n15
    income's inability to predict, 29
    increases in poor households, 102
    lack of data on, 107–108
    as more accurate gauge of living
        standards, 106–107
    OPR's assumptions, 29, 33–34
    OPR's disconnection with, 4
cost of living, see consumer expendi-
    tures; consumption levels
Council of Economic Advisers (CEA), 6
CPI (Consumer Price Index), see
    Consumer Price Index (CPI)
crime and quality of life for lower-
    income families, 85, 103–104
Current Population Reports, 10
Current Population Survey (CPS), 20,
    36–37, 60–61, 137n19,
    143–144n18

Danziger, Sheldon, 77
debt/liabilities and expenditure/income
        gap, 49, 51–52, 73
dental health, improvements in, 92–93,
        150n23
durable goods and consumer spending
        measures, 35–36, 42

Earned Income Tax Credit (EITC), 62,
        133n10
economic growth as determinant of
        poverty rate, 18–20
Economy Food Plan, USDA, 7, 8
educational attainment
    improvements in, 99
    and mortality rate, 89, 148–149n15
    vs. OPR, 17, 21, 23, 25–26, 114,
        116–119
    spending in excess of income by, 38
EITC (Earned Income Tax Credit), 62,
        133n10
elderly vs. working-age population, 12,
        14, 52, 53–54, 55
Ellwood, David, 18–19, 77
employment conditions, 1, 18, 20–21
    See also unemployment rate
employment-to-population ratio, 21
Engel, Ernst, 7
Engel coefficient, 8
episodic vs. chronic poverty, 63–66
equivalence scale for family size in
        OPR, 8, 31, 32
ethnicity and race, see race and ethnicity
European vs. U.S. attitudes on relative
        poverty, 151n6
expenditures vs. income
    assets and net worth, 49–57, 141n6
    CE survey method changes, 57–59,
        62, 73
    definitional issues, 33–36
    discrepancies in, 36–40, 44–47
    introduction, 28–29, 48–49

OPR's inability to account for,
        28–33, 46–47, 49
    summary of factors, 73–75
    transitory income variance, 63–73,
        74, 100, 145–146n33
    underreporting of income, 59–62,
        73–74, 142–143n15, 144n23
    See also consumer expenditures

families
    median income measure, 18–20,
        68–70
    OPR-based trends in poverty, 12, 14
    quality of life issues for poor, 85,
        103–104
    size and structure in OPR calculation,
        8, 9, 31, 32
    spending in excess of income by, 39
farm vs. nonfarm households, OPR
        calculation for, 8
Federal Reserve Board, SCF survey,
        50–51, 71
female-headed households, chronic
        poverty share of population, 64
food and nutrition expenditures
    and living standards, 78, 79,
        80–83, 97
    in OPR calculation, 6–8
foreign-born individuals, 12

gender factor in mortality rates, 89
Gottschalk, Peter, 66
government antipoverty programs, see
        antipoverty policies and programs
government transfers, inclusion in
        alternative income measure, 123
    See also means-tested public benefits
Graduate Equivalence Degree (GED),
        119

Hacker, Jacob S., 66–68
Hassett, Kevin, 41–42

health and medical care
    as component of public benefits, 22
    dental health improvements,
        92–93, 150n23
    expenditures and living standards,
        78, 79, 88–95
    food and nutrition, 78, 79, 80–83,
        97
    means-tested public benefit effects,
        91–95, 97
    out-of-pocket medical expenses,
        30, 32
    PCE/CE discrepancies in consumer
        expenditures, 42, 43
hemoglobin count and children's
    health, 82, 83
Hispanic Americans, 15, 64–65
historical period, shifts in OPR by, 13
home appliances, expenditures and
    living standards, 78, 79, 83–87
home ownership, imputed value of
    and asset appreciation, 52, 53, 54,
        55
    OPR's failure to account for, 30, 31
housing
    expenditures and living standards,
        78, 79, 83–87
    floor space increases, 83–84
    prices and net worth increases, 52,
        53, 54, 55

immigrants, OPR-based trends in
    poverty, 12
in-kind benefits, statistical neglect of,
    22, 43, 97
income
    alternative metrics for calculating,
        29–30, 31–33, 106, 109, 119–125
    CE survey vs. CPS data on, 59–61,
        137n19, 143–144n18
    as measure of poverty, 1, 2, 6, 33,
        102, 106–107

median income measure, 18–20,
        68–70
    OPR's exclusive reliance on, 9, 96
    spending in excess of income by
        level of, 39
    underreporting of, 59–62, 73–74,
        142–143n15, 144n23
    See also expenditures vs. income;
        per-capita income; pretax money
        income
inequality, economic
    lower-income households' gains in
        wealth, 55–56
    and transitory income variance
        increases, 70, 72
infant mortality rate, 89–92,
        149nn17–18
international perspective, 10–11, 151n6
intertemporal adjustments to cost of
        living, OPR's failure to deflate
        correctly, 30, 31, 32
    See also Consumer Price Index (CPI)

Jencks, Christopher, 58–59
Johnson, Lyndon B., 1, 6

Krueger, Dirk, 72

labor force participation rates, changes
        in, 20–21
liabilities/debt and expenditure/income
        gap, 49, 51–52, 73
life expectancy, 88
lifecycle-income hypothesis, 34
living standards
    actual improvement in, 4–5, 16,
        78, 95–97, 101–102
    food and nutrition, 78, 79, 80–83, 97
    health and medical care, 78, 79,
        88–95
    housing and home appliances, 78,
        79, 83–87

income as inadequate measure of, 96

introduction, 76–78

long- vs. short-term planning for, 34

OPR's ability to measure, 3, 4

transportation, 78, 79, 86–88

long-term vs. transitory poverty, 63–66

longitudinal data, value in analyzing living standards, 107

low–birth weight babies and infant mortality, 90–92

macroeconomic indicators vs. OPR, 17–27, 111–125

marital status, spending in excess of income by, 39

material deprivation, measurement of, see expenditures vs. income; living standards; official poverty rate (OPR)

Mathur, Aparna, 41–42

means-tested public benefits
  CE survey exclusion of, 43–44
  EITC, 62, 133n10
  inclusion in alternative income measure, 123
  increase in, 21–22
  medical care effects on health, 91–95, 97
  method for calculating spending on, 138–139nn31–32
  non-officially poor recipients of, 151n5
  reliance upon OPR, 2–3
  spending on vs. OPR, 21
  See also cash benefits; noncash benefits

median family income, 18–20, 68–70

medical care, see health and medical care

men, mortality rate, 89

middle class vs. poor households, transitory income variance, 69–70, 145–146n33

Moffitt, Robert A., 66, 68–70

mortality and living standards, 88–91, 148–149n15, 149nn17–18

motor vehicle ownership, increases in, 86–88

National Center for Health Statistics (NCHS), 80–81, 88–95

National Income and Product Accounts (NIPA), 41–42

net worth, 49–57, 71, 141n6

New York City, initiative for replacing OPR, 109

noncash benefits, publicly funded
  OPR's failure to account for, 30, 31, 97
  statistical neglect of, 22, 43, 44, 97

nondurable goods and consumer spending measures, 35–36, 42

nonfarm vs. farm households, OPR calculation for, 8

nutritional health of population, 78, 79, 80–83, 97

obesity, lower-income household increases in, 81

Office of Economic Opportunity (OEO), 2

official poverty rate (OPR)
  and absolute vs. relative poverty, 10, 76–77, 95–96, 100–101, 147n3
  and antipoverty policies and programs, 2–3, 15, 18, 21, 23–26, 114, 116–118
  authority and credibility of, 2
  case against, 98–107
  cash benefits in, 30, 31, 43, 44, 62, 97

and consumption levels, 4, 29,
    33–34
current framework for, 9–11
evaluation of effectiveness, 3–4
historical perspective, 1–2, 4, 6–9
and income/expenditure discrepancy,
    28–33, 46–47, 49
vs. other indicators of material
    deprivation, 17–27, 107–110,
    111–125
poverty trends according to, 12–16
See also Consumer Price Index (CPI)
Orshansky, Mollie
on absolute vs. relative poverty
    measure, 76, 147n3
on importance of consumption
    tracking, 47
original metric for OPR, 6–9,
    129–130n 7, 130nn9–10
on purpose for measuring poverty,
    95
and standard of living threshold for
    poverty, 77–78
out-of-pocket medical expenses, OPR's
    failure to account for, 30, 32
outlays vs. expenditures, 35–36
owner-occupied housing
and asset appreciation, 52, 53, 54,
    55
OPR's failure to account for value of,
    30, 31

Panel Study of Income Dynamics (PSID),
    66–70, 145n25
PCE (personal consumption expendi-
    tures) vs. CE survey data, 41–44
per-capita income
as alternative poverty measure,
    122–123
and antipoverty program spending,
    152n2
increase in, 20, 99

vs. OPR, 17, 21, 23–26, 114,
    115–116
permanent-income hypothesis, 34, 63
permanent vs. temporary income and
    expenditures in excess of
    income, 34
Perri, Fabrizio, 72
personal consumption expenditures
    (PCE) vs. CE survey data, 41–44
persons living alone, 14, 64
physical data for living standards
housing and home appliances,
    83–87
motor vehicle ownership, 86–88
value of, 107
post-tax, post-transfer family income,
    transitory variance in, 67
poverty
continuation of quality of life
    issues, 85, 103–104
median duration of, 65, 144n24
OPR-based trends in, 12–16
persistence of, 50–51
as transitory state for most house-
    holds, 63–64
See also absolute vs. relative
    poverty; living standards; official
    poverty rate (OPR)
poverty guidelines, 127–128n4
poverty thresholds, 134n2, 139n34
pretax money income
arbitrariness of, 10
CE vs. CPS data on, 60–62
inability to predict material depri-
    vation, 100, 150n25
inability to predict spending, 37,
    45–47
as measure for OPR, 9, 10
ratio of spending to, 39–40
transitory variance increases,
    58–59, 66–67
private philanthropy, increase in, 22

propertyless-ness among poor, decline in, 54–55

proportional vs. absolute income variability, 68–70

PSID (Panel Study of Income Dynamics), 66–70, 145n25

public assistance programs, see antipoverty policies and programs

purchasing power, see living standards

quality of life vs. material living standards, 85, 103–104, 108

race and ethnicity
  African Americans, 12, 14, 64
  Hispanic Americans, 15, 64–65
  spending in excess of income by, 38
  whites, 12, 15, 38, 64, 90, 91

regional differences and OPR-based trends in poverty, 14–15, 30, 32

relative vs. absolute poverty, see absolute vs. relative poverty

Residential Energy Consumption Survey (RECS), 83

risk tolerance/preference and transitory income variability, 72–73

SCF (Survey of Consumer Finances), 50–51, 71

second-order overspending hypothesis, 51

services, spending on, 35–36, 42

SIPP (Survey of Income and Program Participation), 50, 63–64, 72

Slesnick, Daniel, 58

Smith, Adam, 105

social well-being, need for measurement of overall, 108

spending down of assets, lack of evidence for, 50–52

spending patterns, see consumer expenditures; consumption levels

standard of living, see living standards

Summers, Lawrence, 18–19, 77

Survey of Consumer Finances (SCF), 50–51, 71

Survey of Income and Program Participation (SIPP), 50, 63–64, 72

Task Force on Economic Growth and Opportunity, 29–30

taxes and tax credits
  EITC, 62, 133n10
  inclusion in alternative income measure, 122–123
  OPR's failure to account for, 9, 30, 31

thresholds, poverty, 134n2, 139n34

time-series variable in OPR vs. other indicators analysis, 114–116

transitory income variance, 58–59, 63–73, 74, 100, 145–146n33

transportation expenditures and living standards, 78, 79, 86–88

underreporting of income, 59–62, 73–74, 142–143n15, 144n23

underweight status of U.S. population, 81–83

undocumented immigrants, OPR-based trends in poverty, 12

unemployment rate
  and alternative poverty measures, 122
  and antipoverty program spending, 152n2
  changes in, 20–21, 99
  vs. OPR, 17, 21, 23, 25–26, 114, 115–118
  unrelated individuals in OPR calculation, 8

U.S. Department of Agriculture (USDA), food plan data and OPR, 7, 8

U.S. vs. European attitudes on relative poverty, 151n6

variability in income over time, 58–59, 63–73, 74, 100, 145–146n33

War on Poverty, 1–2, 6, 105
wealth position (net worth), 49–57, 71, 141n6
Welfare programs, *see* antipoverty policies and programs
Welfare reform, 22, 104

whites
  chronic poverty share of population, 64
  infant mortality rate declines, 90, 91
  OPR-based trends in poverty, 12, 15
  spending in excess of income among, 38
women, mortality rate, 89
working-aged vs. elderly population, 12, 14, 52, 53–54, 55

year-to-year income variability, 58–59, 63–73, 74, 100, 145–146n33

# About the Author

Nicholas Eberstadt holds the Henry Wendt Chair in Political Economy at the American Enterprise Institute (AEI), and is senior adviser to the National Bureau of Asian Research (NBR). He has served on the Board of Scientific Counselors for the U.S. National Center for Health Statistics, and is currently a member of the President's Council on Bioethics. Mr. Eberstadt's previous books on poverty issues include *The Poverty of Communism* (1988), *The Tyranny of Numbers* (1995), *Prosperous Paupers and Other Population Problems* (2000), and *Health and the Income Inequality Hypothesis* (coauthor, 2004). Mr. Eberstadt earned his AB, MPA, and PhD from Harvard University, and his MSc from the London School of Economics.